CREATIVE SCHEDULING
for Diverse Populations
in Middle and High School

To the teachers and learners of the world who strive to create the best of times

CREATIVE SCHEDULING
for Diverse Populations
in Middle and High School

**Maximizing
Opportunities
for Learning**

Elliot Y. Merenbloom | Barbara A. Kalina

CORWIN
A SAGE Company

CORWIN
A SAGE Company

FOR INFORMATION:

Corwin

A SAGE Company

2455 Teller Road

Thousand Oaks, California 91320

(800) 233-9936

www.corwin.com

SAGE Publications Ltd.

1 Oliver's Yard

55 City Road

London, EC1Y 1SP

United Kingdom

SAGE Publications India Pvt. Ltd.

B 1/I 1 Mohan Cooperative Industrial Area

Mathura Road, New Delhi

India 110 044

SAGE Publications Asia-Pacific Pte. Ltd.

3 Church Street

#10-04 Samsung Hub

Singapore 049483

Acquisitions Editor: Jessica Allan

Development Editor: Julie Nemer

Editorial Assistant: Lisa Whitney

Production Editor: Cassandra Margaret Seibel

Copy Editor: Melinda Masson

Typesetter: C&M Digitals (P) Ltd.

Proofreader: Rae-Ann Goodwin

Indexer: Joan Shapiro

Cover Designer: Karine Hovsepian

Permissions Editor: Karen Ehrmann

Printed in the United States of America.

A catalog record of this book is available from the Library of Congress.

ISBN 978-1-4129-9525-2

This book is printed on acid-free paper.

12 13 14 15 16 10 9 8 7 6 5 4 3 2 1

Contents

List of Figures

List of Tables

Acknowledgments

Many researchers contributed to our thinking and writing. We are indebted to their scholarship that provided the basis for our many scheduling frameworks and instructional models that appear in this book. Their individual recognition appears throughout the book and in the bibliography.

Our gratitude extends to the dedicated people at Corwin: Lisa Cuevas Shaw, Jessica G. Allan, Cassandra Seibel, Allison Scott, Lisa Whitney, and Julie Nemer, whose dedication to the world of education and learning supported us throughout the process. We appreciate the thorough and timely work of Melinda Masson who guided us patiently through the editing stage. Finally, we treasure the confidence placed in us by Hudson Perigo at the outset of this project. Her encouragement and support energized our creativity.

Gratitude extends not only to our publishing family but to our immediate families. We appreciate the support of our family cheerleaders: our spouses, Ilene Merenbloom and Richard Kalina, as well as our children, who gave us encouragement, and our grandchildren, who inspired us.

Corwin gratefully acknowledges the contributions of the following reviewers:

Cynthia Church
Principal
G. Stanley Hall, Marquardt School District 15
Glendale Heights, IL

Michelle Kocar
District Level Administrator
North Olmsted City Schools
N. Olmsted, OH

About the Authors

After 33 years of service in the Baltimore County (Maryland) Public Schools, **Elliot Y. Merenbloom** chose to pursue a career as an educational consultant. During his career in that district, Elliot served as a classroom teacher, a school counselor, an assistant principal, a principal, a director of middle school in instruction, and an area director. This is his 20th year as a full-time educational consultant.

A graduate of Towson University and Loyola University of Maryland, his areas of expertise include the following topics: creative scheduling, the restructuring/change process, teaching strategies for variable-length time periods, team/small learning communities, and curriculum implementation.

In collaboration with Barbara A. Kalina, Elliot coauthored *Making Creative Schedules Work in Middle and High Schools* (Corwin, 2007). The book focuses on three phases of school reform: scheduling, teams or small learning communities, and teaching in variable-length time periods. His previous publications include *The Team Process: A Handbook for Teachers* and *Developing Effective Middle Schools Through Faculty Participation* (published by the Association for Middle Level Education, formerly the National Middle School Association).

In addition to leading workshops and seminars for the Association for Supervision and Curriculum Development, Silver Strong & Associates, the International Renewal Institute, the National Association of Secondary School Principals, the Association for Middle Level Education, the New England League of Middle Schools, and the New York State Middle School Association, he has served as a consultant for school districts in 45 states as well as Guam; Vienna, Austria; and Vancouver, British Columbia.

Barbara A. Kalina combined the careers of registered nurse working in surgery and emergency response with motherhood to prepare for the excitement of teaching middle school students. She received her bachelor's and master's degrees in British literature and philosophy from Mundelein College in Chicago and taught at Sam Rotolo Middle School of Batavia, Illinois.

Barbara's interest in writing and reading led her to become an active member, trainer, and assessment developer for various Illinois State Board of Education language arts committees. For 20 years, she served in that capacity, during which she provided professional development in writing throughout Illinois.

As a teacher, she held a variety of district leadership positions and served as an adjunct professor at Benedictine University and National Louis University in Illinois. Her consulting areas of expertise include teaching strategies especially for extended-time periods, initiating or maintaining teams/small learning communities, and literacy.

Barbara's 21-year collaboration with Elliot Y. Merenbloom led to the publication of their first book in 2007 published by Corwin: *Making Creative Schedules Work in Middle and High Schools*. The book addresses the restructuring process of schools through the development of comprehensive master schedules, the implementation of small learning communities, and maximizing instruction in extended time.

Barbara is a board member for the Association of Illinois Middle-Grade Schools. She has presented workshops and professional development for the Association of Illinois Middle-Grade Schools, the Illinois Association for Supervision and Curriculum Development, the New York State Middle School Association, and the New York Association for Supervision and Curriculum Development. Besides workshops, she has presented at national conferences for the Association for Middle Level Education, formerly the National Middle School Association; the Association for Supervision and Curriculum Development; the National Staff Development Council; and Learning Forward.

Introduction

It was the best of times, it was the worst of times,
it was the age of wisdom, it was the age of foolishness . . .

Charles Dickens, *A Tale of Two Cities*

Recently, at lunch a woman posed the question of history's view of the many crises in today's world. Several people quickly responded, each from a different vantage point and interest. Eventually, the discussion addressed the apparent escalating problems plaguing the educational world. Again, each person defined the situations from particular vantage points and experiences. To each, the issue seemed to suggest the "worst of times."

While too often it seems like the worst of times, many educational visionaries provide suggestions that, for some students and schools, these may be the best of times. The challenge remains for educators to follow the recommendations of these visionaries. Not unlike successful athletic coaches, Michael Schmoker (2011, pp. 10–11) encourages the world of education to return to the basics of simplicity and diligence in how and what is taught within an authentic literacy base. Doug Reeves (2010) and Charlotte Danielson (2002) emphasize the importance of consistency between the mission/vision statement and decisions. Each of these experts discusses the impact of decisions and the mission statement on student achievement through the classroom experience (Danielson, 2002, p. 118; Reeves, 2010, p. 4).

Our earlier book, *Making Creative Schedules Work in Middle and High Schools* (Merenbloom & Kalina, 2007), makes a case for change in the educational focus of the 21st century. Since the book's publication, the world of education has experienced even more assaults on its integrity. Demands for reform arise from citizens as well as from government leaders. The merits and faults of public schools, charter schools, and voucher systems are tossed about as though the discussion alone will bring about change.

In this book, we intend to continue to add a perspective on change that solely ranges from instructional practice to the fundamental structure that provides the framework for instructional decisions: the schedule. Each chapter will focus on different issues confronting the educational curriculum and programs as well as how the schedule can play a role in meeting the challenges.

In Chapter 1, we will explore the definition and expectations of a schedule. Like instruction, the best schedules begin with the end in mind. In part, that end is contained in the school or district's mission/vision statement. Consequently, the process becomes a shared vision with faculty and administration in accord with content and directives of the mission/vision statement and to form decisions based on those understandings.

Chapters 2 and 3 take us into the world of diverse populations: response to intervention (RTI), special education, English-language learning (ELL), credit recovery, career and technical education, gifted and talented, Advanced Placement (AP), and International Baccalaureate (IB). This book does not attempt to define the criteria for admission to each of these programs. Rather, the book serves as a guide for the development of a school schedule that is fully inclusive. One size does not fit all. The ability to modify or adapt is essential.

Chapters 4, 5, and 6 present a wide variety of fixed and variable scheduling frameworks, including models to integrate fixed and variable possibilities into one comprehensive schedule.

In order to meet the needs of students, much has been written on the merits of small learning communities (SLCs). Chapter 7 offers scheduling frameworks for the SLC as well as magnets, houses, and academies to accommodate those needs. This chapter also offers research-based flexible scheduling frameworks that create opportunities for SLCs and teams to function within the scheduled day. Further, a positive correlation is presented between flexibility and student achievement. To build the preceding schedules, specific steps are offered for middle and high schools in Chapters 8 and 9.

If mission statements are reflected in choices of schedules, the instruction that occurs within those schedules must also be true to the statements. Chapter 10 provides a template for effective teaching in variable-length time periods. Based on research and best practices, the model encourages bell-to-bell teaching.

Finally, no educational or instructional plan to address the needs of diverse populations and to increase student achievement functions without supportive professional development. Chapter 11 provides guidelines for professional development that leads to successful implementation of a schedule and instructional strategies used to make the schedule work. Continuous discussion, monitoring, and assessment contribute to the comfort level desired for a faculty. A discussion guide appendix follows Chapter 11. To soften effects of "the worst of times," scheduling decisions guided by the mission of the school and focused instruction can make students' educational experiences "the best of times."

1

Schedules

The Springboard for Action

If you want change, you have to make it.
If we want progress, we have to drive it.

Susan Rice, *Stanford University Commencement, 2010*

Although the word *change* drips easily from the lips, its embodiment in action often remains frozen. In *Leading Change in Your School*, Reeves (2009) continually reminds us that sustainable change occurs only when behaviors lead, especially the behaviors of those who seek the change. Those behaviors take their cues from the vision of the leaders and the mission/vision statements they espouse.

Developing a new master schedule embodies change. Danielson (2002) recommends that we consider the influence of a schedule on the pace of teacher and student interactions as well as class length, which in turn determines the nature and depth of instruction (p. 45). Since schedules provide organizational structure for schools and the intended curriculum, the actions of teachers to deliver curriculum validate the schedule and move change forward. Because schedules vary in form and complexity, they are developed to meet the level of understanding held by those who use them to effectively meet student needs.

A well-considered schedule incorporates eight aspects:

- A schedule is a means to an end and not an end unto itself.
- Based upon a fixed curriculum, the schedule includes offerings that are required or elective.

- Actual student requests, including needs-based placements, contribute to the student-centered approach of the schedule.
- Subject to opportunities for flexibility, the schedule becomes the order of the day for teachers and students.
- The student experience that arises from the schedule defines the school.
- All students' needs warrant consideration.
- Teachers' needs for professional collaboration should be included.
- Discussions about schedules begin with the mission/vision statement of the school and, ultimately, mesh with it.

■ MISSION/VISION

Like the target learning in instruction, the mission/vision statement of a school or district guides the efforts and subsequent behaviors to the desired result. Improved student achievement and a comprehensive method to meet student needs form the basis of the mission/vision statement. Within the statement, clearly stated goals coincide with the actions necessary to meet those goals as well as how they will be monitored. In formulating the statement, the writers "must begin with a vision of what school staff want the school to become" (Protheroe, Shellard, & Turner, 2003, as cited in Protheroe, 2011, p. 1). Professional dialogue aids the direction of the mission/vision statement, but care needs to be taken to stay focused on the essential needs of the students and the school as well as what can be accomplished without piling on initiatives and causing "initiative fatigue" (Reeves, 2009, p. 14). In fact, too many intitatives remain a major reason that change fails to occur as imagined by the leader (Fullan, 2001; Reeves, 2009). If a new format for a school schedule is chosen, the inititative for the year must focus on making the schedule work for instruction and address the student needs that were the catalyst for the schedule change.

Rather than add another three-ring binder of multiple goals and initiatives to the overladen shelves in teachers' classrooms and administrators' offices, this process can be completed in what Reeves (2009) refers to as the "plan on a page" (p. 83). He describes the work of Joe Crawford in the Freeport, Illinois, school district that developed the "plan on a page" for all of its schools. The one-page plan resulted in a 30% increase in the number of students who met or exceeded state standards. It contains the vision, the goals and measures, and the action necessary to accomplish the vision of the school.

■ CATALYST FOR CHANGE

In the scheduling committee's desire to meet student needs, a variety of issues and programs are to be considered. Programs possess particular criteria specific to that program but must be able to exist within the schedule as an independent entity that is simultaneously dependent. For example, a master schedule can be built for the entire school to follow. Within that schedule, subsets can coexist. For instance, a freshman academy can exist within the school schedule but operate independently. Increasingly, schools find themselves meeting mandates that address specific populations within the school or district.

Opposition to any change will certainly occur (Fullan, 2001; Reeves, 2009). Reeves (2009) maintains that if no opposition occurs, perhaps the measures being presented do not represent meaningful change. Within districts, opposition to change may arise within the community as well. The opinions of community members, like those of the staff, should be respectfully heard and addressed through transparent and inclusive information. In the beginning, resisters may see aspects of the plan that the leader does not; consequently, their views may strengthen the change initiative. The respect afforded them allows the dialogue to continue on a more positive basis (Fullan, 2001). Encouragingly, Fullan (2001) and Reeves (2009) agree that once positive results are noted, those who resisted begin to value the change.

Rather than seeing the schedule as an empty framework that exists on its own and has only a simplistic impact on the life of the school, today's educational leaders need to know the direct correlation that exists between the schedule and instruction. A well-developed schedule provides the right set of circumstances to apply Marzano's (2003) conviction that all students deserve the "opportunity to learn" and that teachers need time to deliver the intended curriculum (pp. 22, 24). Darling-Hammond (1995) echoes the premise that schedules and the organizations they serve need to be "structures for caring" rather than simply divisions of labor. When developed with the end of serving students in mind, the schedule can incorporate those opportunities for diverse populations as well.

USING THE SCHEDULE EFFECTIVELY ■

The schedule in itself, however, is not the proverbial silver bullet. In order to bring about increased student achievement, effective instruction that works within the schedule needs to occur. Whether the schedule includes short- or extended-time class periods, research-based best practices can be implemented. Incremental engagements throughout the class period incorporate not only the three Rs of recall, rehearsal, and reflection but also ample experiences of formative assessment. In Chapter 10, detailed steps for bell-to-bell instruction guide teachers through a research-based lesson plan.

When the schedule includes extended-time class periods, teachers have additional time to create a greater depth of understanding in their lesson. Students have more opportunities to practice recall, rehearsal, reflection, and formative assessment. Consequently, when the school schedule considers the delivery of instruction, all students benefit.

Provision of adequate time for professional dialogue within the schedule enables teachers to devote time to discuss data. The investigation of data directly affects the development and delivery of the curriculum and has a positive effect on student achievement.

Further, through the inclusion of extended-time periods and a period for an advisory, homeroom, or seminar experience, the schedule accommodates the personalization that enhances a student's sense of belonging and provides the supportive environment advocated by the authors of

Breaking Ranks II (National Association of Secondary School Principals [NASSP], 2004). Experiences that the authors encourage to incorporate personalization within the school include creating structures and practices so that all students are well known by at least one adult and establishing schedules and priorities so that students' abilities are known to and appreciated by teachers (NASSP, 2004, p. 68). Each of the identified practices has a definitive impact on schedule building. Therefore, when the schedule provides adequate time, the teacher is better able to open the lines of communication. Through that process, a better understanding of each student's needs emerges.

Curriculum integration is another aspect of instruction influenced by the schedule. When the schedule provides time for professional dialogue, teachers use their curriculum maps and team weekly plan guides to see the natural connections that may exist within their respective curricula. In middle school, not only teachers of core courses but also teachers of exploratory/encore courses can be scheduled so that they have common planning time. During that time, they are able to plan to integrate aspects of their curriculum. Integration can take the form of skills as well as content. For instance, if the small learning community (SLC) or team, grade level, or school chooses a skill of the week on which to focus, all subject areas can integrate that skill into their instruction. Through the schedule's provision of common planning time for teams, houses, or academies, it sets the stage for curriculum integration.

■ FLEXIBILITY

Flexibility emerges as another benefit of a well-planned school schedule. Some middle school, freshman academy, and career pathway schedules promote the concept of teachers flexing time and classes. Research indicates several areas in which flexing time benefits the learner. For instance, midway between waking and sleeping, people experience diminished energy levels (Sousa, 2001, p. 101). Additionally, the neurotransmitters that carry information to the brain are most active in the morning and tend to level off in the afternoon (Sousa, 2001; Sylwester, 1995). Consequently, if the schedule allows it, teachers can take advantage of students' increased alertness by altering the sequence of classes so that students may be seen in the morning or in the afternoon. Sousa (2001) explains, however, that this phenomenon runs about an hour later in the adolescent than in the preadolescent or adult (p. 101). Therefore, decisions about flexing schedules in high school need to consider this developmental characteristic.

When classes are so arranged, the sequence can be altered without disturbing the rest of the school. For instance, an entire team can meet at one time to hear a speaker without affecting the schedule of an individual student or the entire school. Flexibility also allows teachers to group and regroup students for enrichment, remediation, or interest.

Although flexibility is desirable in the schedule for an academy or career pathway program, the existence of these programs is more important even if flexibility must be sacrificed. Career pathways have changed from the time that schools simply wanted a program that would interest low-level learners and keep them in school. Today, these classes are filled with college-bound students as well. In 2005, 8% of high school students completed three or more Carnegie units in CTE (career and technical education) as well as a full program of college prep classes, including two years of a foreign language (Hoachlander, 2008, p. 22). In the new format, the originally targeted population gains equity in learning. The courses often are connected with academic courses. The involved teachers create an integrated curriculum to be studied. The positive aspect of integrated study and connection of teachers creates a scheduling challenge. The teachers involved need common plan time, and the students need to have those specific teachers in their class schedules.

Another impact on the scheduling committee includes the movement of students. Students enrolled in the advanced CTE courses often travel off campus to study, work, or observe in their chosen academy or career pathway. In this case, the schedule needs to free the students from the campus with an amount of time that will allow them to travel and be involved in the off-campus element of the program.

ROLE OF THE SCHEDULING COMMITTEE ■

Considering the above programs and concerns, scheduling committees have complex issues to weigh and balance when developing a new schedule. Not to be forgotten, the schedule impacts student-teacher interactions as well as the nature and depth of instruction. It also covertly indicates the values placed on various subjects according to their time allocation (Darling-Hammond, 1995).

In the beginning, the school or district mission/vision statement sets the stage for research on schedules. If the data accumulated by committee members do not coincide with the existing mission/vision statement, the statement should be rewritten prior to making final decisions about the schedule. Using the data collected and the mission/vision statement, the committee continues with the pursuit of scheduling frameworks. Where appropriate, the following questions should be considered:

- What size of team is beneficial for fifth- or sixth-grade students?
- Should rising ninth-grade students have a freshman academy experience?
- Is the school interested in implementing a career academy approach?
- Will a flex/advisory period be included?
- How would the design of an intervention period look?
- How will flexibility be achieved?
- What electives will be offered?
- How many full-time-equivalent (FTE) teachers are available?
- What guidelines exist for class size?
- How long is the school day?
- How many periods should be in the school day?
- What issues are involved in determining the length of a period?
- How will the schedule accommodate Tier 2 and Tier 3 interventions?
- What effect will remedial courses have on the elective/exploratory courses?

- Do programs such as response to intervention (RTI), English-language learning (ELL), Advanced Placement (AP), career pathways, or credit recovery need special consideration in developing the schedule?
- Will cohorts of teachers have a common plan period?

The scheduling committee can answer some of these questions. Additional questions may require the solicitation of opinions from others, including the community. As stated earlier, resisters can be won over if their ideas are respectfully heard and considered (Darling-Hammond, 1995, p. 538).

■ TEACHER CONTRACTS

At times, the teaching contract affects the detail of the schedule. Today's antiunion climate makes this element even more delicate from both sides of the equation. From the schedule builder's perspective, contract language needs to be clear and to fit the specific type of schedule being studied. Lunch is an example. If the schedule includes periods that are divisible by 40 or 45, lunch would be a 40- or 45-minute period. If, however, the contract language says teachers are to have one period for lunch and the scheduling committee is considering 80- to 90-minute periods, a conflict may arise. Typically, the lunch period in schedules that feature 80- to 90-minute instructional periods is approximately 30 minutes.

In another scenario, contracts often state the number of consecutive periods that a teacher may teach. If a teacher cannot teach more than 135 consecutive minutes, a schedule may not be able to include extended-time class periods. Some contracts indicate a specific number of classes a teacher may teach. Scheduling committees may discover that additional periods in a day are necessary to accommodate programs chosen for the school's population or to meet state-mandated requirements. Consequently, additional FTEs would have to be hired to make the schedule work.

Even the process of contract negotiations may impact the study or acceptance of a new schedule. When the schedule has been created, in some instances it is to be voted upon by either the teachers or the board of education or both. A few of the previously discussed dissenters can block the acceptance of a schedule seen as beneficial for the remainder of the school and its staff.

■ PROGRAMS FOR DIVERSE POPULATIONS

As discussed earlier in this chapter, a variety of mandated and chosen programs emerged to fill what seems to be a void in meeting student needs. These programs require the scheduling committee's close monitoring of how the programs mesh with the school's mission/vision statement and how the programs will correspond to the schedule frameworks under consideration.

The ramifications of the Individuals with Disabilities Education Act (IDEA) of 1975 have caused many schools to reevaluate how the needs of all students are met. RTI is one. Following the implementation of IDEA, districts discovered that the number of students with special needs in general as well as the number of minority students in special education increased. Minority students' representation in learning disability programs appeared in a higher percentage than general population representation (Brown-Chidsey, 2007, p. 40). Consequently, in 2004 Congress reauthorized IDEA by including the guidelines for the RTI component. This part of IDEA intends to develop early interventions and to avoid assigning students to special education classes when they are simply lacking the reading and writing skills to be at grade level. A new schedule explores opportunities to implement the three tiers of RTI classes with minimum disturbance to other student programs in place.

Districts struggle with finding time within the schedule to meet the needs of incoming students who read far below their grade level. When students are not on grade level at the secondary level, making the switch in reading from a learning-to-read to a reading-to-learn instruction model poses a challenge. Consequently, the existing schedule needs to be reconsidered. The principal as the instructional leader of the school is responsible for rethinking the master schedule.

Besides RTI considerations, accommodations to other special programs challenge the construction of a school's schedule: special education, gifted and talented, credit recovery, and small learning communities. To ensure effective implementation, these programs need to occur within a contractually determined time.

SUMMARIZING SCHEDULES: THE SPRINGBOARD TO ACTION

Because of the many mandates and needs of students, districts have recognized the need for change in the schedule and the scheduling process. Districts often find, however, that action and implementation do not follow the vision. Returning to the admonition by Reeves (2009) that actions can lead, the following chapters will identify and explain paths that can be taken to facilitate the change necessary and the actions that must accompany that change.

Special Programs for Educational Success

RTI, Special Education, and ELL

*A human being is not attaining his full
heights until he is educated.*

Horace Mann

As discussed in Chapter 1, today's schools exist in an era of multiple mandates as well as an increased understanding of how people learn. Consequently, schools and districts focus their attention on programs that meet the educational needs of their particular community of students. Largely, their decisions on what programs to include and the schedule that will accommodate those programs may be directed by the economic condition of the district and the teachers' contract language. Those decisions require the scheduling committee to seriously consider the chosen programs before a schedule can be developed.

Numerous programs to be considered meet the needs of students requiring specialized action plans: response to intervention (RTI) and credit recovery for struggling students; special education for academically challenged students; English-language learning (ELL) for language-challenged students; career and technical education (CTE) and work study for those in career academies or pathways; gifted and talented, including Advanced Placement (AP) for the high-achieving student; and International Baccalaureate (IB) for those schools seeking a more rigorous curricular offering.

Once the curricular programs are determined, logistical issues need to be considered. In some cases, this requires the schedule to accommodate student absences from the school campus to pursue programs like CTE. In other instances, students with physical limitations may need additional time to move within the school complex, necessitating the scheduler to place sequential classes in close proximity.

RESPONSE TO INTERVENTION ■

One of today's most far-reaching mandates that contribute to the need for change arises from the 2004 reauthorization of the Individuals with Disabilities Education Improvement Act: Response to Intervention (RTI). In 1975, Congress passed the Individuals with Disabilities Education Act (IDEA). Intended to address the needs of all students, IDEA seemed to cause a rise in the identified special education population with a disproportionate number of those students coming from minority groups (Brown-Chidsey, 2007, p. 40). Consequently, the reauthorization of IDEA in 2004 included RTI that introduced a different method for identifying students in need of interventions.

Previously, the IQ discrepancy model determined the need for interventions. If a large discrepancy was noted between the student's school performance and intellectual ability, the student was recommended for special intervention services. Often this identification did not occur until after the student was deeply mired in failure and may have led to a special education placement without intervention strategies applied first.

Although it was originally initiated to address special education and reading development issues, the more contemporary intent of RTI is on general education reform in which the needs of all students are continually assessed. The requisite for interventions is determined through a composite of factors that describe student progress: classroom observation through ongoing formative assessment, looking at student work, Measures of Academic Progress (MAP) and other comprehensive tests, and state tests. Therefore, the result of RTI is not primarily to reduce the number of special education students but to address need for support. As more RTI principles and interventions occur, the numbers in special education should decrease (National Association of State Directors of Special Education [NASDSE], 2008). Samuels (2011) indicates this decrease is true and has been occurring since 2005. Samuels cites Alexa E. Posny, assistant secretary overseeing the U.S. Department of Education's Office of Special Education and Rehabilitative Services, as indicating that RTI has not changed special education but rather has changed education itself and will continue doing so (Samuels, 2011).

The RTI premise encourages interventions at the earliest evidence of student struggles and failure. Brown-Chidsey (2007) compares the new method to that of medical prevention. Medical prevention includes three stages: Primary intervention seeks to stop a pernicious outcome from occurring; secondary intervention addresses the problem at first signs of symptoms; tertiary intervention takes action after the problem surfaces. Applied to education, this method emerges as the process and levels identified in RTI (Brown-Chidsey, 2007, p. 40).

To address the needs of all students, RTI uses a three-tier diagram (see Figure 2.1). Tier 1 includes 80%–90% of students; Tier 2 consists of 10%–15% of students to receive intervention in small groups; Tier 3 comprises the 1%–5% of the student body that requires intensive interventions perhaps on an individual basis (Howell, Patton, & Deiotte, 2008, p. 11; Protheroe, 2011, pp. 2–3).

Howell et al. (2008, p. 24) describe Tier 1 as the "lynchpin" for change. They contend that effective instruction and consistent behavior management need to be hallmarks of Tier 1 teaching. In their view, effective instruction addresses the needs of 80%–90% of students in the classroom. Without this occurring, Tiers 2 and 3 will be overwhelmed in numbers (Howell et al., 2008, p. 60). The minutes allotted for class periods influence the degree to which intensive and effective instruction can take place. When lessons are scaffolded and instruction is built on prior knowledge, students progress through a series of learning engagements that include formative assessment. Due to the time essential for deep processing, this lesson plan format is more likely to occur in an extended-time class period (see Chapter 10). Bransford, Brown, and Cocking (2000, p. 58) affirm that students need time to process information and that instruction cannot be rushed.

Figure 2.1   RTI Tiers and Population Percentages

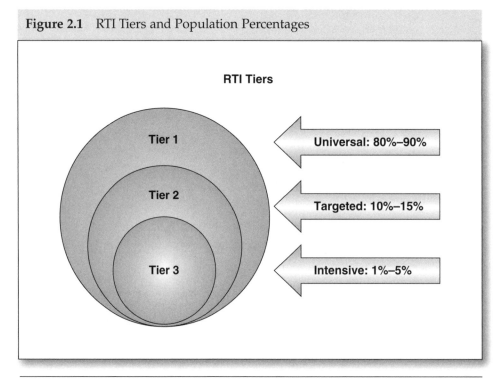

Source: Adapted from Howell et al., 2008.

One strategy that meets this prescription appears in Chapter 10: the lesson plan prototype. It describes the process for scaffolding instruction in incremental steps or engagements. When it is used effectively, students are continually and actively engaged, which often eliminates disruptive behaviors. The lesson plan also encourages depth of instruction to meet the needs of the 80%–90% of students who have met grade-level expectations.

Tier 1 interventions take many forms. Differentiation is one that aids the teacher to meet varied student needs in the classroom. One of the most beneficial teacher-focused strategies is looking at student work (LASW). When collaborative groups of teachers review samples of student work, evaluate the work with a rubric, and discuss their findings, they have a greater understanding of where student learning gaps may be. In other words, the connection between the intended curriculum, the delivered curriculum, and the learned curriculum becomes more apparent.

David Allen, a Harvard Project Zero researcher and one of the authors of *Looking Together at Student Work: A Companion Guide to Assessing Student Learning* (Blythe, Allen, & Powell, 1999, 2008), maintains that the process allows teachers to monitor their own teaching and to uncover reasons for students' levels of achievement in assignments. Allen emphasizes the importance of professional dialogue: "Time with colleagues spent in focused inquiry about teaching and learning is a necessity, not a luxury" (interviewed in *Education World*, 2000).

Consequently, to incorporate the components of an effective Tier 1, time for planning needs to be allocated. Allen recommends an hour or more a week for collaborating teams to meet on a regular basis (*Education World*, 2000). Finding the time to honor this step requires creativity by the school leadership. Some possibilities exist within the daily school schedule, after school, and in place of or included in faculty meetings, team/department plan time, or redirected professional development time.

The schedule in Table 2.1 shows how, in a Day 1/Day 2 schedule, an opportunity becomes apparent for teachers to meet with their interdisciplinary team and their departmental team. For example, by placing LASW on the agenda of both meeting formats, teachers gain a horizontal grasp of students' achievement in a particular subject area as well as in integrated/interdisciplinary subjects. Further, if the departmental meetings are able to cross grade levels, a vertical perspective of student work is revealed.

Table 2.1   Team and Department Meetings in a Secondary School Schedule

	Day 1				Day 2			
	1	2	3	4	5	6	7	8
English	TM/P	01	02	03	DM/P	04	05	06
Math	TM/P	01	02	03	04	DM/P	05	06
Science	TM/P	01	02	03	04	05	DM/P	06
Social Studies	TM/P	01	02	03	04	05	06	DM/P
Special Ed	TM/P							

From a student's perspective, Tier 2 instructional success depends on the frequency, intensity, and duration of instruction (Howell et al., 2008, p. 68). Although this process in the most effective format begins in first grade, students requiring this level of intervention are diagnosed in the middle grades as well. Howell et al. (2008, p. 8) assert that students who are two or more years behind their peers usually fail to catch up to their on-grade peers. Therefore, secondary interventions become essential.

In a regular school day, those students who have been identified as needing Tier 2 interventions are scheduled for additional instruction. NASDSE (2008, p. 34) recommends a core reading block of 90 minutes plus 30-minute daily supplements. Prior to actualizing a Tier 2 program, teachers discuss the instructional practices that were most and least effective. In that way, different strategies can be employed in the intervention to avoid a plateau experience for the targeted student's needs (Buffum, Mattos, & Webber, 2010, p. 15). As evidence of progress emerges, the time allotted for interventions diminishes. Once students have shown sufficient progress, they move into Tier 1 status. If no progress is noted, reevaluation takes place (Brown-Chidsey, 2007, p. 41).

While placement is determined through a sifting of multiple criteria such as MAP, standardized tests, past performance, and attendance, progress in the identified tiers appears most emphatically through examining student work by the intervention team. Intervention teams typically consist of literacy and mathematics specialists as well as special education teachers. This intervention team then works in conjunction with the student's interdisciplinary team. Therefore, a functioning schedule provides time for teacher collaboration and student assignments for interventions.

Besides allowing for sufficient time periods for the tiered interventions, the successful schedule accommodates fluidity so that students can move between the tiers as data indicate. Some Tier 2 interventions might take place in a well-differentiated core classroom. Other forms of teaching and learning take place in the flex period of a school schedule. The design of the flex period meets multiple needs: RTI, gifted and talented, band, special study, and intense interest classes. Two interdisciplinary schedules that include a flex period appear in Tables 2.2 and 2.3.

Table 2.2   Interdisciplinary Team With Flex Period: High School or Middle School

	1	2	3	4	5	6	7	8
English	H-01	01	02	03	04	Flex-Advisory	TM	Plan
Social Studies	01	H-01	02	03	04	Flex-Advisory	TM	Plan
Math	M8-01	M8-02	ALG I-01	M8-03	ALG I-02	Flex-Advisory	TM	Plan
Science	01	02	03	H-01	04	Flex-Advisory	TM	Plan
Spanish	I-01	I-02	II-01	I-03	II-02	Flex-Advisory	TM	Plan
Special Education	ICS	ICS	ICS	ICS	ICS	Flex-Advisory	TM	Plan

In Table 2.2, the same teachers have the same students for the same time periods. Therefore, they are free to flex the schedule further as needed. Periods 1–5 can be compressed to create a longer period of time for the flex period. Student needs and their RTI placement during the flex period are discussed at a team or small learning community (SLC) meeting. Sometimes the teachers on the team are assigned to provide the necessary intervention instruction. In that case, the student does not have to leave the team area, and the team can operate independently from the rest of the school. When students stay within their team for RTI, they can more easily move in and out of the subject matter intervention experiences offered without complicating their schedule. If it is necessary for students to leave the team area to meet with students from other teams for the intervention experience, the cohort schedules need to coincide. In this schedule, ICS refers to the in-class support given by the special education teacher.

Table 2.3 illustrates a flex period for a K–8 or Grades 6, 7, and 8 middle school structure. The teachers in Table 2.3 are licensed in two content areas. The intervention period occurs during the same period so that students may be grouped and regrouped for maximum fluidity. The special education teacher co-teaches (CT) with the regular education teacher.

Fluidity is important so that students are not locked into an intervention time when it is no longer needed. In Table 2.4, a middle school student is scheduled for one quarter of Tier 2 interventions outside of the core team

Table 2.3 Interdisciplinary Team With Flex Period: K–8 School

	1	2	3	4	5	6	7	8	9
ELA/SS	RLA 01	RLA 01	SS 01	TM	Flex/ Advisory	RLA 02	RLA 02	SS 02	Plan
Math/ Science	M 02	M 02	Sci 02	TM	Flex/ Advisory	M 01	M 01	Sci 01	Plan
Sp Ed CT	CT	CT	CT	TM	Flex/ Advisory	CT	CT	CT	Plan

Table 2.4 Middle School Student Schedule With Tier 2 Intervention Period

Period	Course
1	English
2	Social Studies
3	Math
4	Lunch
5	Science
6	Spanish
7	PE/Band
8	Q1: Tier 2 Interventions; Q2: Art; Q3: Tech; Q4: FCS

schedule. The remaining three quarters are scheduled for exploratory courses. If, however, the student needs an additional intervention, the exploratory course (art, technology, or family consumer science) gives way to the intervention. Team meetings are the key for managing student placement and progress within the three tiers.

Tier 3 interventions are the most intense. If all Tier 1 and Tier 2 interventions have been implemented and the student continues to struggle, a comprehensive reevaluation of the student's educational history takes place. The results may indicate that the student is a true candidate for special education services. But the results may also indicate that a different format or curriculum for interventions will serve the student better (Brown-Chidsey, 2007, p. 41; Howell et al., 2008, p. 68).

To meet student needs and promote student success in Tier 3, NASDSE (2008, p. 34) recommends 90 minutes of intervention-supportive instruction in addition to core instruction. At this level, the additional instruction is provided for an individual student or a small group of students. In a high school, a student's schedule could have a period designated for Tier 3 interventions.

The schedule in Table 2.5 does not include 90 minutes of intervention time but does allow the student to have one elective as well as a daily intervention period. Period 4 in Table 2.5 is designated in the school schedule as an intervention period and can accommodate more than one student. Care needs to be taken to keep the group at the recommended small instructional level. Depending on the student's progress, the student can be assigned to that period for a semester or a year.

Table 2.5   High School Student Schedule With Tier 3 Intervention Period

Period	Course
1	English 10
2	Social Studies 10
3	Geometry
4	Tier 3
5	Lunch
6	Spanish II
7	Biology
8	Art II

The elements in the above discussion of RTI directly require an operative schedule. Without a well-designed schedule, the identified levels of intervention cannot be provided effectively. A first step in building the schedule includes a close look at the mission/vision statement of the school/district. A positive correlation between the statement and RTI principles and beliefs should be apparent. Because of that correlation, the schedule ensures all supplemental and incidental instruction can be and is provided to all students in need of this form of instruction (NASDSE, 2008, p. 12).

Different scheduling frameworks are available to meet the requirements of the program format adopted by individual schools and districts. Besides the sample schedules included in this chapter, Chapters 4, 5, and 6 provide a wide variety of schedule frameworks from which to choose for RTI interventions.

SPECIAL EDUCATION ■

Since the reauthorization of IDEA in 2004, the form and format of special education instruction has assumed a dramatically different face. Rather than isolating or grouping special education students in a self-contained classroom, IDEA directs schools to place students in the least restrictive environment. Within that environment, the special education services provide supports so that students can be successful within the general curriculum whenever possible. This premise that all students can learn echoes the RTI goal of meeting the needs of all students.

Weber (2009, p. 729) affirms that IDEA is the backbone of special education law. Consequently, it is of importance for schedulers to know the seven basic concepts of IDEA that may impact building a schedule.

1. Zero exclusion: All children, regardless of conditions, are entitled to an education.

2. Free public education: Districts are obliged to adapt education to the needs of the child.

3. Related services: Any necessary services beyond ordinary classroom instruction are provided, including supports of materials, adaptations, or aides.

4. Least restrictive environment: Children with disabilities are to receive the same educational opportunities as children without disabilities.

5. Free education: No charges for services are to be given to parents of the child receiving them.

6. Parental rights: Parents are to be involved in the decisions about the services their child is to receive.

7. Individualized Education Plan (IEP): This document lays out the goals for the child and the specific educational and related services that will be provided.

Eligibility for special services has become a focus for discussion. Concerns include the administration of IQ tests and the discrepancy model. Both have been held responsible for the disproportionate number of minority students in special education. Intending to eliminate any cultural biases, the more scientific and research-based process promoted by RTI addresses individual students' levels of success with a variety of testing instruments. In fact, some researchers maintain that some previously identified students had simply been deprived of adequate classroom instruction (Harry & Klingner, 2006, cited in Harry & Klingner, 2007; Weber, 2009, p. 730).

According to the provisions in IDEA, the first placement to be considered for any child is the regular classroom. For the special education student, that placement is often an inclusion placement. The Association for Supervision and Curriculum Development (ASCD, 2011) *Lexicon of Learning* defines inclusion as the practice of educating all children in the same classroom, including children with physical, mental, and developmental disabilities. An aide or special assistant is frequently assigned to the classroom or a specific child. If the school is fully inclusive, all children follow the same schedules, including field trips, extracurricular activities, and assemblies (ASCD, 2011). When schools have procedures in place to meet the needs of their heterogeneously grouped students, inclusion merges seamlessly into place. Villa and Thousand (2003, p. 20) suggest some of the best practices that well serve inclusive classrooms: transdisciplinary teaming, block scheduling, multi-age grouping, looping, positive behavior support and discipline approaches, de-tracking, and school-within-a-school family configurations of students and teachers. Each of their suggestions requires scheduling considerations.

The different needs of students require different teaching models. If students are assigned aides or paraprofessionals, those persons should be perceived as a part of the team rather than attached only to a particular student. Citing the National Center on Educational Restructuring and Inclusion (1995), Villa and Thousand (2003, p. 22) name five models:

- Consultation: Support personnel who care for a particular student's needs allow the general educator to teach all students in the class.
- Parallel teaching: Support personnel such as special education teachers, psychologists, or speech therapists circulate the classroom with the general education teacher to meet different heterogeneous sections of the class.
- Supportive teaching: The general education teacher leads the instruction, while support personnel rotate among the students.
- Complementary teaching: The support person performs tasks within the classroom that complement the instruction (e.g., note taking on a whiteboard).
- Co-teaching: Support personnel co-teach with the general education teacher. See Tables 2.6, 2.7, and 2.8.

Schedules are created to accommodate these models as well as the logistics they present. The National Education Association (NEA) recommends a capacity mark of 28 students per inclusion class and that no more than 25% of the students in the class need special education or accommodation for a learning disability (Hines, 2001). If schools use co-teachers as defined by Villa and Thousand (2003), following this recommendation would require the hiring of additional faculty. The use of co-teachers does, however, meet the requirements of No Child Left Behind (NCLB) and IDEA as long as both teachers are highly qualified in their respective areas. Little and Dieker (2009) present case studies of co-teaching in a Kansas City, Missouri, middle school and a Milwaukee, Wisconsin, high school. In both schools, using a co-teaching model, student achievement increased significantly. The authors maintain that the success of these schools arose from the schools' diligence in providing "planning, continued

Table 2.6 Two Regular Education Teachers, One Special Education Co-Teacher

	1	2	3	4	5	6	7	8	9
English/ Social Studies	TM	Reading 01	*LA 01	*SS 01	Lunch	Plan	Flex	LA 02	SS 02
Math/ Science	TM	* Reading 02	Math 02	Sci 02	Lunch	Plan	Flex	*Math 01	*Sci 01
Special Education Co-taught	TM	*Co-taught	*Co-taught	*Co-taught	Lunch	Plan	Flex	*Co-taught	*Co-taught

skill development, instruction that is tailored to students' learning and behavioral needs, resource support (including planning time), and continual progress monitoring" (Little & Dieker, 2009, p. 46).

In Table 2.6, the asterisk implies a co-taught class. All teachers teach reading; the special education teacher co-teaches reading with the math/ science teacher. In Periods 3 and 4, the special education teacher co-teaches with the English/social studies teacher. In Periods 8 and 9, the special education teacher co-teaches with the math/science teacher. During the team meeting, teachers coordinate the RTI program plus the details of the co-teaching process. All students are in exploratory or encore classes in Periods 1 and 6.

Table 2.7 has two special education teachers operating on a continuum basis: One is completely responsible for co-taught classes; the other is responsible for replacement classes as well as some co-taught classes. The replacement classes in the resource room meet the needs of the students whose IEPs require specialized small group instruction beyond the general classroom. To fully implement the planning and decision making for

Table 2.7 Four Regular Education Teachers, Two Special Education Co-Teachers

	1	2	3	4	5	6	7	8
English	*Read	*01	*02	03	04	Flex/ Advisory	TM	Plan
Social Studies	Read	01	*02	03	04	Flex/ Advisory	TM	Plan
Math	Read	Alg 01	Math 01	*Math 02	*Math 02	Flex/ Advisory	TM	Plan
Science	Read	01	02	03	*04	Flex/ Advisory	TM	Plan
Sp. Ed. Co-taught	*CT Read	*CT Eng.	*CT Eng.	*CT Math	*CT Math	Flex/ Advisory	TM	Plan
Sp. Ed. Replacement	Read Replace	Eng. Replace	*CT SS	Math Replace	*CT Sci	Resource Room	TM	Plan

Tiers 1 and 2, special education co-teaching, and resource room referrals, team plan time is essential. In this schedule, lunch is a module of time rather than a full period.

High schools as well as middle schools benefit from schedules that focus on the needs of their special education population. Table 2.8 illustrates how a freshman academy merges two teams to form one educational family. By combining the teams, cross-teaming can occur without losing the necessary opportunities for personalization within the team. This limited cross-teaming model provides balance by staying within the 25% special education representation within the classes. The fluidity of the schedule accommodates the needs of the student in special education, regular education, and honors or gifted education. Whenever a student with an IEP has an individualized schedule based on details within the IEP, the schedule provides opportunities for advanced students to take honors English and science.

Table 2.8   Freshman Academy With Special Education Co-Taught and Replacement

		1	2	3	4	5	6	7	8
9A	English	H-01	*01	02	TM	Plan	Flex	03	04
	SS	* 01	02	03	TM	Plan	Flex	*04	05
	Math	Alg. 01	Geo. 01	*Alg. 02	TM	Plan	Flex	Geo. 02	*Alg. 03
	Science	* 01	02	H-01	TM	Plan	Flex	*03	04
	Spanish	I-01	I-02	II-01	TM	Plan	Flex	I-03	II-02
	Sp. Ed. CT	CT SS	CT Eng.	CT Alg.	TM	Plan	Flex	CT SS	CT Alg.
	Sp. Ed. CT/ Replace.	CT Sci.	Repl. Eng.	Repl. Math	TM	Resource Room	Flex	CT Sci.	Plan
9B	English	H -02	05 X	06	TM	Plan	Flex	07	08
	SS	06	07	08	TM	Plan	Flex	09	10
	Math	Alg. 04	Geo. 03	Alg. O5 X	TM	Plan	Flex	Alg. 06	Geo. 04
	Science	05	06	H-02	TM	Plan	Flex	07	08
	Spanish	II-03	I-04	I-05	TM	Plan	Flex	II-04	I-06

A continuum of instruction appears during the same period in three forms: a replacement section, a co-taught section, and a regular education section with no support services. During Periods 4 and 5, a sufficient number of electives and other required courses must be available for students in both freshman academy teams, 9A and 9B. Foreign language students can take Spanish I or II. Period 6 allows multiple frameworks for Tiers 2 and 3 as well as use of the resource room. If a student is not taking Spanish, the resource room can be used in Period 5.

Periods 2 and 3 on Team 9B are designated (X) as regular sections of English and algebra in which students receiving special education may be enrolled if they do not require support in those subjects. Creating a schedule with these various frameworks contributes to the fluidity necessary to meet the multiple needs of diverse populations.

In order to monitor the number of students receiving special education co-taught in regular education classrooms, a separate course number is assigned. Table 2.9 illustrates how two different course numbers can be assigned to the same class so that the 25% recommendation is met.

Table 2.9   Computer Encoding of Co-Taught Classes

Period 3	Mrs. Smith	Capacity—25 seats
Course 3417	Section-01	18 seats—regular education
Course 3419	Section-01	7 seats—special education inclusion

Some classes will not require separate special education course numbers to provide the least restrictive environment. In middle school, those classes could be physical education, art, choir, band, and family and consumer science. At the high school level, physical education, art, band, choir, agricultural electives, or career pathway courses may be openly scheduled so that students who need special education have opportunities similar to those for students on the regular education track.

As indicated in the discussion of RTI, today's approach to meeting the needs of all students requires meticulous planning of the schedule. Directed by the mission/vision statement, the construction of the schedule should have a positive impact on student achievement as well as provide fluid placement of classes. In Chapter 9, a conflict matrix technique guides the de-tracking process so that student placement is least restrictive and spread over the greatest number of sections of a course.

ENGLISH-LANGUAGE LEARNER PROGRAMS   ■

IDEA addresses the needs of another population: the English-language learner (ELL). Like students receiving RTI and special education, ELL students are a heterogeneous group whose English language deficiencies arise from many factors: They may be children of new immigrants; long-term English learners who have been in American schools since kindergarten but who have not received adequate English-language instruction; students whose education is interrupted as families follow agricultural work; transnational students who return to their native countries for a period of time and then return to the United States; students who have been moved into general education classes but are not proficient in the four domains of language (reading, writing, speaking, and listening); and refugee children. Even the new immigrants have subgroups: Some students who have strong academic backgrounds need to learn academic English rather than core concepts; others have had interrupted education in their native countries or inadequate educational experiences (Calderon, Slavin, & Sanchez, 2011, pp. 104–106).

ELL students represent 11% of the students in the K–12 population. Of these, 80% are Spanish speakers (Plank, 2011, p. 20). This group of students represents the fastest-growing student population today (see Batalova & McHugh, 2010; Plank, 2011, p. 20).

Although many states have established forms of English language acquisition in their school systems, many more are experiencing an influx for which they are unprepared. The literature identifies conflicting theories and reveals inconsistent identification and instruction of ELL students. Depending on the geographic area and school district formulating the intervention programs, even the title by which these students are identified changes. Some of the alphabet soup in which the programs are mired include ELL, EL, LEP, ESL, ELD, and ESOL. The variety of titles alone can muddy the communication between the ELL specialist and the rest of the school or district personnel.

Rossell (2004–2005, p. 32) identifies six different approaches to meet the needs of the ELL students:

- Structured immersion, or sheltered English immersion, a self-contained classroom of ELL students in which nearly all instruction is given in English (The terms *structured* and *sheltered* are often interchanged in the literature.)
- ESL pullout programs supplementing mainstream classroom instruction with a focus on developing English skills within a small group
- Mainstream instructon with no supports, referred to by Rossell as sink or swim
- Transitional bilingual education that begins instruction and literacy in the student's native language but emphasizes the development of English language skills
- Two-way bilingual or two-way immersion delivered to a class of native English speakers and non-English speakers, using two languages
- Bilingual maintenance programs that place equal emphasis on developing English proficiency and maintaining students' primary language

Rossell (2004–2005) indicates that she has listed the programs in hierarchal order from what she believes to be the most effective to the least effective. She indicates, however, that determining the effectiveness of any of the implemented programs is difficult if not impossible. Statistical records do not specifically describe the variations of each program in their academic achievement reports. Some of the programs have elements of several formats, depending on the class makeup and the existence of differing approaches to ELL in the same school (Rossell, 2004–2005, p. 34).

Districts need to identify the programs that best meet the needs of their populations. Recently, however, voters in five states were presented with initiatives on the education of ELL students: California, Arizona, Massachusetts, Oregon, and Colorado. In California, Arizona, and Massachusetts, the intiative became law. That law states that ELL students will be taught in structured (also referred to as sheltered) English immersion classes. In these classes, all instruction is completed in English. After one year, students are placed in mainstream and sheltered classes with support and timelines to improve proficiency. Proponents of this format maintain that students learn English more quickly when immersed in it alone.

Clark (2009) rejects the double labeling of the *structured* program, which is often referred to as *sheltered*. He attributes the term *structured English immersion* (SEI) to Keith Baker and Adriana de Kanter (1983) who first described the intense immersion of students into learning the English language (Clark, 2009, p. 43). When members of the Arizona English Language Learners Task Force began developing their program and curriculum, they discovered that many educators did not share a similar definition of SEI. Some believed it to be submersion, the sink-or-swim process described by Rossell; others thought it to be the same as sheltered or specially designed academic instruction in English, or SDAIE. Sheltered instruction uses various strategies to help students of intermediate or higher language proficiency to access grade-level material (Clark, 2009, p. 44). Much of today's literature uses the terms *sheltered* and *structured* interchangeably, leading to misunderstandings through lack of a common reference.

Table 2.10 illustrates a high school student's schedule in which the student is placed in some structured classes and a heterogenous physical education class. By meeting prerequisites, the student is placed in non-structured Spanish II and Art II.

Table 2.10   High School Structured ELL Instruction With Electives

Period	Class
1	Structured English
2	Structured Social Studies
3	Structured Algebra I
4	Structured Science
5	Lunch
6	Physical Education
7	Spanish II
8	Art II

Clark (2009) makes a case for this emerging form of instruction, implying that teachers can maximize instruction if delivered in English and adapted to the level appropriate for the students. To highlight the program's efficacy, he presents the ideal framework for SEI:

1. A significant amount of the school day is dedicated to teaching English language. Students are grouped by level of proficiency. In Arizona, students receive English instruction 4 hours daily; in Massachusetts, the minimum is 2 hours, 30 minutes.

2. Learning the English language is the focus of instruction. While the academic content supports the instruction, it is subordinate to the learning of language.

3. Teachers are to speak, read, and write in English only.

4. English is taught as a foreign language.

5. Discrete grammar skills are focal points with 25% of the teaching time devoted to learning verbs and tenses.

6. Rigorous timelines exist for exiting the program (Clark, 2009, pp. 44–45).

In some cases, a student may be placed in an intense reading and language arts program for as many as three periods per day with no electives other than physical education (see Table 2.11).

Table 2.11   High School Structured ELL Instruction With PE Elective

Period	Class
1	Intense Structured Reading and Language Arts
2	
3	
4	Lunch
5	Structured Algebra I
6	Structured Biology
7	Structured Social Studies
8	Physical Education and Health

Schools that have implemented SEI as originally defined report improved levels of student achievement.

Opponents of SEI suggest that while students may learn English as their second language, the content that they are to learn at their grade level has been "watered down" (Thomas & Collier, 2003, p. 62). Advocating a bilingual approach, Thomas and Collier (2003) contend that bilingual programs honor the student's culture and native language while providing the student with the tools for second-language proficiency. Through the use of both languages, students receive enriched content instruction with support in their first language while learning another (Thomas & Collier, 2003, p. 63). The authors present two forms of bilingual instruction: one- and two-way.

One-way instruction encompasses bilingual immersion in which instruction occurs in two languages for speakers of one language. In Canada, using both French and English, teachers instruct only English speakers (Thomas & Collier, 2003, p. 61). Two-way instruction occurs in a class composed of ELL students and native English speakers and is taught in both languages. Its purpose is to "provide cognitive stimulus of schooling two languages" and present a rich mainstream curriculum for both

(Thomas & Collier, 2003, p. 61). Thomas and Collier (2003, pp. 62–63) suggest recommendations for effective delivery of bilingual instruction that will promote student achievement:

1. A minimum of six years of instruction must occur before the student achieves parity with the average native speaker.

2. Instruction must focus on the core curriculum.

3. High-quality language arts instruction occurs in both languages and is taught in thematic units.

4. A separation exists between the two languages during instruction, and no translation or repetition is provided in the other language.

5. Non-English instruction occurs 50% of the time for most levels except for 90% of the time in early grades.

Table 2.12   High School Dual-Immersion Student Schedule

Period	Class
1	Social Studies
2	English 10
3	Physical Education
4	Algebra I
5	Lunch
6	Spanish II
7	Biology
8	Chorus

In the bilingual student schedule, all core classes are to be taught in two languages (see Table 2.12). The physical education and chorus classes are in English. The division of the language instruction may be applied in three different ways:

1. Time: Instruction in each language can occur during half-day, alternate-day, or alternate-week intervals.

2. Content: The subject matter determines which language will be used (e.g., Spanish for math, science, and social studies; English for literacy).

3. Staff: Two teachers co-teach with one being fluent in the majority language and the other in the minority language. Class work is done in the language spoken by the teacher instructing (Hadi-Tabassum, 2004–2005, p. 51).

Besides the three models specifically presented, a hybrid model is suggested: the cluster model. This model combines aspects of SEI and bilingual. Content teachers are trained in the theories of second-language acquisition and the methods to teach the English language. The class contains 25%–33% ELL students; the remainder are native English speakers. Content mastery and skills are taught in English while aides may explain the instruction in the student's native language. Students may use their native language to clarify any part of instruction (Rance-Roney, 2009, p. 35). Calderon and colleagues (2011, p. 107) conclude that the ultimate determination of a successful program is the quality of the instruction that occurs within it.

Placement of ELL students is subject to the part of IDEA referred to as the exclusionary clause. Prior to the student's placement, schools need to determine if the student has had sufficient opportunity to learn, including instruction in a language that the student understands. If the exclusionary clause applies, additional testing must take place with a realization that the test results may be influenced by levels of language proficiency (Klingner & Artiles, 2003, p. 68). For instance, a student who has a solid academic background in his own language may not have sufficient language proficiency to be able to test at his academic ability level. This student needs a program or schedule different from that assigned to the student who has little academic background (Rance-Roney, 2009, p. 37).

Plank (2011) reaffirms the concern about how students' language difficulties skew testing and assessment of academic program effectiveness. Without language proficiency, students are unable to demonstrate their academic ability when tested. Often their scores are unfairly depressed, causing misplacement within the program and the use of incorrect instructional content and strategies. Plank (2011, p. 21) further suggests that the testing results that determine Adequate Yearly Progress (AYP) are misconstrued.

ELL programs are often fluid with students moving in and out as they enter the school or gain language proficiency. Therefore, the students with higher proficiency may no longer be in the program when the testing takes place, allowing the scores of the students with lower proficiency to determine the basis of the testing scores. The NCLB report focuses on the program but not the individual students, so the program appears to lack progress. Unfortunately, no long-term study of students is employed to determine the true success of the program in the form of graduation rates, college access, or other forms of success data (Plank, 2011, p. 21).

When the challenges for scheduling RTI and special education are mixed with those of ELL, the scheduling committee needs to seek frameworks that best accommodate all stakeholders. As with students in special education, appropriate testing practices identify student needs, which eventually translate into detail of the student's schedule. The student schedule in Table 2.13 places the student in structured ELL classes in the morning and provides an opportunity for a resource room experience and mainstreamed math and science in the afternoon.

Where possible, district and school leaders should consider the prevailing culture of the community and have the freedom to choose the program that best fits: SEI, bilingual, or some other format (Mora, 2009, p. 19). They need to avoid the "implementation gap" described by Garcia, Jensen, and Scribner (2009, p. 12). That gap persists in areas where a mismatch exists between what is done and what works. Whatever program is chosen, the curriculum should be viable with a detailed developmental sequence for learning the English language in social and academic

Table 2.13   Middle School Structured ELL With Special Education Resource Room

Period	Class
1	Structured English and Social Studies
2	
3	
4	Physical Education
5	Lunch
6	Resource Room
7	Math 8
8	Science 8

contexts. Further, allocating time is essential: Students must have adequate time in which to learn the language, and teachers or cross-curricular team members need to have adequate time for planning and discussing student progress (Rance-Roney, 2009, p. 35).

SUMMARIZING SPECIAL PROGRAMS FOR EDUCATIONAL SUCCESS: THE IDEA EFFECT

The Individuals with Disabilities Education Improvement Act of 2004 impacts the educational programs of students who require interventions, generally referred to as RTI; special education services as modified instruction to meet students at their learning level; and ELL students who need some level of instruction in the English language. In order to meet these demands, the scheduling committee must create a schedule that is as inclusive as possible, looking at each student as an individual who contributes to the whole of the school culture. The master school schedule should enable the student to be placed in the variety of experiences required by that student. Some students may require a combination of services (e.g., RTI and ELL or special education and ELL). Therefore, an effective schedule demands to be flexible and fluid. The schedule should be sensitive to the students who are able to move from one tier of RTI to another, to the students who move through the levels of English proficiency at varying rates, and to the students who move from special education to fully inclusive or mainstreamed classes.

Challenges exist for the success of contemporary educational experiences. In an unsettled social and economic climate, the educational family has been given the mission to educate and socialize today's youth for success in the present and for the future. In order to fulfill that mandate, schools need to take to heart the words of Horace Mann and nourish their educational programs so that each student is educated and attains full height as a human being.

3

Special Programs for Educational Success

Credit Recovery, Career and Technical Education, Gifted and Talented, Advanced Placement, and International Baccalaureate

Destiny is not a matter of chance, but of choice.
Not something to wish for, but to attain.

William Jennings Bryan

While IDEA (Individuals with Disabilities Education Improvement Act) addresses the special needs of students who require interventions in order to support their education, schools are also responsible for providing programs for students who have other needs: credit recovery, career and technical education (CTE), and gifted and talented. Each of these programs undertakes a different mission: Credit recovery allows students the opportunity to recapture credit for a class that was failed; CTE brings the world of work into the school, allowing a student to learn the fundamentals of specific careers; gifted and talented programs meet the needs of the advanced student in various ways within the school schedule such as Advanced Placement (AP) programs that furnish additional rigor within the classroom so that students may test out of particular collegiate classes, and International Baccalaureate (IB) programs that present a comprehensive rigorous program beyond a school's traditional curriculum.

CREDIT RECOVERY   ■

Since school dropouts have become an increasing issue in the United States, more attention has focused on credit recovery. The dropout statistics alarm the nation. Each day 7,000 students drop out of high school. The 50 largest cities in the United States have a 53% graduation rate. Only 70% of high school students in the United States graduate with a diploma; for African American and Hispanic students, the rate is 50% (Dessoff, 2009; Butrymowicz, 2010). To quantify these issues, districts need consistent reliable data. Today's methods of acquiring data do not supply reliable figures that arise from similar collection methods. Consequently, to provide an even playing field for quantifying data, the guidelines of No Child Left Behind (NCLB) in part address the way dropout statistics are calculated. By 2012, all schools and districts are advised to use a common formula to calculate the dropout rate.

These dropout statistics not only create concern over the state of our educational system but also place stress on our economic system: Students without adequate education have difficulty finding jobs. Without jobs, these dropout students are unable to assume productive roles in their communities. According to Cecilia Rouse (2005), professor of economics and public affairs at Princeton University who is cited in the Alliance for Excellent Education (2007) *Issue Brief*, each dropout over a lifetime costs the nation approximately $260,000. Looked at differently, if the students who dropped out of school in 2007 had graduated, they would have contributed $329 billion in income to the nation's economy (Editorial Projects in Education, 2007).

Beyond the economic costs of the nation's low graduation rates, other factors influence a district's desire to provide a program for credit recovery: Higher school attendance brings higher reimbursement for schools, principals' evaluations and salaries often contain an appraisal of student achievement, and states are beginning to raise their graduation requirements (Butrymowicz, 2010). In support of credit recovery as a program to meet the above factors, Joel I. Klein, former schools chancellor for New York City, supports the concept of credit recovery as "a legitimate and important strategy for working with high school students" (Gootman & Coutts, 2008).

Originally, credit recovery most often took place during summer school. At this time, while credit recovery may occur in the summer, more focus has been placed on its format and offerings during the school year. Basically, three different formats exist: online, using a variety of software programs from commercial vendors; face-to-face, having direct instruction by a certified teacher; and a blended combination of both forms.

Online programs seem most prevalent. The National Dropout Prevention Center at Clemson University reports that nearly one third of the states have developed or endorsed online programs (Gootman & Coutts, 2008). Florida and Georgia have established state-funded virtual schools. As is the case with other credit recovery programs, however, few guidelines exist, and consistency among districts does not occur. In Florida, a student works independently and is expected to complete the online work within the same time frame as a regular semester—18 weeks. If the student needs more time, an extension of 9 weeks is allowed. The program focuses on interactive work, has little text, and requires the completion of many assignments (Dessoff, 2009).

Omaha Public Schools allows students to choose a time frame for their online experiences in credit recovery: during school time in their own school or another school or after school. Rather than a particular program, the district creates its own credit recovery experience with available free material. Teacher facilitators are present for help during the 18-week sessions that are scheduled in a computer lab once a week for three hours (Dessoff, 2009).

Even the face-to-face format often contains an online component. In Jackson, Michigan, the credit recovery program operates in an alternative school setting. To complete this program, the student meets high expectations in behavior as well as in academic achievement. Attendance is rigorous; hours are long—3:30 p.m. to 8:00 p.m. During the first half, students receive face-to-face instruction. The second half takes them into the computer lab to work with the Michigan Virtual School program. Regular classroom teachers as well as a special education teacher and behavior coordinator are also present in the lab to assist students (Dessoff, 2009).

In New York City, a credit recovery experience may be a five-day crash session over a school break, an interactive computer program format that has online tests as well, or an independent study that includes varied quality study packets (Gootman & Coutts, 2008). While these formats have come under scrutiny and criticism, some argue that seat time is not the objective for credit recovery; mastery of the subject matter is. Gootman and Coutts (2008) cite Joel I. Klein's defense of New York City's approach to improving student achievement and credit standings: "We do students no favors by giving them credit they haven't earned." New York students must still pass the Regents Exams in order to graduate.

Little true data exist to show the effectiveness of one format over another or how widely and completely implemented each is. Tension exists between the need to improve the abysmal graduation rates and the push for rigorous and high academic standards. Teachers argue that credit recovery students are not learning the same content in the same depth as students with a regular classroom experience. Joanne Jacobs, an educational blogger and author of *Our School: The Inspiring Story of Two Teachers, One Big Idea, and the School That Beat the Odds,* suggests that the way credit recovery exists today is ineffective: "I see potential for a game of let's pretend. Students pretend they've learned, online providers pretend they've taught, and schools pretend all their graduates have a high school education" (Butrymowicz, 2010).

With a focus on credit recovery as a formal class within the schedule, credit recovery can gain some consistency and legitimacy. If the schedule offers flexibility, a student seeking credit recovery can complete the failed course and the on-track course in the same year. In order for this process to be beneficial, the teacher must be experienced in using extended time effectively as well as in teaching a standards-based curriculum. Table 3.1 shows how a schedule can accommodate this form of credit recovery.

Table 3.1   Credit Recovery: Student Schedule for Two Courses in Same Year

Period	Course
1	CR English 9 and English 10
2	
3	World History
4	Lunch
5	CR Algebra I and Geometry
6	
7	Biology
8	Biology Lab/Physical Education
9	Spanish I

In the combined English and math credit recovery shown in Table 3.1, students have the benefit of having the same teacher for both classes, English 9 and English 10 or Algebra I and Geometry. When a student experiences the danger of not graduating, having the same teacher for both courses increases the personalization factor between the student and the teacher and establishes a positive level of confidence. The teacher knows the scope and sequence of the course and can move the student through the material at the student's own pace. By passing both courses, the student's likelihood of graduating on time improves. If the student has failed both English 9 and Algebra I, however, it is not feasible for the student to take both English 9 and English 10 or Algebra I and Geometry classes at the same time. The student should successfully complete the work for English 9 or Algebra I before moving to the next level.

From the beginning of school until December 1, the student is enrolled in the two courses failed in Grade 9: English 9 and Algebra I. Assuming that the student passes the courses, the student takes English 10 and Geometry from December 1 until the end of the school year. Depending on the credits earned during the first two years of high school, the student could achieve junior status by the end of the school year. By using this format, students experience the curriculum as intended to be delivered, the teacher is able to focus on the standards failed by the student, and consistency as well as continuity of instruction occurs.

Although not specifically for students with special needs, credit recovery courses can provide support based on a student's Individualized Education Plan (IEP). In Table 3.2, a special education teacher and a regular education teacher co-teach credit recovery courses.

Table 3.2   Credit Recovery: Student Schedule That Includes Co-Taught English 9 and Algebra I

Period	Course
1	CR English 9 and English 10
2	(Co-taught)
3	World History
4	Lunch
5	CR Algebra I and Geometry
6	(Co-taught)
7	Biology
8	Biology Lab/Physical Education
9	Spanish I

Some districts have established a trimester schedule in which a student may be assigned immediately to a credit recovery course in the following trimester. A trimester is 12 weeks long and generally has classes of 70-minute duration. A student has the opportunity to earn 7.5 credits each year. In a traditional schedule, one full year of study is completed in two trimesters. In a Semester 1–Semester 2 schedule, one semester of study is also completed in two trimesters. Therefore, each course of that duration will have an A and B course entry (e.g., Geometry A and Geometry B). The Table 3.3 student schedule shows the student taking two credit recovery courses in the first trimester. Those courses were courses failed in the previous year. If successful, the student follows through the rest of the year with on-track classes. If not successful, adjustments are made in the following trimester.

Additional support for struggling students appears in the form of a small learning community and the incorporation of a flex/advisory period in the schedule. Teachers of noncredit recovery courses and special education should be included in the small learning community (SLC). Table 3.4 illustrates a schedule in which one English teacher and one math teacher form a combination team within the trimester model. Special education teachers are available for co-taught classes to address IEP and response-to-intervention (RTI) needs.

The schedule in Table 3.4 centers on students who need additional support to be successful in school or have failed either English 9, Algebra I, or both as ninth-grade students. For this reason, English and math become the focal point for instruction. This team serves students who need extra support: students who need credit recovery, students who may have

Table 3.3   Credit Recovery: Trimester Student Schedule

Trimester	Period	Class
1	1	CR English 9 B
	2	CR Algebra I B
	3	Biology A
	4	Spanish II A
	5	Social Studies 10 A
2	6	English 10 A
	7	Geometry A
	8	Biology B
	9	Art II A
	10	Physical Education 10 A
3	11	English 10 B
	12	Geometry B
	13	Spanish II B
	14	Social Studies 10 B
	15	Art II B

passed English 9 or Algebra I but have been identified as needing three trimesters to complete the English 10 or Geometry work, and students with special needs whose IEPs fit this model and who need this support. Flex/advisory is a significant aspect of this schedule. It not only provides time for mentoring support for these students, but it can accommodate the scheduling of Tier 2 and Tier 3 interventions as well.

If the intent is to have the student graduate on time, the instructional program needs to be altered to accommodate the completion of required core classes. For example, if the student needs both English 11 and English 12 in the same year in order to fulfill graduation requirements, the schedule facilitates that adjustment. Table 3.5 shows a traditional schedule in which a double period for English 11 is scheduled for Semester 1 and a double period for English 12 is scheduled for Semester 2. The key is to avoid having the student take two English classes concurrently. To meet the needs of the student in these cases, the curriculum may need to be adjusted by eliminating those units or topics that are not essential learning; appropriate lengths of time for reading and comprehension are necessary and should be considered when revising the curriculum; and teachers must be able to teach effectively within the extended time (see Chapter 10).

Table 3.4   Credit Recovery: Teachers' Schedule for Trimester Combination Team

Trimester	Period	English	Special Education Co-taught	Math	Special Education Co-taught
1	1	CR 9A	CT	Geometry A	CT
	2	CR 9B	CT	CR Algebra IA	CT
	3	English 10A	CT	CR Algebra IB	CT
	4	Plan	Plan	Plan	Plan
	5	Flex/Advisory	Flex/Advisory	Flex/Advisory	Flex/Advisory
2	6	English 9B	CT	Geometry B	CT
	7	English 10A	CT	Geometry A	CT
	8	English 10B	CT	Geometry A	CT
	9	Plan	Plan	Plan	Plan
	10	Flex/Advisory	Flex/Advisory	Flex/Advisory	Flex/Advisory
3	11	English 9A	CT	Geometry C	CT
	12	English 10B	CT	Geometry B	CT
	13	English 10C	CT	Geometry B	CT
	14	Plan	Plan	Plan	Plan
	15	Flex/Advisory	Flex/Advisory	Flex/Advisory	Flex/Advisory

Table 3.5   Credit Recovery in a Traditional Grade 12 Student Schedule

Period	Course
1	English 11 (Sem. 1)
2	English 12 (Sem. 2)
3	Pre-calculus
4	Lunch
5	Spanish III
6	Government/Economics
7	Chemistry
8	Health/PE
9	Band

While the student dropout rate is real and frightening, schools and districts must not lose sight of their mission/vision statements in striving to meet this challenge. Statements related to credit recovery should be included in the mission/vision statement. Additionally, districts struggle to solve their dropout problems economically as well as educationally. If a common philosophy about the purpose of credit recovery and the means to attain it existed across the nation, that philosophy would be beneficial in solving the problem. The reality is that none exists.

Some reasoning about the value of credit recovery, however, does exist. If the purpose is to meet the needs of the whole student, serious consideration must be given to incorporating credit recovery classes into the schedule. Students benefit most when they are able to immediately repeat a failed class. In this way, the student faces the real consequences of having failed but remains able to graduate on time. Most important, the intended curriculum maintains its integrity. Further, the credit recovery schedules shown in this chapter contain opportunities for Tier 1, 2, and 3 interventions to be embedded in credit recovery and to support efforts of teachers to meet the needs of students with IEPs.

Some caveats arise when planning a credit recovery program: Teachers must be carefully selected in order for the program to succeed, continuous evaluation of student progress should take place to determine program effectiveness, and a conflict matrix is essential in developing the composite school schedule (see Chapter 9).

CAREER AND TECHNICAL EDUCATION ■

The 20th century saw great strides in America's concern for education and its recognition that learning best occurs when students learn in context. The various approaches to career education have made this initiative one of the oldest and most established high school reforms in the United States (Kemple & Snipes, 2000). In the beginning, however, the focus for real-world learning was to prepare students for the world of work only. The term *vocational* was used to describe the program. Its intent was to prevent students from dropping out and increase preparation for the workplace among high-risk students. In 1917, the requirements for a vocational education program indicated that any such education would be of less than precollege grade. At that time, only 10% of the 14- to 17-year-olds attended high school. In fact, it was not until 1918 that all states even required students to have a free public elementary education (National Center for Education Statistics, 2006, cited by Wise, 2008, p. 9).

During the 1970s and 1980s, career programs were intended to curb the dropout problem and focus on the job needs of the high-risk students as well as the requirements of employment after high school. In the late 1980s, the philosophy began to shift from solely vocational to a combined program, providing preparation for work and college as well as serving a wide range of students (Kemple & Snipes, 2000). The School-to-Work Opportunities Act of 1994 increased rigor in school- and work-based learning and encouraged the development of partnerships between schools and employers. Still, in 1998, the federal vocational education (VE) law stated that any vocational preparation would not be for careers that required a baccalaureate, master's, or doctoral degree. In order to accommodate this requirement, schools continued to set up college prep and vocational tracks for students.

The impetus toward combining precollege and career coursework began gaining ground. In 1982, 28% of high school students completed a combination of academic and career coursework. In 2000, the number increased to 88% (Stern, 2010). According to the U.S. Department of Education's National Center for Education Statistics, in 2005, the average high school student took four Carnegie units of credit in CTE courses (Hoachlander, 2008, p. 22). In 2006, the term *vocational* was replaced by *career and technical*, eliminating the prohibition against preparation for careers that might require a bachelor's or advanced degree (Wise, 2008, p. 9).

Today the United States has about 7,000 career academy–type programs (Stern, 2010). Although different school districts approach the makeup of their academies differently, such as their choices of career themes, they all embrace three objectives: to create a school-within-a-school framework in which students stay with a group of teachers over a period of three to four years, to combine academic and occupational-related curricula integrated by a career theme but not focused on a specific job, and to establish partnerships with local employers to allow work-based learning (Kemple & Snipes, 2000).

Table 3.6 illustrates an interdisciplinary approach to the schedule that provides possibilities for curriculum integration, focusing on careers in technology. The technology teacher is a member of the team and teaches three different technology classes within this academy pathway. All teachers meet during Period 6 to discuss student needs, curriculum and pedagogy, and schedule adaptations for Periods 1–5. Students are individually scheduled and have opportunities to take honors classes as well as co-taught classes based upon their IEPs. During Periods 6 and 7 (see Tables 3.7, 3.8, and 3.9), students take additional courses or electives away from the academy. Not all

Table 3.6 Career Academy or Pathway: Technology

	1	2	3	4	5	6	7
English	Honors 01	01	02	03 Co-taught	04	Team Meet	Plan
U.S. History	01 Co-taught	Honors 01	02	03	04	Team Meet	Plan
Math	Honors Geom. 01	Honors Geom. 02	Pre-calc. 01 Co-taught	Honors Geom. 03	Pre-calc. 02	Team Meet	Plan
Physics	Honors 01	01 Co-taught	02	Honors 02	03	Team Meet	Plan
Tech	Programing 01	Intro. to Computing 01	Programing 02	Networking 01	Networking 02	Team Meet	Plan
Sp. Ed.- Eng. & SS	Co-taught U.S. History			Co-taught English		Team Meet	
Sp. Ed.- Math & Sci.		Co-taught Physics	Co-taught Pre-calc.			Team Meet	

Table 3.7　Career Academy or Pathway: Technology, Student Schedule A

Period	Course
1	Programing
2	English 11
3	U.S. History
4	Honors Geometry
5	Physics
6	Physical Education (Day 1)/Band (Day 2)
7	Spanish III

Table 3.8　Career Academy or Pathway: Technology, Student Schedule B

Period	Course
1	Honors English 11
2	Physics
3	Pre-calculus
4	Networking
5	U.S. History
6	Physical Education (Day 1)/Chorus (Day 2)
7	Graphic Design I

Table 3.9　Career Academy or Pathway: Special Education Co-Taught, Student Schedule C

Period	Course
1	U.S. History Co-taught
2	Intro. to Computing
3	Pre-calculus
4	English 11 Co-taught
5	Physics
6	Physical Education (Day 1)/Resource Support (Day 2)
7	Spanish I

academy schedules will be able to include all honors classes, so students must be able to access singleton courses offered by a teacher in another career pathway. This SLC format encourages an atmosphere of personalization so that students have the necessary support for success. Students with special needs can be accommodated in academy frameworks.

Occasionally, a stigma of low expectations seems to remain from vocational education's original impetus of deterring high-risk student dropouts. The leaders in the CTE movement are emphatic on this point: The curriculum does not lower the expectations of achievement but rather alters how core academic courses are taught (Hoachlander, 2008, p. 23).

The schedule in Table 3.10 places the student in the agriculture section of the building in the morning. The afternoon courses meet in the main part of the high school building.

Table 3.10   Career Academy or Pathway: Agriculture, Student Schedule

Period	Course
1 2 3	Animal Science Agricultural Finance
4	Honors English
5	Pre-calculus
6	Government & Economics
7	Physical Education (Day 1)/Chorus (Day 2)
8	Spanish III

As the career academy reform approach evolves, several practices emerge as vital to its success:

- The development of personalized learning environments that include additional support in the manner of counseling and supplemental instruction
- The alignment of increasingly similar skills necessary for work/careers, college readiness, and life (e.g., working collaboratively, thinking critically, and solving problems)
- The embedding of common, high expectations to match the skills and knowledge necessary to succeed in college, the workplace, and life through the use of an engaging curriculum, project-based learning, and field-based opportunities (Hoachlander, 2008, p. 34; Saunders & Hamilton, 2010; Wise, 2008, p. 10)

The freshman academy schedule shown in Table 3.11 introduces the program concept of career education to students via a rotational schedule as a required portion of the ninth-grade curriculum. At registration, each rising freshman student chooses four CTE introductory courses from an array of course offerings. These offerings will vary from district to district depending on local interest or business support. Themes for the academies might include engineering, multimedia design, marine biology, veterinary science, agriculture, health careers, sports marketing, building and environmental design, or culinary arts. The student will have a one-quarter introductory experience in each of the courses chosen.

Table 3.11 Freshman Academy With CTE Exploratory Rotation

Period	Cohort 1	Cohort 2	Cohort 3	Cohort 4
1	English	English	English	English
2	Social Studies	Social Studies	Social Studies	Social Studies
3	Phys. Ed./Health	Phys. Ed./Health	CTE Exploratory Rotation	
4	CTE Exploratory Rotation		Phys. Ed./Health	Phys. Ed./Health
5	Math	Elective	Elective	Math
6	Science	Elective	Elective	Science
7	Elective	Math	Math	Elective
8	Elective	Science	Science	Elective

Each freshman academy cohort has four teachers, four sections, and four academic core subjects. As noted in Table 3.11, the schedule must provide teachers with common plan time to align, coordinate, and integrate instruction between the core subjects and the career introductory courses. Since all students do not take all introductory courses or are not in the same course at the same time, content integration will of necessity be general in scope. Common skills, however, should be integrated throughout the curriculum.

In some cases, students' course offerings for academic core and career courses exist in different physical locations. Except for the freshman academy exploratory rotation, the career locale can be in a separate part of the building or on a different site. In either case, the schedule must address the issue of time for student movement and accessibility to required courses. This issue is especially critical when a work-study program is part of the district's intended curriculum. Sample student and teacher schedules in Tables 3.12 and 3.13, respectively, illustrate the two dimensions of the work-study experience.

Table 3.12 Work-Study Student Schedule

Period	Course
1	English 12
2	Government/Economics
3	Senior Art Seminar
4	Lunch
5	AP Calculus
6	Work-study experience at an art supply store that is supervised by a work-study coordinator
7	
8	

Table 3.13   Work-Study Teacher Schedule

Period	Course
1	Marketing II-01
2	
3	Computer Applications II-01
4	Lunch
5	Teacher prep
6	Work-study supervision
7	
8	

In order to document the effects and importance of the career academy program, the Manpower Demonstration Research Corporation (MDRC) in New York City began a longitudinal study in 1993. The organization compared students who had been randomly chosen to be in a career academy with students who were not in a career academy. The results are mixed for all the outcomes measured, but they do indicate several positive outcomes for students in well-defined career academy programs: more regular school attendance, fewer dropouts, an increased number of credits earned toward graduation, and improved preparation for postsecondary experiences (Kemple & Snipes, 2000).

Beyond the positive effects demonstrated in the educational environment, career academy students experience positive effects in the world of work. The MDRC research found that after four years, the career academy students earned 18% more salary than the nonacademy students (Kemple, 2004).

■ HONORS, GIFTED AND TALENTED, ADVANCED PLACEMENT, AND INTERNATIONAL BACCALAUREATE

Improved student achievement exists as the ultimate goal of all of the previously discussed programs. Proponents of gifted education maintain that advanced students, however, are not being served in the manner they require in order to achieve at their level or to improve their level of achievement commensurate with their ability. Callahan, Tomlinson, Reis, and Kaplan (2000) point to the Trends in International Mathematics and Science Study that compares our high-achieving 12th-grade students with comparable students in other countries. According to the authors, AP courses in the United States are more rigorous than other coursework, but the exams in the United States are not as rigorous as those in other countries, and fewer students take the AP exams. In England, Wales, France,

Germany, and Japan, 25%–50% of high school students take the exams, and the majority pass. In 1995 in the United States, 8% of high school students took the exams, and 5% of those students passed. The authors further argue that since the publication of *A Nation at Risk* in 1983, nearly all efforts to improve education have focused on at-risk students and general improvements in education rather than the high-performing students.

High-stakes testing has become the magnet toward which our education policies and strategies are drawn. Much has been written about teaching to the test, but little has surfaced into the public's view on the goals of the tests. While purporting to measure student progress, Wade Nelson (1998) suggests that standards are mandated minimums that become maximums (Callahan et al., 2000). Sternberg (2008, p. 15) offers a more severe observation: "The law discourages schools from providing special services for gifted students because they will pass the test anyway." In his thorough report based on National Assessment of Educational Progress (NAEP) scores, Loveless (2008, p. 18) reports that between 2000 and 2007 the lowest-achieving students made solid progress in fourth-grade reading and math and eighth-grade math, but the top 10% of students made minimal gains.

As in other educational dilemmas to meet special population student needs, gifted education can be addressed through programs that regroup students in a variety of ways. Schedules that accommodate this action are not unlike the schedules that accommodate other special populations. Karen B. Rogers (1993) has conducted meta-analysis research on ways of grouping gifted students and the types of academic outcomes each grouping offers. Each of her categories can be adapted to a functioning schedule. Holloway (2003) and the National Association for Gifted Children (NAGC, 2009a) review the literature on grouping gifted students and list Rogers's (1993, p. 3) findings in order of most to least effective:

1. Full-time gifted program

2. Cluster grouping within heterogeneous classrooms

3. Acceleration

4. Regrouping in specific subjects

5. Cross-grade grouping or nongraded classrooms

6. Enrichment pullouts

7. Within-class ability grouping

8. Cooperative grouping for regular instruction

In her analysis of the research, Rogers (2002) determined that full-time programs demonstrate the strongest benefits for this population (cited in Holloway, 2003, p. 89). By definition, *full-time* implies a program of services for a group of gifted children of the same or multiple grade levels that are housed in a single school in which all the curricular areas are challenging and complex (NAGC, 2009a, p. 1). A full-time gifted program has several housing variations. A self-contained gifted class has homogeneous grouping that is distinct from other general classrooms at each grade level.

In this schema, all curricular areas are challenging and complex. In a special or magnet school for gifted students, the entire building is dedicated to addressing the needs of gifted children.

Cluster grouping is a variation on the theme of a full-time program. In a clustered group, the top five to eight students at a grade level are placed in a mixed-ability class. They experience differentiated instruction in proportion to their numbers in the class from a teacher with gifted education training. For instance, if a class of 26 has eight gifted students, the gifted students would receive one third of the teacher's instructional time (Rogers, 2002, cited in Holloway, 2003, p. 89; NAGC, 2009a, p. 1). This practice is similar to the instruction in an ELL immersion class, indicating that the schedule meets a variety of needs. In the case of a middle or high school schedule, the criteria of proportional instruction and teachers trained in gifted education remain the same. In order to maintain the integrity of the program, cluster teachers must meet consistently to compact and differentiate the program.

Acceleration refers to a process that allows students to progress through an educational program at rates faster than a conventional pace based on the student's ability, readiness, and motivation. Although inconsistently practiced, content and grade acceleration provide additional methods for districts and schools to meet the needs of their gifted populations. Unfortunately, acceleration is inconsistently practiced and often discouraged through state or district prohibitions (Institute for Research and Policy on Acceleration, National Association for Gifted Children, & Council of State Directors of Programs for the Gifted, 2009, p. 1).

Content acceleration includes single-subject acceleration, curriculum compacting, dual enrollment in high school–and college-level courses, credit by exam or experience, AP, and enrollment in an IB program. Students who receive content acceleration for a single subject may be with their peer group for most of the instructional day but receive advanced instruction in their single-subject coursework. This instruction occurs in an advanced-grade classroom or in a regular classroom in which the student's work is on a more advanced level than grade-level work. This format works for the student who presents an uneven achievement profile and needs grade-level work as well as more challenging work in a particular subject or subjects.

In Table 3.14, the sixth-grade student is in grade-level gifted classes for English and social studies, in Grade 7 gifted classes for Spanish and science, and in a Grade 8 geometry class for math. This schedule can also be labeled as a cross-grade or regrouping program. Not all such programs have the student in all advanced classes.

Within content acceleration, the curriculum can be compressed via grade telescoping so that two levels of content are completed in one year, with each level completed in one semester. In Table 3.15, the student completes two levels of English and social studies in one year as well as an

Table 3.14   Content Acceleration: Grade 6 Student Schedule

1	2	3	4	5	6	7
G/T English 6	Spanish I (7th-grade course)	G/T Social Studies 6	Art 6/ Tech 6/ FCS 6/ Health 6	PE 6/ Band 6	G/T Science 7	G/T Math 8 (Geometry)

Table 3.15 Content Acceleration: Curriculum Telescoping, Grade 10–11 Student Schedule

	1	2	3	4	5	6	7
Semester 1	English 10	World History	French III	Pre-calculus	Honors Physics	Band/ PE	AP Probability & Statistics
Semester 2	English 11	U.S. History					Art Seminar

AP math course in one semester, leaving an opening for an elective in the second semester. In part, a distinguishing feature of the curriculum delivery for gifted and talented students is to compact their in-school experiences for Grades K–12. As an outcome of the telescoping of curriculum, the student represented in Table 3.15 will have an opportunity for dual enrollment, taking college-level courses while still in high school. Some students may opt to leave high school early and enroll in college.

Tables 3.14 and 3.15 also illustrate grade acceleration by placing middle school students in advanced-grade classes and scheduling high school students to complete two levels of a subject in one year. In elementary grades, students might be able to skip an entire grade either in the beginning of the school year or at midpoint.

Similar to the student in Table 3.14, students can be regrouped into an advanced class for specific subjects but stay with their grade-level heterogeneous group for other classes. Table 3.16 shows a middle school student's schedule in which the student is regrouped for gifted and talented math and science.

Table 3.16 Regrouping for Middle School Gifted Math and Science

1	2	3	4	5	6	7
Social Studies 7	German 7	G/T Math	G/T Science	English 7	Chorus/ PE: Day 1/Day 2 rotation	Technology/ FCS/ Music/ Art: Quarter rotation

In another example of cross-grade grouping, Table 3.17 presents two middle school teams, each of a different grade. In this schedule, teams can mix students across grade levels according to individual needs. The teams share a common plan time so that any student movement or concern can be discussed during the team meeting. Students of these two teams are in encore/exploratory classes at the same time.

To further illustrate how cross-grade grouping can be accomplished, the schedule in Table 3.18 allows a student's movement from one grade-level class to another to address the specific needs of these students.

Although the research on the frequency of gifted class meetings indicates that those classes that meet daily show substantial academic growth (Rogers, 2002, cited in NAGC, 2009a, p. 2), not all districts or schools can or do offer daily gifted experiences. In this case, pullout enrichment programs can be implemented. The students assigned to a pullout program are out of

Table 3.17   Cross-Grade Middle School Teams

Team 7A	1	2	3	4	5	6	7
English	H-7-01	G/T 7-01	7-01	7-02	7-03	TM	Plan
Social Studies	G/T-7-01	H-7-01	7-01	7-02	7-03	TM	Plan
Math	PA 7-01	PA 7-02	H Alg. I 7- 01	G/T Alg. I 7-01	PA 7-03	TM	Plan
Sci.	7-01	7-02	G/T 7-01	H-7 01	7-03	TM	Plan
Spanish 7	7-01	7-02	7-03	7-04	7-05	TM	Plan
Sp. Ed. (inclusion)						TM	Plan
Team 8 A							
English	G/T 8-01	H 8-01	8-01	8-02	8-03	TM	Plan
Social Studies	H 8-03	G/T 8-01	8-01	8-02	8-03	TM	Plan
Math	Alg. I 8-01	Alg. I 8-02	G/T Geom. 8-01	H 8-01	Alg. I 8-03	TM	Plan
Science	8-01	8-02	H 8-01	G/T 8-01	8-03	TM	Plan
Spanish	8-01	8- 02	8-03	8-04	8-05	TM	Plan
Sp. Ed. (inclusion)						TM	Plan

Table 3.18   Cross-Grade Middle School Student Schedule

1	2	3	4	5	6	7
G/T Soc. Studies 7-01	G/T English 7-01	G/T Geom. 8-01	G/T Science 8-01	Spanish 8-01	PE 7/ Orch: Day 1/ Day 2	Art 7/Tech 7/FCS 7/ Health 7: Rotation

their regular classroom for a period of time each week to work on a more challenging and complex curriculum.

As discussed earlier, RTI can also exist as a pullout program. NAGC encourages districts and schools to include gifted education students in their implementation of RTI pullout periods. These students, like below-grade-level learners, are exceptional and require services that are fluid and flexible because the students do not progress at the same rate (NAGC, 2009b, p. 3). To illustrate the similarities between these populations, NAGC (2009b, p. 2) lists common components that should be in place when evaluating students for services:

1. Universal screening, assessments, and progress monitoring

2. Established protocols for students who need additional support and services

3. Problem-solving parental involvement

4. A tiered system of intervention based on level of need and support

Further, some gifted education students are "twice exceptional" learners. These students have disabilities that put them in need of more than one level of intervention. It is feared, however, that these students' additional needs may be overlooked because the students present an adequate performance in a "less-than-challenging curriculum" (NAGC, 2009c). Each of the exceptional needs identified here can be addressed with a flex/advisory period.

Tables 3.19 and 3.20 are similar in appearance. In Table 3.19, gifted and talented students meet during the flex/advisory period for more advanced instruction. This meeting can be daily but more than likely would be one or two times per week. In Table 3.20, the gifted students are pulled out of their math and science classes during Periods 1 and 2 for more advanced instruction on a daily basis and out of the flex/advisory period on a less frequent basis.

Table 3.21 reflects a Day 1/Day 2 schedule. In this model, classes meet for 90 minutes each on an alternate-day basis enabling teachers to use best practices in instruction for extended-time periods. During the 90-minute flex/advisory period, students meet with a variety of teachers for differentiated enrichment experiences.

By creating a schedule in which the gifted education students are able to meet in a homogeneous group, they experience fewer repetitive drills in the pullout class than in regular classrooms. Bolstering the importance of more advanced curriculum and engagements, James Kulik's (1993, p. 3)

Table 3.19   Pullout Enrichment in Flex/Advisory

1	2	3	4	5	6	7
Math 7	Science 7	English 7	Social Studies 7	Flex/ Advisory Including G/T Pullout for STEM* Supplement	PE 7/Orch 7: Day 1/ Day 2	Art 7/Tech 7/ FCS 7/ Health 7

*STEM: Science, Technology, Engineering, Math

Table 3.20   Daily Pullout and Weekly Enrichment

1	2	3	4	5	6	7
Math 7: G/T pullout	Science 7: G/T pullout	English 7	Social Studies 7	Flex/Advisory Including G/T Pullout for STEM* Supplement	PE 7/ Orch 7: Day 1/ Day 2	Art 7/Tech 7/ FCS 7/ Health 7

*STEM: Science, Technology, Engineering, Math

Table 3.21   Day 1/Day 2 With In-Class Ability Grouping and Heterogeneous Cooperative Grouping

Day 1				Day 2			
1	2	3	4	5	6	7	8
Art Elective	Social Studies 8	Geometry	Science 8	Flex/ Advisory	Spanish II	Phys. Ed.	Eng. 8

research on ability grouping indicates that when gifted students are required to do routine work at a routine pace their achievement drops dramatically.

The two remaining group forms occur in the regular classroom. In one, students are consistently grouped according to their ability within the classroom. Their cooperative groups are solely ability based. These students are assigned different work and assessed differently than the rest of the class. As stated earlier in the section on cluster grouping, this process will work for gifted students only if the teachers have gifted education training or access to specialists.

The final grouping occurs randomly within the classroom, is not necessarily ability based, and has no demonstrable research that indicates benefit for gifted students. Rogers (1991, 1993) recommends that mixed-ability cooperative learning be sparingly used for academic goals but notes that it has merit when used for social skill development.

To meet the needs of high school students who seek a more challenging curriculum, many schools offer AP courses. Fewer schools offer an IB program, which is available for lower grades as well. Both programs present schedule challenges. In part, these programs enjoy increasing popularity because schools lack other rigorous and challenging frameworks, the perception of school quality is influenced by their presence in a school's repertoire, and the programs enjoy governmental support (Callahan, 2003).

Introduced in the 1950s as an opportunity to earn college credit while still in high school, AP seems to fit the concept of giftedness as a function rather than an identity resulting from testing (Callahan, 2003). The identification of gifted students in ways other than intelligence tests closely resembles Joseph Renzulli's (1978) three-pronged premise in his definition of giftedness: above-average intelligence, high levels of task commitment, and high levels of creativity.

AP programs purport to increase factual knowledge, interpretive understanding, and transferable skills that are beneficial in higher education experiences (Tomas Rivera Policy Institute, 2006, p. 2). Thirty-five college-level courses in 20 subject areas are available to be offered in the 14,000 or 60% of American high schools that offer AP. Although each course is designed to be an introductory college-level course, some high-level colleges such as Yale, Harvard, and MIT require students to take their introductory courses regardless of the students' scores on the AP tests. These universities suggest that in order to prepare students to earn high scores on the tests, the AP curriculum focuses on coverage rather than student interaction with the concepts (Macklein, 2006). Other concerns about AP offerings include their predominance in upper-middle-class student districts and lack of availability in low-income or rural districts (Tomas Rivera Policy Institute, 2006).

In spite of socioeconomic status, any school can include AP courses because they coexist with other course offerings. In Table 3.22, the student takes a combination of AP courses, an honors course, and heterogeneous courses.

As presented in Table 3.23, teachers can teach a mix of classes: AP, heterogeneous, and elective.

In some schools and districts, a teacher's assignment may focus on teaching AP courses. Table 3.24 presents a Day 1/Day 2 schedule in which the AP teacher's assignment focuses on AP courses with pre-calculus as another rigorous course.

Unlike AP courses that can be taken on a course-by-course basis, IB is a comprehensive program that has specific sequential requirements that result in an IB diploma. Begun in 1968 at the International School of Geneva, Switzerland, IB's rigorous educational program emphasizes a global education. Students uprooted from their native countries found the educational curriculum in another country did not coincide with the curriculum from that of their previous location. Therefore, the founders reasoned that a rigorous curriculum was needed so that as students moved they would have a consistent education. Callahan (2003) describes the IB

Table 3.22 Advanced Placement Student Schedule: Grade 12

1	2	3	4	5	6	7	8
AP English 12	Pre-calculus	Honors Government/ Economics	AP Psychology	Chorus	Physics	Spanish V	Robotics

Table 3.23 Advanced Placement Teacher's Schedule

1	2	3	4	5	6	7
English 12-01	AP English 12-01	English 12-02	Duty/ Data Meeting (Day 1/ Day 2 rotation)	Plan	English 12-03	Yearbook

Table 3.24 Advanced Placement Teacher's Schedule: Day 1/Day 2

Day 1				Day 2			
1	2	3	4	5	6	7	8
AP Calculus 01	AP Probability and Statistics 01	Duty/ Data Meeting (45 minutes each day)	Pre-calculus 01	AP Calculus 01	AP Probability and Statistics 02	Duty/Data Meeting (45 minutes each day)	Pre-calculus 02

curriculum as one that has cross-disciplinary requirements and encourages an increased student interaction.

In most IB schools, either the entire school follows IB requirements, or a part of the school is devoted to IB. If the school is a partial IB school, students are able to take other courses. In high school, the curriculum includes introductory IB courses for Grades 9 and 10 and the full IB diploma-focused curriculum in Grades 11 and 12. Students can take the Grade 11 and 12 program without the introductory courses but may find the curriculum and expectations too rigorous. Because the student generally follows a complete IB curriculum, few scheduling conflicts exist. The IB school that exists within a traditional school can follow its own individual schedule without interfering with the schedule of the remainder of the school.

In the 11th and 12th grades, students take six major subjects, including study of a second language chosen by the student. In the program, 70 first languages are studied, and 21 languages are offered as second languages. Students choose at least one subject from the following categories: individuals and society, experimental sciences, and mathematics. Arts subjects are not mandatory but are recommended. Three additional requirements fill the curriculum: an extended-research essay, a theory-of-knowledge course, and activities that promote personal development such as community service. Each requirement contributes to the interdisciplinary bent of the program and requires coordinated scheduling.

An IB program exists for middle school as well. Table 3.25 illustrates a middle school team's schedule in which the teachers may create interdisciplinary units that focus each quarter on one of the four exploratory

Table 3.25   Middle School International Baccalaureate Interdisciplinary Team

Team 7A	1	2	3	4	5	6	7
English	01	02	03	04	05	Team Meet	Plan
Social Studies	01	02	03	04	05	Team Meet	Plan
Mathematics	Alg. I-01	Alg. I-02	Alg. I-03	Geom. 01	Geom. 02	Team Meet	Plan
Science	01	02	03	04	05	Team Meet	Plan
Art: Q 1	Q1-01	02	03	04	05	Team Meet	Plan
FCS: Q 2	Q2-01	Q2-02	Q2-03	Q2-04	Q2-05	Team Meet	Plan
Tech: Q 3	Q3-01	Q3-02	Q3-03	Q3-04	Q3-05	Team Meet	Plan
Music: Q 4	Q4-01	Q4-02	Q4-03	Q4-04	Q4-05	Team Meet	Plan

Table 3.26 Middle School International Baccalaureate Exploratory Rotation

	Period 1	Period 2	Period 3	Period 4	Period 5
Art	Q1-7A	Q1-7A	Q1-7A	Q1-7A	Q1-7A
FCS	Q1-7B	Q1-7B	Q1-7B	Q1-7B	Q1-7B
Tech	Q1-8A	Q1-8A	Q1-8A	Q1-8A	Q1-8A
Music	Q1-8B	Q1-8B	Q1-8B	Q1-8B	Q1-8B

courses that rotate in the schedule. Teachers have individual and common plan time while students attend exploratory or elective courses. Table 3.26 more specifically illustrates the rotations. Over a two-year cycle, each student will have two quarters of each of the four exploratory courses to be included in an interdisciplinary study.

SUMMARIZING SPECIAL PROGRAMS FOR EDUCATIONAL SUCCESS: ATTAINING OUR DESTINY

Today's schools face a dilemma of meeting a wide variety of student needs. The complexity of meeting those needs challenges school leaders, especially when creating the master schedule. Each special population has its own characteristics that need to be accommodated. A well-developed schedule can provide opportunities for student needs to be met, whether those needs are to recover credit, to pursue a career interest, or to experience a curriculum that challenges high achievers. Schools and districts must orchestrate the delivery of educational experiences that provide students with opportunities to determine their own destiny through individualized choices.

4

Inclusive Scheduling Frameworks

Fixed

When you come to a fork in the road, take it.

Yogi Berra

Seeking answers to the challenges of meeting students' needs with pertinent programs sometimes feels as ambiguous a route as Yogi Berra's advice to take the fork in the road. The ambiguity, however, may encourage decisions to be made after studying a variety of ways a schedule can be built to address the issues. Then the fork in the road becomes a clearer destination.

The following three chapters present varied conceptual frameworks of schedules: fixed, variable, and hybrids of the two. For each schedule, three major components appear: a definition with examples; benefits for students, including special populations discussed in Chapters 2 and 3; and points or issues to consider when developing the schedule. This chapter highlights fixed schedules. In a fixed schedule, the entire school follows the same bell schedule. The administration holds the locus of control and sets the start and stop times for each class session. Potentially, teachers control time within the allocated class period.

SEMESTER 1/SEMESTER 2 ■

Generally, Semester 1/Semester 2 (S1/S2) is the traditional 4 × 4 block schedule. In each semester, students take four classes, and teachers are responsible for teaching three classes. This schedule originated as an effort to reduce the number of classes taken by a student each semester, to increase instructional time, and to reduce passing time. Lunch is usually a 30-minute module during Period 3 of Semester 1 and Period 7 of Semester 2. Table 4.1 illustrates high school teachers' schedules.

Table 4.1 Semester 1/Semester 2: High School Teachers' Schedules

		Semester 1				Semester 2			
		1	**2**	**3**	**4**	**5**	**6**	**7**	**8**
1	Mrs. Jabar	10-01	10-02	X	Journalism	10-03	Honors 11-01	Honors 11-02	X
2	Mr. Toor	AP Eng. 12-01	X	AP Eng. 12-02	11-01	11-02	X	11-03	Yearbook
3	Mr. Lipsitz	9-01	9-02	9-03	X	Drama 1-01	X	Honors 9-01	9-04
4	Ms. Jackson	Honors 11-01	Honors 11-02	12-01	X	X	12-02	Speech 01	Speech 02

A variation of the 4 × 4 block appears in a 5 × 5 block. The 5 × 5 splits one or two periods each semester to form A and B subsets. Approximately 40 minutes long, these subsets, referred to as skinnies, accommodate tutorial, enrichment, remedial, and certain yearlong classes. Yearlong classes might include band, orchestra, chorus, or yearbook. Lunch takes place in the subset opposite a skinny class. The teachers' schedules in Table 4.2 illustrate skinnies in Periods 3 and 8 during which tutorial, Advanced Placement (AP) tutorial, yearbook, SAT preparation, and advisory classes are offered.

If necessary to have more than two lunch periods, Periods 4 and 9 can be split as well.

Most benefits for S1/S2 schedules are similar for the traditional 4 × 4 or the 5 × 5.

- Teachers have a reduced teaching schedule and fewer students per semester.
- Teams, houses, academies, and magnets can be formed.
- Opportunities exist to implement the research on teaching in extended-time periods.
- The extended time opens the possibility for a balance of content and skills to be delivered in lessons.
- Career pathways and freshman academies can be implemented in either 4 × 4 or 5 × 5 schedules.

Table 4.2 Semester 1/Semester 2: 5 × 5 Teachers' Schedules

		1	2	3A	3B	4	5	6	7	8A	8B	9	10
					Semester 1						**Semester 2**		
1	Mrs. Jabar	10-01	10-02	Lunch	Tutorial	X	Journalism1-01	10-03	Honors 11-01	Lunch	Tutorial	Honors 11-02	X
2	Mr. Toor	AP Eng. 12-01	X	Year-book	Lunch	AP Eng. 12-02	11-01	11-02	X	Year-book	Lunch	11-03	Yearbook
3	Mr. Lipsitz	9-01	9-02	Lunch	SAT Prep	9-03	X	Drama 1-01	X	Lunch	SAT Prep	Honors 9-02	9-04
4	Mrs. Jackson	Honors 11-01	Honors 11-02	AP Tutorial	Lunch	12-01	X	X	AP 12-02	Adv.	Lunch	Speech 01	Speech 02

- Opportunities exist for integrating the curriculum.
- Excellent possibilities occur to build personalization experiences between teacher and student.
- The extended-time allocation increases the possibility of embedding Tier 1 interventions.

The 5 × 5 model offers some additional benefits within the skinny periods:

- Tutorial time
- A supplement to AP courses in the semester opposite to the one in which the course is offered
- Tier 2 and 3 interventions
- Special education support as called for in a student's Individualized Education Plan
- Advisory periods
- Credit recovery

Among the points and issues to be considered is the importance of sufficient training for teachers to teach in extended-time periods. This training needs to move beyond the familiar "sit and get" experience. Adequate amounts of follow-up training also need to occur. In this framework, the number of courses taught by teachers may be limited by the teachers' contracts. In the 4 × 4 model, teachers need to teach three courses in Semester 1 and three courses in Semester 2. In the 5 × 5 model shown in Table 4.2, teachers teach three courses and a skinny each semester.

When creating either schedule, the schedule builder includes one nonteaching period in each semester for each teacher. Unless limited by contract, the nonteaching period can be used for personal plan and professional meetings on an interdisciplinary or a disciplinary basis for discussion of data, teaching strategies, Common Core State Standards (CCSS), or student needs.

DOUBLE ENGLISH/DOUBLE MATHEMATICS ■

In the mid-20th century, a more intense scrutiny of educational outcomes, objectives, and standards appeared on the scene. Districts sought to develop a unified intended curriculum. In part, that curriculum integrated the four areas of English-language arts (ELA): reading, writing, speaking, and listening. In order to deliver the intended curriculum in those areas, some schools incorporated extended-time periods as a possible solution. Post–No Child Left Behind, schools began looking more closely at their students' achievement proficiencies in all areas, especially English and mathematics. Often, they discovered that students were deficient in math as well as in English, which manifested itself in low reading achievement. Consequently, the number of schools using a double English and double math period increased.

In the double English/double mathematics (EEMM) schedule, a student has two periods or 80–90 minutes of English, two periods or 80–90 minutes of math, one period of social studies, and one period of science daily. Table 4.3 illustrates an interdisciplinary team that consists of two

Table 4.3 Double English/Double Mathematics: Interdisciplinary Team Schedule

	1	2	3	4	5	6	7	8
ELA	01	01	Team Meeting	02	02	Plan	03	03
ELA	04	04	Team Meeting	05	05	Plan	06	06
SS	03	06	Team Meeting	01	04	Plan	02	05
Sci.	06	03	Team Meeting	04	01	Plan	05	02
Math	02	02	Team Meeting	03	03	Plan	01	01
Math	05	05	Team Meeting	06	06	Plan	04	04
Sp. Ed.	Replacement ELA		Team Meeting	In-Class Support ELA		Plan	In-Class Support Social Studies	
Sp. Ed.	Replacement Math		Team Meeting	In-Class Support Math		Plan	In-Class Support Science	

English teachers, two math teachers, one social studies teacher, one science teacher, and two special education teachers.

In Table 4.3, the double English and double math periods are consecutive so that instruction is not interrupted. The science and social studies periods are scheduled so that those teachers can have double periods whenever they choose. In this case, they would operate on an alternate-day schedule and see a class of students every other day for 80–90 minutes. This arrangement for double periods could continue for a longer time frame: a three-week period to complete a particular unit, a quarter, or a semester. If desired, the school could add a flex/advisory period as a ninth period in the example in Table 4.3. This schedule format can be used for a two-teacher team as well.

In Table 4.4, each of the two teachers teaches English or math for a double period. Their teaching assignments also include two single-period classes of social studies or science. Because they have control of

Table 4.4 Double English/Double Mathematics: Grade 5 or 6 Two-Teacher Team

	1	2	3	4	5	6	7	8	9
Mrs. Griffin	ELA-01	ELA-01	SS-01	Team Meet	Lunch	ELA-02	ELA-02	SS-02	Plan
Mr. Boyd	Math-02	Math-02	Sci.-02	Team Meet	Lunch	Math-01	Math-01	Sci.-01	Plan

Table 4.5   Double English/Double Mathematics: Student and Teacher Schedule

	Student Schedule	Teacher Schedule
1	ELA	ELA 01
2	ELA	ELA 01
3	PE	Team Meeting
4	Math	ELA 02
5	Math	ELA 02
6	Social Studies	ELA 03
7	Science	ELA 03
8	Art, Music, Tech, Health	Plan

time, they can flex their periods to deliver an integrated curriculum that meets student needs.

Table 4.5 shows a schedule for a student and a teacher on the same team. Note that when the student is in an exploratory class, the teacher has either team plan or personal plan.

Many of the benefits of a double English/double mathematics schedule arise from increased instructional time as well as teacher control of time. Specific needs of students can be addressed in the teacher-controlled time. Examples of these benefits follow:

- Double English/double mathematics is primarily a middle school framework but can be effectively used in a freshman academy.
- English and math are the more frequently tested courses, so schools and districts allot more instructional time.
- A greater opportunity exists to integrate the reading and language arts programs.
- Extended time for social studies and science occurs if offered on an alternate-day basis.
- Double periods provide opportunities to implement the research on teaching in extended time.
- Double periods provide more opportunity for Tier 1 interventions to take place via effective teaching and the use of differentiation.
- The double periods and teacher-controlled time allow the potential for lessons to include a balance between content and skill instruction.
- Teaming increases the likelihood of curriculum integration.
- Double English/double mathematics fits a two- or six-teacher teaming model.
- Replacement and in-class support programs for special education students can be an integral part of the schedule.
- Students with special needs can be included in exploratory courses during Periods 3 and 6 (Table 4.3).
- Double periods provide increased possibilities to build personalization.
- A flex period can be the ninth period.

Schools considering double English/double mathematics need to recognize that extended-time teaching presents issues that influence the decision. Although the scheduling framework may be chosen because of the increased amount of time for instruction, all parties must be aware that the schedule itself does not improve achievement; the instruction that occurs within the scheduled time must be effective to improve achievement. Teaching in extended time requires intense professional development for teachers that is not limited to an initial presentation but includes follow-up sessions. Further, in the six-teacher team, the ELA and math teachers have fewer total students than the social studies and science teachers.

When building the schedule, the double English and double math periods as well as the social studies and science periods should be consecutive periods to allow for greater flexibility. That flexibility is more easily accomplished in a two-teacher team used for Grades 5 and 6.

■ QUARTERS

The quarters schedule looks quite like an S1/S2 schedule with quarter segments embedded in semesters. In this schedule, class periods are 90 minutes long with semester courses being divided into two quarter courses. Built as a yearlong schedule, courses exist on a quarter, semester, or yearly basis.

Table 4.6 Quarters: Grade 9 Student Schedule

	Semester 1		Semester 2	
	Quarter 1	Quarter 2	Quarter 3	Quarter 4
1	English 9 A	English 9 B	Social Studies 9 A	Social Studies 9 B
2	Algebra I A	Algebra I B	PE 9 A	PE 9 B
3	Biology A	Biology B	Spanish II A	Spanish II B
4	Art	Tech	FCS	Computer Applications

Table 4.6 shows a ninth-grade student schedule in which the student takes the four core courses, physical education (PE), and foreign language on a semester basis and four electives on a quarterly basis.

Several benefits occur in this schedule for both the advanced student and the student who needs additional academic support. Table 4.7 illustrates an AP student's schedule that coincides with the dates of the AP exam, allowing the student to take an elective during the fourth quarter.

Similarly, course placement can accommodate the student who needs extra support. Table 4.8 shows how a student who has had difficulty with the first half of a course can repeat that first half rather than moving into the next half of the course before mastery is attained. Through this process, the student achieves credit recovery.

As in S1/S2 and EEMM schedules, teachers need preparation for teaching in extended-time periods that occurs not just in an initial presentation but in follow-ups with review and observed practice. Additionally,

Table 4.7   Quarters: Grade 12 Advanced Student Schedule

	Semester 1		Semester 2	
	Quarter 1	Quarter 2	Quarter 3	Quarter 4
1	French IV A	French IV B	French V A	French V B
2	English 12 A	AP Chemistry A	AP Chemistry B	English 12 B
3	AP Calculus A	AP Calculus B	AP Calculus C	Robotics
4	AP U.S. History A	AP U.S. History B	AP U.S. History C	Creative Writing

Table 4.8   Quarters: Credit Recovery Student Schedule

	Semester 1		Semester 2	
	Quarter 1	Quarter 2	Quarter 3	Quarter 4
1	English 9 A	Credit Recovery English 9 A	English 9 B	English 10 A
2	World History A	World History B	Geometry A	Geometry B
3	Chemistry A	Chemistry B	Spanish III A	Spanish III B
4	PE 10 A	PE 10 B	Computer App. II	FCS II

the teachers' contract plays a role in how this schedule is implemented. Teachers teach three courses in Quarters 1 and 2 or Semester 1 and three courses in Quarters 3 and 4 or Semester 2. When building the schedule, the schedule builder needs to include one nonteaching period in Semester 1 and one nonteaching period in Semester 2. Unless limited by contract, the nonteaching period can include professional meetings that are arranged on an interdisciplinary or a disciplinary basis for professional discussions on data, teaching strategies, CCSS, or student needs.

DAY 1/DAY 2   ■

As a variation on the theme of extended-time periods, a Day 1/Day 2 schedule includes eight periods, but only four meet on each day. The teacher is responsible for three classes on Day 1 and three classes on Day 2. This arrangement, however, depends on the teachers' contract. Table 4.9 demonstrates teachers' schedules that resemble an S1/S2 arrangement but operate on a Day 1/Day 2 basis.

The schedule shown in Table 4.10 includes a flex/advisory period on Day 2. In this period, response-to-intervention (RTI) Tiers 2 and 3 can be scheduled.

All of the benefits of extended-time teaching appear in this framework so Tier 1 instruction can be accomplished. As seen in Table 4.11, teams, houses, magnets, or academies operate effectively within this framework, allowing departments or data groups as well as teams to meet. Special education teachers and students are an integral part of the team or small learning community (SLC).

Table 4.9   Day 1/Day 2: High School Teachers' Schedule

		Day 1				Day 2			
		1	**2**	**3**	**4**	**5**	**6**	**7**	**8**
1	Mrs. Jabar	10-01	10-02	Plan	Journalism 1-01	10-03	Honors 11-01	Honors 11-02	Plan
2	Mr. Toor	AP Eng. 01	Plan	AP Eng. 02	11-01	11-02	Plan	11-03	Yearbook 01
3	Mr. Lipsitz	9-01	9-02	9-03	Plan	Drama 1-01	Plan	Honors 9-01	9-04
4	Ms. Jackson	Honors 11-01	Honors 11-02	12-01	Plan	Plan	12-02	Speech 01	Speech 02

Table 4.10   Day 1/Day 2: Middle or High School Teaching Team or SLC Schedule

	Day 1				Day 2			
	1	**2**	**3**	**4**	**5**	**6**	**7**	**8**
English	01	02	03	Team Meet	04	05	Flex/ Advisory	Team Meet
Social Studies	01	02	03	Team Meet	04	05	Flex/ Advisory	Team Meet
Math	Alg. I-01	Alg. I-02	Geom. 01	Team Meet	Alg. I 03	Geom. 02	Flex/ Advisory	Team Meet
Science	01	02	03	Team Meet	04	05	Flex/ Advisory	Team Meet
Spanish	I-01	II-01	I-02	Team Meet	II-02	I-03	Flex/ Advisory	Team Meet
Special Ed.: Eng. & SS	Replace Eng.	ICS Eng	ICS SS	Team Meet	ICS Eng.	ICS SS	Flex/ Advisory	Team Meet
Special Ed.: Math & Sci.	ICS Math	Replace Math	ICS Sci.	Team Meet	ICS Math	ICS Sci.	Flex/ Advisory	Team Meet

Further, because all core classes meet on alternate days throughout the year, the framework is state and national "test friendly." Data or department meetings provide opportunities for subject matter coordination, including specific focus on the CCSS. When teachers are in team or data meetings, "sections away" means that the schedule must include enough seats for electives or other required courses in those designated periods.

In high school, magnet or academy programs can exist. Table 4.12 illustrates a communications magnet in which the special communications courses appear on either Day 1 or Day 2. Core and magnet teachers attend

Table 4.11   Day 1/Day 2: Team and Department Meetings

	Day 1				Day 2			
	1	**2**	**3**	**4**	**5**	**6**	**7**	**8**
English	TM/P	01	02	03	DM/P	04	05	06
Social Studies	TM/P	01	02	03	04	DM/P	05	06
Math	TM/P	01	02	03	04	05	DM/P	06
Science	TM/P	01	02	03	04	05	06	DM/P
Special Ed.	TM/P							
Sections Away	6	2	2	2	3	3	3	3

Table 4.12   Day 1/Day 2: Communications Magnet

	Day 1				Day 2			
	1	**2**	**3**	**4**	**5**	**6**	**7**	**8**
English	01	02	Team Meet/Plan	03	04	05	Team Meet/Plan	06
Social Studies	01	02	Team Meet/Plan	03	04	05	Team Meet/Plan	06
Math	Alg. I-01	Alg. I-02	Team Meet/Plan	Geom. 01	Alg. I-03	Geom. 02	Team Meet/Plan	Alg. I-04
Science	01	02	Team Meet/Plan	03	Honors 01	04	Team Meet/Plan	05
Broadcasting	01		Team Meet/Plan		02		Team Meet/Plan	
Journalism		01	Team Meet/Plan			02	Team Meet/Plan	
Acting: TV/ Film			Team Meet/Plan	01			Team Meet/Plan	02
Sections Away	1	1	6	1	1	1	6	1

the team meeting, providing teachers the opportunity to integrate the curriculum. During the team's professional discussions, teachers can share strategies for connecting the curriculum to real-life situations.

Just as issues exist with other frameworks, the Day 1/Day 2 schedule has some as well. Students have twice the number of courses to maintain than they would in S1/S2 or quarters, and teachers have a double load. If the teachers' contract indicates that teachers can only teach five courses, they must be scheduled for two nonteaching periods on either Day 1 or Day 2.

TRIMESTERS

Since *Making Creative Schedules Work in Middle and High Schools* (Merenbloom & Kalina, 2007) was published, an increased interest in trimester scheduling has occurred. Designed to maximize the number of credits a student receives, trimesters are a variation of a six- or seven-period traditional schedule. The school year is divided into three 12-week periods in which a student takes five courses and a teacher teaches four sections per trimester. Each period is approximately 72 minutes in length. In Table 4.13, a high school student's schedule shows band as a yearlong course and the other courses as two-trimester courses designated by A and B (e.g., English 9 A and English 9 B).

Table 4.13   Trimesters: High School Student Schedule

Trimester 1		Trimester 2		Trimester 3	
1	Band A	6	Band B	11	Band C
2	English 9 A	7	Algebra I A	12	Algebra I B
3	Social Studies 9 A	8	English 9 B	13	Social Studies 9 B
4	Spanish I A	9	Phys. Ed. 9 A	14	Phys. Ed. 9 B
5	Biology 9 A	10	Biology 9 B	15	Spanish I B

Students are able to earn 7.5 credits per year. If a student fails a course, the student repeats the course in the following trimester. Special education and English-language learning (ELL) classes are possible, and the end of Trimester 2 is closer to the AP exam date than Semester 1 in the S1/S2 schedule. Although high school teams and SLCs can exist within this schedule, not all teachers in a cohort will have each of the students during a particular trimester.

The teachers' schedules in Table 4.14 demonstrate the placement of A and B courses through the trimesters to accommodate the student's pace through the curriculum.

As is apparent in Table 4.14, issues include the nonconsecutive nature of some classes. A trimester may intervene between the A and B sections of a particular course, creating a possibility that the student will not have the same teacher for both courses. Consequently, a clear pacing guide is essential so that students receive the intended curriculum in all courses. Further, careful decisions must be made about the number of trimesters in which a course will be offered. Most traditional yearlong courses are completed in two trimesters. When too many courses are allocated a three-trimester length, the schedule lacks the ability to include sufficient elective courses.

In building the trimester schedule, each segment of a course such as English 9 A or English 9 B is a single entry. Therefore, the placement of singletons and doubletons on a master schedule may involve two or three entries. This schedule needs to be built as a yearlong schedule and the process begun early in the year preceding its implementation.

Table 4.14 Trimesters: Teachers' Schedules

	Trimester 1					Trimester 2					Trimester 3				
	1	2	3	4	5	6	7	8	9	10	11	12	13	14	15
Dr. Griffin	Eng. 9 A 01	Eng. 9 A 02	Eng. 9 A 03	Eng. 9 A 04	Plan	Eng. 9 B 01	Eng. 9 B 02	Eng. 9 A 05	Eng. 9 A 06	Plan	Eng. 9 B 03	Eng. 9 B 04	Eng. 9 B 05	Eng. 9 B 06	Plan
Dr. Davis	U.S. Hist. A 01	Plan	U.S. Hist. A 02	U.S. Hist. A 03	U.S. Hist. A 04	U.S. Hist. A 05	Plan	U.S. Hist. B 01	U.S. Hist. B 02	U.S. Hist. A 06	U.S. Hist. B 03	Plan	U.S. Hist. B 04	U.S. Hist. B 05	U.S. Hist. B 06
Mr. Bolster	Plan	Alg. I A 01	Alg. I A 02	Geom. A 01	Geom. A 02	Plan	Alg. I B 01	Geom. B 01	Alg. I A 03	Geom. A 03	Plan	Alg. I B 02	Geom. B 02	Alg. I B 03	Geom. B 03
Mr. Harris	Sp. I A 01	Sp. I A 02	Plan	Sp. IV A 01	Sp. I A 03	Sp. I B 01	Sp. I B 02	Plan	Sp. IV B 01	Sp. IV A 02	Sp. I B 03	Sp. IV B 02	Plan	Sp. II A 01	Sp. V A 01

In middle school, trimesters present a different look. The core classes meet all year, but the encore/exploratory classes change each trimester. In Table 4.15, PE meets every other day for the year, alternating each trimester with one of the exploratory classes: art, music, or technology.

In this schedule, teachers teach 80% of the time, leaving 72 minutes for planning. Common plan time occupies a portion of the 72 minutes. If the high school is on a trimester schedule and staff must be shared with the middle school, the middle school needs to be on a similar bell schedule.

Table 4.15   Trimesters: Team Schedule for Middle School

	Trimester 1					Trimester 2					Trimester 3				
	1	2	3	4	5	6	7	8	9	10	11	12	13	14	15
Eng.	P	01	02	03	04	P	01	02	03	04	P	01	02	03	04
SS	P	04	01	02	03	P	04	01	02	03	P	04	01	02	03
Math	P	03	04	01	02	P	03	04	01	02	P	03	04	01	02
Sci.	P	02	03	04	01	P	02	03	04	01	P	02	03	04	01
PE	7A					7A					7A				
Art	7A					7A					7A				
Music	7A					7A					7A				
Tech	7A					7A					7A				

■ CREDIT RECOVERY

Credit recovery can be implemented in most high school schedules. Its format depends on the major structural framework chosen: quarters, Day 1/Day 2, trimesters, single subject, rotational, or traditional. Table 4.16 shows how a student can make up the lost credit and remain on track for graduation.

Table 4.16   Credit Recovery: Student Schedule

1	English 9 and English 10
2	
3	Chorus
4	Algebra I and Geometry
5	
6	Social Studies
7	Physical Education
8	Physical Science

When scheduling the student for credit recovery, it is important that the student is not scheduled to take two levels of a subject at the same time. In Periods 1 and 2, the student begins with the failed course, English 9. When the standards that were failed are mastered, the student moves into English 10 with the same teacher. Similarly, in Periods 4 and 5, the student recovers the Algebra I credit before moving into Geometry. By retaining the same teacher for the credit recovery course, the integrity of the course prevails, and the focus on standards is evident.

If the student is on a credit recovery team, the teachers collaborate on the student's progress during a daily plan time. The team focuses on interventions, the CCSS, and formative assessments during their plan time and class instruction. In addition to responsibility for the two sections of the credit recovery course as in Table 4.17, the teachers teach two other sections apart from the credit recovery schedule.

Table 4.17   Credit Recovery: Team Schedule

	1	2	3	4	5	6	7	8
Mr. Johnson: English	English 9/10-01		Team Meet	English 9/10-02		Plan	English 11-03	English 11-04
Mrs. Browning: Math	Algebra/ Geometry-02		Team Meet	Algebra/ Geometry- 01		Plan	Pre-calculus 01	Pre-calculus 02

The creation of a credit recovery team allows for increased opportunities for personalization, an element often missing in the academic experience of students who need extra support to pass a course. Most important, the credit recovery process as illustrated minimizes dropouts and increases the chances of the student graduating on time.

ROTATIONAL   ■

The rotational schedule extends instructional time beyond the traditional time but not as much as the S1/S2, quarter, or Day 1/Day 2 schedules. Instead of 80- to 90-minute periods, the rotational schedule provides 60- to 65-minute periods. Teachers generally teach three or four classes daily. Although students have six classes daily, classes do not meet each day or in the same sequence each day. Table 4.18 shows how a rotational schedule works within a nine-period day.

Table 4.19 includes two time frames for teachers: the traditional time frame of 40 minutes and the rotational variation with 60-minute classes. The placement of teachers' nonteaching periods in the master schedule controls the number of classes that they teach each day of the rotation. The number of nonteaching periods may vary each day.

Because of the number of schools on an eight-period day excluding lunch, the schedules in Table 4.20 and Table 4.21 may be more realistic. In these schedules, lunch appears twice: One lunch period occurs before the first afternoon class; the second lunch period occurs after the first afternoon

Table 4.18 Rotational: Nine-Period Day

	Day 1 (60-Minute Classes)	Day 2 (60-Minute Classes)	Day 3 (60-Minute Classes)
1			
2	1 2	3 1	2 3
3			
4			
5	4 5	6 4	5 6
6			
7			
8	7 8	9 7	8 9
9			

Table 4.19 Rotational: Teacher's Schedule

	Periods (40 Minutes)	Day 1 (60 minutes)	Day 2 (60 Minutes)	Day 3 (60 Minutes)
1	Geometry-01	Geometry-01 Geometry-02	Plan Geometry-01	Geometry-02 Plan
2	Geometry-02			
3	Plan			
4	Geometry-03	Geometry-03 Study Hall	Geometry-04 Geometry-03	Study Hall Geometry-04
5	Study Hall			
6	Geometry-04			
7	Plan	Plan Honors Geometry-01	Algebra II-01 Plan	Honors Geometry-01 Algebra II-01
8	Honors Geometry-01			
9	Algebra II-01			

Table 4.20 Rotational: Eight-Period Day

Period	Day 1	Day 2	Day 3	Day 4
1				
2	1 2 3	4 1 2	3 4 1	2 3 4
3				
4				
Period	Day 1	Day 2	Day 3	Day 4
	Lunch			
5	5	8	7	6
	Lunch			
6				
7	6 7	5 6	8 5	7 8
8				

Table 4.21 Rotational: Eight-Period Teacher's Schedule

Period	Course	Period	Day 1	Period	Day 2	Period	Day 3	Period	Day 4
1	English 10-01	1	10-01	4	Plan	3	SH	2	10-02
2	English 10-02								
3	Duty-Study Hall	2	10-02	1	10-01	4	Plan	3	SH
4	Plan	3	SH	2	10-02	1	10-01	4	Plan
5	Plan	5	Plan	8	10-03	7	H10-02	6	H10-01
6	H English 10-01	6	H10- 01	5	Plan	8	10-03	7	H10-02
7	H English 10-02	7	H10- 02	6	H10-01	5	Plan	8	10-03
8	English 10-03								

class. Some schools have only one lunch period. The class periods are longer in the eight-period rotation than in the nine-period rotation.

The rotational schedule takes advantage of the students' biorhythms that change as the day progresses. Therefore, S1/S2 and Day 1/Day 2 classes can rotate but must remain as 80- to 90-minute classes. In the rotation schedules introduced in this section, additional instructional time is gained by eliminating some passing time. Freshman academies and career pathways can be established within this structural framework.

Concerns exist, however, about the ability to test on the same day. Teachers would have to create two versions of tests. Additionally, protocols for homework completion or collection need to be created through consensus.

SINGLE SUBJECT ■

A single-subject team capitalizes on the expertise of two content-area teachers and possibly a special education teacher. It centers the instruction on mastery of a subject with flexibility for the teachers to group and regroup students based on formative assessment feedback of student understanding. These teachers have two sections of the same course that are scheduled to meet at the same time and have a common planning period. This framework can be implemented in any of the fixed structural frameworks with a focus on implementing CCSS.

Through the single-subject team, an opportunity exists for mastery learning in a specific subject area. Grouping of students within the team occurs by determining learning styles, mastery levels, and pretesting. As a unit is taught, adjustments of the grouping are made through formative assessments. If necessary, students can be regrouped at any time for reteaching or enrichment. Since special education and ELL teachers can be a part of this team, Tier 2 RTI instruction as well as Tier 1 takes place. By placing two teachers and a special education teacher together, the stage is set for

Table 4.22   Single-Subject Team: High School

Math	1	2	3	4	5	6	7	8
Mr. Bolster	Algebra I-01	Algebra I-03	Team Meeting	Pre-calculus-02	Lunch	Geometry 01	Geometry 03	Plan
Mrs. Geisz	Algebra I-02	Algebra I-04	Team Meeting	Honors Geometry-02	Lunch	Geometry 02	Geometry 04	Plan
Miss Nolan	Co-T	Co-T	Team Meeting		Lunch	Co-T	Co-T	Plan

Table 4.23   Single-Subject Team: Middle School

Math	1	2	3	4	5	6	7	8
Mr. Bolster	Pre-Algebra 01	Pre-Algebra 03	Team Meeting	Math 8-01	Lunch	Algebra 01	Algebra 03	Plan
Mrs. Geisz	Pre-Algebra 02	Pre-Algebra 04	Team Meeting	Math 8-02	Lunch	Algebra 02	Algebra 04	Plan
Miss Nolan	Co-T	Co-T	Team Meeting	Co-T	Lunch	Co-T	Co-T	Plan

teacher mentoring. Table 4.23 shows a middle school schedule that fits the need for improved student achievement in subjects, especially math.

Whether the single-subject team appears in high school or middle school, teachers and students consider themselves as a team with a team identity. In this way, teachers group and regroup students on a fluid basis based on decisions made in their team plan period.

■ TRADITIONAL

Change in instruction and the implementation of special programs can occur within a traditional six-, seven-, eight-, or nine-period schedule as well. A number of fixed frameworks that appear above as well as variable frameworks in Chapter 5 fit within the format of a traditional schedule. Further, any SLC, team, or academy suits a traditional framework as shown in Tables 4.24 and 4.25.

Table 4.24   Traditional: Eight-Period Schedule for a Small Learning Community

	1	2	3	4	5	6	7	8
English								
Social Studies								
Math	Small Learning Community: Technology Career Pathway Required Courses							
Science								
Tech								
Physical Education								
Elective						Courses Outside of Career Pathway		
Elective								

Table 4.25   Traditional: Schedule for Career Pathway or Freshman Academy

	1	2	3	4	5	6	7	8
English	TM	01	02	03	Plan	Lunch	04	05
Social Studies	TM	01	02	03	Plan	Lunch	04	05
Math	TM	Geom. 01	Alg. II 01	Geom. 02	Plan	Lunch	Alg. II 02	Pre-calc. 01
Science	TM	01	Honors 01	02	Plan	Lunch	03	04
Tech	TM	I-01	II-01	I-02	Plan	Lunch	I-03	II-02
Sp. Ed.	TM				Plan	Lunch		

When designing the school schedule, the scheduling committee considers the staff that is available and the teachers' contract before determining the number of periods in a day. Reductions in staff may necessitate fewer periods and fewer offerings for students.

SPECIAL POPULATIONS AND FIXED SCHEDULE MATRIX ■

Table 4.26 illustrates the compatibility of the fixed frameworks discussed in this chapter with the special populations discussed in Chapters 2 and 3. The ability of teachers to differentiate instruction within the class period determines the consideration of some of the frameworks such as EEMM.

Multiple possibilities exist for implementing frameworks to meet the needs of special populations. For several frameworks, however, it is essential that teachers have adequate professional development in differentiating curriculum as well as teaching in extended time.

Table 4.26   Correlation of Fixed Frameworks and Special Populations

	S1/S2: 4 × 4	S1/S2: 5 × 5	EEMM (MS)	Qrtr (HS)	D1/D2 *	Tri.	Credit Rec.	Rota.	Single Subj.	Trad.
RTI	Tier 1	Tiers 1, 2, 3	Tiers 1, 2	Tier 1	Tiers 1, 2, 3	Tiers 1, 2	Tiers 1, 2	Tiers 1, 2, 3	Tiers 1, 2	Tiers 1, 2, 3
Sp. Ed.	X	X	X	X	X	X	X	X	X	X
ELL	X	X	X	X	X	X	X	X	X	X
Cred. Rec.		X		X	X	X	X	X	X	X
CTE	X	X		X	X	X	X	X **	X	X
Gift./Tal.	X	X	X	X	X	X		X	X	X
AP	X	X		X	X	X		X	X	X
IB	X	X		X	X	X	X	X	X	X

*Tiers 1 and 2 are possible with a flex/advisory period in place.

**Limited to the number of periods in the day and rotation selected.

Table 4.27   Fixed Frameworks and Advanced Placement

Structural Frameworks	Commentary	Recommendations
Semester 1/Semester 2: 4 × 4	• AP tests offered toward end of second semester. • Time gap from end of first semester or inability to cover all material in second semester may preclude students from taking test or choosing this more rigorous course.	• Option 1: Schedule AP courses both semesters. This may remove FTE from other courses in the department. • Option 2: Pair AP courses (AP English with AP Calculus) and offer as a Day 1/Day 2 subset of Semester 1/Semester 2 schedule
Semester 1/Semester 2: 5 × 5	• To accommodate AP testing, some schools opt for a Semester 1/Semester 2: 5 × 5 version. • Lunch and skinny courses are offered for 40 minutes each to make up a fifth period each semester. • Other periods meet for 80 minutes for a semester.	• AP courses offered for a 40-minute skinny one semester with an 80-minute class the complementary semester. • Adequate time provided to complete course and encourage student enrollment in AP courses.
Quarters	• An adaptation of Semester 1/Semester 2, classes meet for 80–90 minutes. • Ideally, the student is enrolled in the course in the quarter closest to the test date. • Quarter electives may be necessary. • Non-AP course is split between Quarters 1 and 4.	• Option 1: Teacher desires course offered for two quarters but requests course be scheduled in Quarters 2 and 3. • Option 2: Teacher wants three quarters to complete the course. • Option 3: Teacher has sufficient curriculum for four quarters and wishes course extended beyond test date.
Day 1/Day 2	• All courses meet every other day for the year. • Because of AP testing, some high schools choose Day 1/Day 2 as a rationale to provide extended time periods.	• Option 1: Alternate days for the year. • Option 2: Daily for the year. This option may reduce FTE for other courses in that department.
Trimesters	• School year divided into three 12-week trimesters. • Most core courses meet for two trimesters in 72-minute class periods.	• Option 1: Some AP courses scheduled intentionally in Trimesters 2 and 3. • Option 2: AP courses can be scheduled for three trimesters. Decision may draw FTE from other courses in department.
Rotational	• Classes meet two of three or three of four days. • Total minutes comparable to standard schedule. • Course not completed at time of test.	• An eight-period day provides greater opportunity for instructional minutes during school year. • Permits students to distribute time to complete home assignments and ongoing reading assignments.
Traditional	• Yearlong course. • Fewer periods in master schedule allows longer time periods. • Course not completed at time of test.	• Eight- or nine-period schedule permits students to take greatest number of AP courses.

Table 4.27 offers more specificity in matching fixed frameworks with AP courses. Because of the current testing-time period for AP, close study of each framework is in order.

SUMMARIZING FIXED INCLUSIVE SCHEDULING FRAMEWORKS: THE FORK IN THE ROAD ∎

Although this chapter presents only examples of fixed schedules, the number of possible combinations available validates Berra's admonition to take the fork in the road. Any of the schedules presented has possibilities to meet the needs of all students, including those with special needs. In Chapter 5, variable schedules will add to the variety of frameworks or roads that may be chosen.

5

Inclusive Scheduling Frameworks

Variable

This time, like all times, is a very good one,
if we but know what to do with it.

Ralph Waldo Emerson, "The American Scholar"

Just as Yogi Berra suggests we take the fork in the road when we come to it, Emerson suggests that time is available if we choose to use it wisely. Both speakers compel us to action. In the early part of the 20th century, John Dewey (1938) promoted serious reform for public education. He foresaw the need for more engaged scholarship on the part of students and more action by teachers to be facilitators of education rather than dispensers of knowledge. In the decades following Dewey's observations, little action occurred to change the scene. Time and its flexible use remain constrained by comfortable habits of "authoritarian classroom management" (Sylwester, 2011, p. 2) and legislative edicts based on high-stakes testing. The scheduling models presented in this chapter focus on the effective use of time and flexibility. In these schedules, teachers have the locus of control, the opportunity to use time effectively for the benefit of their students' education and achievement.

INTERDISCIPLINARY–MAXIMUM FLEXIBILITY ■

In the interdisciplinary–maximum flexibility (I-MF) schedule, the same teachers have the same students for the same periods of the day. Common planning periods form a part of the prerequisite pieces. This format sets the stage for teams, houses, magnets, and academies and the professional collaboration that is essential for these frameworks to succeed. Within the I-MF schedule, teachers control time for class periods—their meeting times, length, and sequence. When teachers are able to make decisions regarding time, their sense of empowerment over curriculum and instruction heightens. They are able to fulfill the purpose of reform and restructuring: to increase student achievement (Hackman, 2002). When a time frame meets the needs of the intended curriculum, teachers are better able to provide students with what Marzano (2003, p. 22) calls the "opportunity to learn" (OTL).

In middle school, the I-MF schedule takes a variety of forms. Teams can consist of two, three, four, five, or six core teachers as well as special education teachers. The two- or three-teacher team with an I-MF schedule presents an efficient and welcoming format for the transition from elementary grades to middle school with its higher expectations and increased number of teachers for student instruction. Table 5.1 demonstrates how a two-teacher team has consecutive time periods to adjust as the need arises. The teachers have a common plan time for team meetings and the vital professional discussion that takes place within it.

A three-teacher team also smooths the transition process by limiting the number of core teachers a student has. These smaller teams create opportunities for personalization essential for successful transition experiences.

In Table 5.2, each teacher teaches a section of English and language arts as well as three sections of another core course. A special education teacher

Table 5.1 Interdisciplinary–Maximum Flexibility: Two-Teacher Team, Grades 5 and 6

	1	2	3	4	5	6	7	8	9
Mrs. Griffin	ELA 01	ELA 01	Social Studies 01	Team Meet	Lunch	ELA 02	ELA 02	Social Studies 02	Plan
Mr. Boyd	Math 02	Math 02	Science 02	Team Meet	Lunch	Math 01	Math 01	Science 01	Plan

Table 5.2 Interdisciplinary–Maximum Flexibility: Three-Teacher Team With Special Education, Grades 5 and 6

	1	2	3	4	5	6	7	8
ELA + SS	ELA 01		Team Meet	Plan	Flex/Advisory	SS 01	SS 02	SS 03
ELA + Sci.	ELA 02		Team Meet	Plan	Flex/Advisory	Sci. 03	Sci. 01	Sci. 02
ELA + Math	ELA 03		Team Meet	Plan	Flex/Advisory	Math 02	Math 03	Math 01
Special Ed.	In-Class Support		Team Meet	Plan	Flex/Advisory	ICS	ICS	ICS

is part of the team and carries out in-class support. As part of the team, the special education teacher can flex the schedule whenever the core teachers choose to reallocate time.

Table 5.3 includes a foreign language teacher on the core team as well as two special education teachers. All of the teachers meet for a common plan time. In this case, the special education teachers are subject-area specialists. This qualification is not always necessary for inclusion purposes. Each of the special education teachers has one resource room section and two sections of inclusion teaching. Resource support can be offered in the flex/advisory period. The work of the two special education teachers indicated in Table 5.3 is not limited to this interdisciplinary team.

Table 5.3 Interdisciplinary–Maximum Flexibility: Five-Teacher Team With Two Special Education Teachers, Grade 8

	1	2	3	4	5	6	7	8
English	Team Meet	01	02	03	Plan	04	05	Flex/ Advisory
Social Studies	Team Meet	01	02	03	Plan	04	05	Flex/ Advisory
Math	Team Meet	Alg. I-01	Alg. I-02	Pre-Alg. 01	Plan	Pre-Alg. 02	Alg. 1-03	Flex/ Advisory
Science	Team Meet	01	02	03	Plan	04	05	Flex/ Advisory
World Lang.	Team Meet	Spanish I-01	Spanish I-02	Spanish II-01	Plan	Spanish II-02	Spanish I-03	Flex/ Advisory
Special Ed.: Eng./Social Studies	Team Meet		Inclusion Social Studies	Inclusion English	Resource			Flex/ Advisory
Special Ed.: Math/ Science	Team Meet				Resource	Inclusion Math	Inclusion Science	Flex/ Advisory

Table 5.4 Interdisciplinary–Maximum Flexibility: Freshman Academy

	1	2	3	4	5	6	7	8
English	Plan	9-01	9-02	Team Meet	9-03	9-04	Flex/ Advisory	Yearbook
Social Studies	Plan	9-01	9-02	Team Meet	9-03	9-04	Flex/ Advisory	AP Psychology
Math	Geometry	Alg. II 01	Alg. II 02	Team Meet	Alg. I 01	Alg. I 02	Flex/ Advisory	Plan
Science	AP Biology	Biology 01	Biology 02	Team Meet	Biology 03	Biology 04	Flex/ Advisory	Plan
Spec. Ed.	Resource	In-Class Support	In-Class Support	Team Meet	In-Class Support	In-Class Support	Flex/ Advisory	Plan

A high school I-MF schedule generally has a four- or five-member small learning community (SLC). In Table 5.4, a freshman academy schedule shows a four-person team plus a special education teacher. Each core teacher has one class outside of the academy team. The consecutive periods on the schedule allow team members to rearrange the periods and time segments as necessary.

As in the two- and three-teacher team model for middle school, the freshman academy I-MF schedule provides for a smooth transition into high school. Personalization can be better created within the cohesive time available.

Personalization becomes increasingly important as the high dropout potential in Grade 9 is recognized. Cited in the National Association of Secondary School Principals' (NASSP) *Principal's Research Review*, Roderick's (1993) study on dropouts indicated that the transition years between elementary and middle school or middle and high school were difficult for some students who dropped out after Grade 9. Roderick's study further comments on the inability of these students to "form positive attachments and become integrated into these larger and more complex environments" (Protheroe, 2009, p. 3). In the same article, Protheroe (2009, p. 4) cites the Allensworth and Easton study (2007) on the importance of freshman-year performance, which emerges as a more important indicator of dropping out than background characteristics and prior achievement.

The beauty of I-MF lies in its ability to provide opportunities for SLCs to flex time in order to meet student needs. In *What the Research Shows: Breaking Ranks in Action* (NASSP, 2002, p. 33), the authors cite Lee and Smith's 1995 observation: SLCs indirectly affect student achievement due to the creation of conditions that facilitate desirable practices. Flexibility is a significant part of those conditions.

Depending on the need of the SLC or team, flexibility can be achieved in several ways. Table 5.5 lists ways a team flexes time. Additional details for incorporating flexibility into the schedule appear in Chapter 7.

Table 5.5   Flexible and Creative Uses of Time

Type of Flexibility	Use and examples
Alter sequence of classes.	Classes can meet in varying sequences to respond to research on biorhythms.
Plan large group instruction.	Entire team meets to see a film or hear a guest speaker.
Adjust schedule to extend instruction.	Short periods of time can be added to classes when necessary. Ninety-minute periods can be created at the request of a team teacher.
Group and regroup students.	Student can be placed in a different section without changing teacher or team.
Create time for interdisciplinary connections.	Special team activities can be placed in the schedule to accommodate interdisciplinary and cross-disciplinary units.
Schedule project time.	Teachers monitor student work on projects during school time.
Implement flex/advisory period.	Opportunities for Tier 2 and Tier 3 interventions can take place within a formal period in the schedule or a time created by the team. Opportunity exists for the guidance function of the team or SLC.

Another condition facilitated through SLCs is curriculum integration. The regular professional meetings of the team allow for discussion of the curriculum to be delivered and how it can be integrated. Through the implementation of integrated concepts, content, and skills, depth is emphasized over breadth (Erickson, 2001, pp. 63–99; Jackson & Davis, 2000, pp. 49–52; NASSP, 2002, pp. 7–9; Voltz, Sims, & Nelson, 2010, p. 83; Zemelman, Daniels, & Hyde, 1998, pp.183–188).

In addition to serving as a model for a freshman academy, I-MF fits other academies and house plans or career pathways. To demonstrate how a technology career pathway uses this schedule, Table 5.6 includes Grades 10 and 11 instead of a single grade.

The technology teacher is a part of the core team and meets with the team members daily. A flex/advisory period allots time for additional focus on the academy theme or can be used to meet other student needs such as tutorials, interventions, or independent studies.

Additionally, a trimester schedule meshes with the I-MF concept. The sample schedule in Table 5.7 earmarks a daily team meeting/plan period as well as another class outside of the freshman academy for each teacher. The four core teachers plus the special education teacher control the three periods or 216 minutes per day.

Table 5.6 Interdisciplinary–Maximum Flexibility: Technology Career Pathway

	1	2	3	4	5	6	7	8
English	10-01	10-02	Team Meet	11-01	11-02	11-03	Flex/ Advisory	Plan
Social Studies	10-01	10-02	Team Meet	11-01	11-02	11-03	Flex/ Advisory	Plan
Math	Geometry 01	Pre-calc. 01	Team Meet	Algebra 01	Algebra 02	Geometry 02	Flex/ Advisory	Plan
Science	Physical Science 01	Physics 01	Team Meet	Physics 02	Physics 03	Physics 04	Flex/ Advisory	Plan
Tech. Careers	I-01	II-01	Team Meet	II-02	III-01	I-02	Flex/ Advisory	Plan

Table 5.7 Interdisciplinary–Maximum Flexibility: Trimester Schedule

	Trimester 1					Trimester 2					Trimester 3				
	1	2	3	4	5	6	7	8	9	10	11	12	13	14	15
Eng.				TM/P	O				TM/P	O				TM/P	O
SS				TM/P	O				TM/P	O				TM/P	O
Math				TM/P	O				TM/P	O				TM/P	O
Sci.				TM/P	O				TM/P	O				TM/P	O
Sp. Ed. Inclu.				TM/P	O				TM/P	O				TM/P	O

When choosing the I-MF framework, several points need consideration. A commitment to I-MF must be of prime importance in building the schedule, including the provision of a common plan period for the SLC/team. The common plan time is essential for professional dialogue that pertains specifically to the delivery of the intended curriculum and attending to student needs. These SLC teams must be the initial entries on the high school master schedule. At both middle and high school levels, consecutive instructional periods set the stage for maximizing flexibility.

Additionally, the extended-time periods make it vital for teachers to have adequate professional development that addresses how to plan for bell-to-bell teaching. The schedule itself cannot improve student achievement; the instruction within the schedule needs to incorporate the practices that engage students.

INTERDISCIPLINARY–LIMITED FLEXIBILITY ∎

In the interdisciplinary–limited flexibility (I-LF) schedule, flexibility is subordinated to the existence of the team. This condition occurs especially in high school due to the number of singletons and doubletons that exist. As in I-MF scheduling, the same teachers have the same students during the same periods of the day and have a common plan period. Some exceptions to the same-periods factor can be made as long as a team control number keeps the same students with the same teachers. Limited opportunities exist, however, to alter the sequence of classes. A flex/advisory period is possible as well as the opportunity to group and regroup students. Most I-LF teams consist of four or five members with a special education teacher included.

In Table 5.8, the students on two Grade 8 teams leave the team to attend Spanish, French, or reading classes. Consequently, the off-team classes curtail the teams' ability to flex the schedule.

Many of the benefits of I-LF echo those of I-MF. The existence of teams creates the conditions necessary for implementation of student-focused strategies: curriculum integration and facilitated transitions between grade levels, as well as providing enhanced communication with parents. Freshman academies, houses, and magnets can use this scheduling framework. Table 5.9 illustrates a communications career pathway in which the placement of the communications courses precludes the ability to flex the rest of the schedule.

Daily, the communications teachers meet with the core teachers for a team meeting. When I-MF is not possible, I-LF should be considered. The points to consider for the two frameworks are similar. Like I-MF, when building the schedule, commitment to I-LF is essential as is a common plan time for the SLC or team to function efficiently. Teachers in this framework need the same type of intense professional development.

INTERDISCIPLINARY–ENCORE/EXPLORATORY ∎

Increasingly, schools are incorporating career exploration opportunities within their curriculum in order to connect curricula with real-life

Table 5.8   Interdisciplinary–Limited Flexibility: Grade 8

8 A	1	2	3	4	5	6	7
English	01	02	Team Meet	03	04	05	Plan
Social Studies	01	02	Team Meet	03	04	05	Plan
Math	Algebra 01	Pre-algebra 01	Team Meet	Algebra 02	Pre-algebra 02	Pre-algebra 03	Plan
Science	01	02	Team Meet	03	04	05	Plan
Off-Team Classes							
Reading	01	02	Team Meet	03			Plan
Spanish	01	02	Team Meet	03	04	05	Plan
French			Team Meet	01	02	03	Plan
8 B							
English	06	07	Team Meet	08	09	10	Plan
Social Studies	06	07	Team Meet	08	09	10	Plan
Math	Pre-algebra 04	Algebra 03	Team Meet	Pre-algebra 05	Algebra 04	Pre-algebra 06	Plan
Science	06	07	Team Meet	08	09	10	Plan

Table 5.9   Interdisciplinary–Limited Flexibility: Communications Career Pathway

	1	2	3	4	5	6	7
English	Team Meet	01	02	03	Plan	04	05
Social Studies	Team Meet	01	02	03	Plan	04	05
Math	Team Meet	Geometry 01	Algebra 01	Algebra 02	Plan	Geometry 02	Algebra 03
Science	Team Meet	01	02	03	Plan	04	05
Broadcasting	Team Meet	01				02	03
Journalism	Team Meet		01		02		
Acting: TV and Film	Team Meet			01			02

experiences. In middle school, the interdisciplinary–encore/exploratory (I-EE) schedule provides time for the encore-exploratory teachers to meet as a team. In order to provide this period, all students must be in core classes. The blueprint in Table 5.10 shows the periods in which students are either in core or in encore-exploratory classes. Two periods emerge in which the students are not in any encore-exploratory classes: Periods 3 and 5. These are periods in which to schedule the encore/exploratory team meeting.

Table 5.10   Interdisciplinary–Encore/Exploratory: Middle School Blueprint

	Grade 6	Grade 7	Grade 8
1	Core	Core	Encore
2	Core	Core	Encore
3	Core	Core	Core
4	Encore	Lunch	Core
5	Lunch	Core	Core
6	Encore	Core	Lunch
7	Core	Encore	Core
8	Core	Encore	Core

If encore-exploratory classes are scheduled in consecutive periods, the teachers can flex their times to provide extended-time periods or alter the sequence of classes by grade level. Table 5.11 shows consecutive periods for each of the grade-level I-EE classes.

Table 5.11   Interdisciplinary–Encore/Exploratory: Middle School

	1	2	3	4	5	6	7	8
Art	6A	6B	Team Meet	7A	7B	Plan	8A	8B
Music	6A	6B	Team Meet	7A	7B	Plan	8A	8B
Technology	6A	6B	Team Meet	7A	7B	Plan	8A	8B
Family Consumer Science	6A	6B	Team Meet	7A	7B	Plan	8A	8B

The establishment of encore-exploratory teams in middle school allows teachers to include interdisciplinary instruction by using a curriculum map and coordinating integration with core teachers.

By using variations of the I-EE framework, Tables 5.12 and 5.13 show how career exploration and introduction to career pathways or academies provide high school students with an opportunity to explore career and technical education (CTE) courses. The teacher's schedule in Table 5.12 blocks three consecutive periods for freshman-level exploratory classes.

The freshman academy schedule in Table 5.13 introduces the program concept of career education to students via a rotational schedule as a required portion of the ninth-grade curriculum. At registration, each rising freshman chooses four CTE introductory courses from an array of course offerings. These offerings will vary from district to district depending on local interests or businesses. Some themes for the career academies might include engineering, multimedia design, marine biology, veterinary science, agriculture, health careers, sports marketing, building and environmental

Table 5.12 Interdisciplinary–Encore/Exploratory: High School Teacher's Schedule

Period	Course
1	Marketing II-01
2	
3	Computer Applications 03
4	Lunch
5	Prep
6	Freshman Exploratory Classes
7	
8	

Table 5.13 Interdisciplinary–Encore/Exploratory: Freshman Academy

Period	Cohort 1	Cohort 2	Cohort 3	Cohort 4
1	English	English	English	English
2	Social Studies	Social Studies	Social Studies	Social Studies
3	Phys. Ed./Health	Phys. Ed./Health	CTE Exploratory Rotation	
4	CTE Exploratory Rotation		Phys. Ed./Health	Phys. Ed./Health
5	Math	Elective	Elective	Math
6	Science	Elective	Elective	Science
7	Elective	Math	Math	Elective
8	Elective	Science	Science	Elective

design, or culinary arts. The student will have a one-quarter introductory experience in each of the courses chosen.

When this conceptual approach is used to introduce careers to students, the high school student gains an initial exposure to several career pathways. The experience becomes enhanced when the same teacher who teaches the introductory course also teaches the career pathway courses.

Points to consider include the scheduling of teachers. As noted in Table 5.12, teachers in the introductory career pathways program teach CTE courses and upper-level courses. Teacher responsibility for the freshman experience as well as the upper-level experiences becomes an important point in maintaining and sustaining the program. Further, scheduling the career-exploratory courses is a high priority. Groups of CTE teachers need to be available for the rotations. At the middle school level, the blueprint guides the scheduling of teams into the encore program.

COMBINATION   ■

A combination team is a mini-version of an interdisciplinary team that exists primarily in high school. Some typical examples would be English and American History or Geometry and Physics. Table 5.14 illustrates a math-science combination team.

On this team, teachers share the same students and control time within their consecutive periods. They have a common plan period in which to address student needs, curriculum integration, interventions, grouping and regrouping of students, and teaching in extended-time periods as well as to discuss any data findings that relate to their subject areas.

The same principle applies to a freshman academy team in which the four core subjects have a subset of an English–social studies combination and a math-science combination. These combinations appear in Table 5.15.

As in the I-MF and I-LF schedules, the combination schedule allows teachers to control time so that extended-time periods are possible.

Table 5.14   Combination Team: High School Math and Science

	1	2	3	4	5	6	7	8
Math	Algebra II 01	Algebra II 02	Team Meet	Algebra II 03	Algebra II 04	Lunch	Probability and Statistics	Plan
Science	Chem. 02	Chem. 01	Team Meet	Chem. 04	Chem. 03	Lunch	Plan	AP Chem. 01

Table 5.15   Combination Team: Freshman Academy

	1	2	3	4	5	6	7
English	9-01	9-02	Team Meet	9-03	9-04	Plan	Honors Eng. 11
Social Studies	9-02	9-01	Team Meet	9-04	9-03	Plan	Social Studies 10
Special Ed.	Co-T	Co-T	Team Meet				
Math	9-03	9-04	Team Meet	Plan	Pre-calculus	9-01	9-02
Science	9-04	9-03	Team Meet	AP Biology		9-02	9-01
Special Ed.			Team Meet			Co-T	Co-T

As with the other schedules that offer flexibility, this framework requires a high scheduling priority. The two classes need to be scheduled consecutively. Care needs to be taken to enroll the students in the same classes. A separate or new course number is needed for these combinations.

■ SUMMARIZING VARIABLE INCLUSIVE SCHEDULING FRAMEWORKS: USING TIME

The variable inclusive schedules introduced place the locus of control in the hands of teachers to make the most of time. From an instructional perspective, the success of the variable frameworks rests with teachers. Their resulting actions answer Emerson's remarks on the availability of time: "if we but know what to do with it."

6

Integrating Fixed and Variable Frameworks Into a Comprehensive Schedule

The key is not to prioritize what's on your schedule,
but to schedule your priorities.

Stephen Covey

School schedules reveal the priorities of a school as determined by its mission/vision statement. Although the schedule is essential to carrying out the identified priorities, it cannot be viewed as the ultimate answer to raising student achievement. What and how instruction occurs in the classroom matters most. To accommodate the needs of students and mesh with special programs identified in Chapters 2 and 3, this chapter focuses on the interchangeability of fixed and variable frameworks as described in Chapters 4 and 5 to complete a comprehensive schedule.

Schools can have a variety of fixed and variable subsets within the structure of the school. Meeting the needs of special populations within a school or district requires scrutiny to make sure that decisions for those populations fit the comprehensive needs of the total school population. As those who make the schedule work, teachers need to understand the potential of various frameworks and have input into the final selections. Moreover, it is essential that they have the necessary professional development to work within the schedule, especially if the schedule includes the possibility of extended-time periods and flexibility. A changing population presents a major influence on scheduling decisions. This factor requires a reevaluation of the schedule from year to year.

The school leadership team assumes a major role in the scheduling discussion and decisions. Once frameworks are determined, leadership needs to control implementation consistent with the mission/vision statement.

Finally, the matrices and schedules presented are samples developed through the authors' experiences in conducting seminars, workshops, and onsite consultations with schools and districts. They are representative of schools and districts seeking to identify their priorities within a master schedule.

■ INTERCHANGEABILITY: FIXED TO FIXED

The greater the interchangeability of chosen frameworks, the more likely a final schedule will be able to meet the needs of all populations within the school. A schedule can contain multiple fixed frameworks. Table 6.1 contains a matrix that demonstrates how the various fixed scheduling frameworks mesh with each other.

Rotational and single subject are the most interchangeable frameworks with nine possibilities each. The least interchangeable frameworks are trimester at three possibilities, as well as Semester 1/Semester 2 (S1/S2)—4 × 4 and double English/double math (EEMM) at four possibilities. When beginning to choose frameworks with which to create the schedule, the number of possibilities for interchangeability becomes a factor. Fewer possibilities endanger the ability to address the priorities established.

■ INTERCHANGEABILITY: FIXED TO VARIABLE

Embedding variable subsets into fixed frameworks promotes the existence of teams and small learning communities (SLCs). These cohort groups are compatible with nearly all of the fixed frameworks. Teams are a form of SLC. When implemented fully and efficiently, they have research-based advantages for students, increased student performance, a positive school climate, a personalized learning environment, teacher collaboration, improved parent involvement, and cost efficiency (National Forum to Accelerate Middle-Grades Reform, 2004). Chapter 7 takes a closer look at various forms of learning communities.

The matrix in Table 6.2 indicates the interchangeability of fixed and variable frameworks.

Table 6.1 Interchangeability: Fixed to Fixed Schedule Matrix

Interchangeability:	S1/S2: 4×4	S1/S2: 5×5	EEMM*	Quarters**	Day1/Day2	Trimesters	Credit Recovery	Rotational	Single Subject	Traditional***	Total
S1/S2: 4×4	O			X	X			X	X		4
S1/S2: 5×5		O		X	X		X	X	X		5
EEMM*			O		X			X	X	X	4
Quarters**	X	X		O	X		X	X	X		6
Day1/Day2	X	X	X	X	O			X	X		6
Trimesters						O	X	X	X		3
Credit Recovery		X		X		X	O	X	X	X	6
Rotational	X	X	X	X	X	X	X	O	X	X	9
Single Subject	X	X	X	X	X	X	X	X	O	X	9
Traditional***			X		X		X	X	X	O	5
Total	4	5	4	6	7	3	6	9	9	4	

*EEMM: Essentially a framework for middle school and freshman academy programs

**Quarters: Presents 80- to 90-minute classes

***Traditional: Based on 45-minute classes

Table 6.2 Interchangeability: Fixed to Variable Schedule Matrix

	I-Max Flex	I-Limited Flex	I-Encore/E	Comb	Total
S1/S2: 4 × 4	X	X	X	X	4
S1/S2: 5 × 5	X	X	X	X	4
EEMM	X	X	X	X	4
Quarters	X	X	X	X	4
D1/D2	X	X	X	X	4
Trimesters	X	X	X	X	4
Credit recovery		X		X	2
Rotational	X (team function)	X	X	X	4
Single subject	X	X	X	X	4
Traditional	X	X	X	X	4
Total	7	10	9	10	

A master schedule can have more than one fixed framework, such as traditional and EEMM in middle school and S1/S2—5 × 5, credit recovery, rotational, and single subject in high school. Additionally, a master schedule can have one or more fixed frameworks along with one or more variable frameworks. From another perspective, grade configurations influence certain structural frameworks.

Table 6.3 illustrates some combinations available to the scheduling team. As the matrix is studied, the appropriateness of some frameworks for selected grade levels becomes more evident and is discussed in scenario form.

In Scenario #1, the entire K–8 schedule uses a traditional framework. Double English and double math are scheduled in Grades 5 and 6, using a two-, three-, or six-person interdisciplinary–maximum flexibility (I-MF) team. Single-subject teams appear in all grade levels to focus on student development in reading and mathematics. In the K–4 schedule, specific times for reading and mathematics can rotate so these courses can be offered at different times of the day. Within the master schedule, common planning time for core teams occurs by scheduling physical education, art, and music as a cohort group. A common planning time also exists for exploratory teachers to orchestrate and integrate the various components of their instructional programs.

Scenario #2 presents a middle school with Grades 5–8 on a traditional framework. An EEMM schedule is featured in Grades 5 and 6. The I-MF model appears in Grade 7 with five teachers, five subjects, and five sections. As a function of the decisions made by each team, the variable rotational framework is used within each of the interdisciplinary teams in Grades 5, 6, and 7. Interdisciplinary–limited flexibility (I-LF) schedules can be used in Grade 8 with students enrolled in reading, French, or Spanish as the fifth core subject. As an extension of interdisciplinary teams, single-subject

Table 6.3 Compatibility: Structural Frameworks and Grade Configurations

	K–8 Sc. #1	5–8 Sc. #2	6–8 Sc. #3	6–8 Sc. #4	High School Sc. #5	High School Sc. #6	High School Sc. #7
Fixed							
S1/S2 4 × 4						X	
S1/S2 5 × 5					X		
EEMM	Gr. 5–6	Gr. 5–6		X			
Quarters						X	
D1/D2				X			
Trimesters				X (encore)			X
Credit Recovery					X		X
Rotational	K–4 alter sequence of reading and math	Within team	X	X		X	X
Single Subject	All grades	X	X	X	X	X	X
Traditional	X	X	X				
Variable							
I-Max Flex	X	X		X		Fr. Acad.	
I-Limited Flex		X			Fr. Acad.	Career Path	Career Path & Fr. Acad.
I-E/E	X	X	X	X		Career Explor.	Career Explor.
Combination							X

cohorts arise as teachers address complex frameworks for flexibility. Interdisciplinary–encore/exploratory (I-EE) scheduling allows common plan time for those teachers when all students are in core classes.

In an effort to raise student achievement scores and implement the Common Core State Standards (CCSS), a traditional model is used in Scenario #3, Grades 6–8, with single-subject teams in all content areas. Students are grouped and regrouped within content teams based on interest, motivation, formative assessments, and achievement. Each core content area has common plan time as do the encore/exploratory teachers. The entire school schedule rotates to enable teachers to see students at different times of the day.

Scenario #4 shows a Grade 6–8 middle school with a Day 1/Day 2 structure. Double English and double math can be used in all grade levels. In this scenario, a student will have English and math each day of the school year. The entire schedule can rotate. Single-subject teams can be organized in mathematics and other subjects. I-MF teams include English, social studies, math, and science; I-EE includes those subjects listed in the encore portion of the program of studies, which rotate on a trimester basis.

A high school schedule with Grades 9–12 appears in Scenario #5 with the 5 × 5 framework of S1/S2. This choice provides opportunities for enrichment and remediation during the skinny block. By scheduling band, chorus, and orchestra in the skinny section, a greater number of student conflicts are eliminated. Credit recovery courses also appear in the skinny portion of the schedule. Using this format, a student can complete English 10 in the second semester after a successful credit recovery of English 9 in the first semester. In an effort to increase the percentage of students successfully completing Algebra I in one semester, Algebra I classes use the single-subject team approach.

Within the S1/S2—5 × 5 framework, a freshman academy program can be created, involving English, social studies, mathematics, and science teachers who are responsible for the same students. Since total flexibility is not possible, the I-LF framework occurs. Transition to high school, the advisory function, and curriculum integration become the emphasis in the freshman academy.

Scenario #6 presents a high school on the 4 × 4 version of S1/S2. Some quarter courses can be created with class meetings of 90 minutes to increase elective opportunities and provide students with Tier 2 or Tier 3 interventions. The remedial frameworks remain fluid so that once the intervention is complete, the student moves into regular elective offerings. If teachers in various subjects choose the concept of single-subject teaming, the schedule facilitates two sections of similar courses so regrouping can occur.

After implementing a freshman academy on the I-MF platform, the faculty might explore a career pathway program, using I-LF. Because of the greater number of courses and levels of those courses, maximum flexibility is not possible. To prepare students to make a choice of a career pathway, the freshman academy experience includes a career exploratory program.

The trimester schedule in Scenario #7 addresses needs made evident when facing reductions in staff allocation. Fixed features of the trimester framework include credit recovery, rotation, and single-subject teams. Within the trimester framework, career pathways, freshman academy (I-LF), and a career exploratory program (I-EE) for ninth-grade students can be put into effect. English and social studies as well as mathematics and science may combine for curriculum integration purposes, including the CCSS.

◼ SUMMARIZING THE INTEGRATION OF FIXED AND VARIABLE FRAMEWORKS INTO A COMPREHENSIVE SCHEDULE: SCHEDULING PRIORITIES

The significance of scheduling priorities reinforces the importance of the mission/vision statement of the school when making decisions that impact student performance. While the schedule alone cannot improve student achievement, it sets the stage for a more comprehensive approach to serving student needs. One size does not fit all. Rather, attentiveness to the frameworks available and their compatibilities influences decisions that address the priorities of the school.

7

Learning Communities and Flexibility

Coming together is a beginning. Keeping together is progress.
Working together is success.

Henry Ford

Previous chapters offered a variety of structural frameworks tailored to meet districts' special student populations. In each case, the schedule functions as a means to an end of raising achievement, not an end unto itself. Many factors enter into the equation of meeting needs and raising the achievement of all students. One major factor is the implementation of learning communities or teams that come in a range of sizes and shapes and appear in the world of business as well as education.

The official beginnings of learning communities occurred early in the 20th century when society was in flux and seeking answers to meet the needs of a growing population in the next step of the Industrial Age. Radical departures from the status quo appeared in many facets of life. Henry Ford initiated the moving assembly line in order to make the ownership of an automobile available to the masses. Theorists and visionaries sought to introduce new ideas that they perceived to be more democratic and valuable to the progress of the country.

Two educational visionaries were Andrew Meiklejohn and John Dewey who worked together at the University of Wisconsin, establishing the Experimental College. Meiklejohn focused on the collegiate educational scene while Dewey's interest lay in the K–12 grouping. Their tenets included the theme of democracy, access to education for all, and classrooms as community. Within the classroom, they promoted active learning, deep engagement of faculty and students, and preparation for responsible citizenship.

Concerned about the increasing compartmentalization in education, Meiklejohn and Dewey advocated an interdisciplinary curriculum taught by teachers who collaborated on curriculum and strategies. Dewey believed that classrooms and what occurred within them needed to reflect how students learn (Smith, 2001, p. 2). A proponent of learning as building on prior knowledge, he sought a balance between a singular focus of delivering content and a consideration of the development, interests, and experiences of the student.

As the 20th century progressed, interdisciplinary schedules did not become commonplace, and the comfort of the status quo prevailed. Affordable cars for the general population remained, but movement toward a democratization of education for the general population faded. When change fails, Dolan (1994, p. 5) suggests the cause to be that the "system-in-place" resists it. Through the years, many in all educational fields and involved in myriad reform processes attest to the truth in Dolan's observation.

Although those early ideas became dormant, they reemerged when the United States entered the Space Age and realized that education is the key to maintaining world status. In spite of this delayed national realization, persons involved in education and learning never stopped developing and evaluating methods that would provide the support contemporary students need.

One of those visionaries was William Alexander, a professor of education at George Peabody College in Nashville, Tennessee. He jump-started the middle school movement in 1963 through an address he delivered at Cornell University. His arguments confronted the junior high practice of scheduling and teaching the early adolescent like a high school student. He proposed that the early adolescent's needs are different from the needs of elementary or high school students. He continued that those needs are best met with mentor relationships between teacher and student, small communities of learners most often referred to as interdisciplinary teams, and a flexible interdisciplinary curriculum that encourages active learning and personalization (Armstrong, 2006, pp. 111–112). Like Dewey, he believed that balance in educational experiences would support the student's development and learning to meet the demands of a highly technological and socially changed society. He and Paul George proposed a model of instruction that contains the integration of major knowledge areas, skills of communication and learning, and personal development with connections to real-life experiences (George & Alexander, 1993, p. 68).

Tables 7.1, 7.2, and 7.3 illustrate three approaches to middle school interdisciplinary–maximum flexibility (I-MF) schedules. They demonstrate the ability of students to have core and exploratory subjects as well as a flex/advisory period that is controlled by the teaching team.

Students are in exploratory classes when teachers have team meetings and personal plan time. Teachers have control over the core periods subject to the special education teachers' assignments. During team meeting

Table 7.1   Two-Teacher Team Plus Special Education Teacher for Grades 5 and 6

	1	2	3	4	5	6	7	8	9
English + Social Studies	ELA 01	ELA 01	SS 01	Team Meet	Flex/ Advisory	ELA 02	ELA 02	SS 02	Plan
Math + Science	Math 02	Math 02	Science 02	Team Meet	Flex/ Advisory	Math 01	Math 01	Science 01	Plan
Special Education	In-Class Support	In-Class Support	In-Class Support	Team Meet	Flex/ Advisory	In-Class Support	In-Class Support	In-Class Support	Plan

Table 7.2   Three-Teacher Team Plus Special Education Teacher for Grades 5 and 6

	1	2	3	4	5	6	7	8
ELA + Social Studies	ELA 01	Team Meet	Plan	Flex/ Advisory	SS 01	SS 02	SS 03
ELA + Math	ELA 02	Team Meet	Plan	Flex/ Advisory	Math 03	Math 01	Math 02
ELA + Science	ELA 03	Team Meet	Plan	Flex/ Advisory	Science 02	Science 03	Science 01
Special Education	In-Class Support	Team Meet	Plan	Flex/ Advisory	I-CS	I-CS	I-CS

Table 7.3   Interdisciplinary–Maximum Flexibility: Grade 8

	1	2	3	4	5	6	7	8
English	Team Meet	01	02	03	Plan	04	05	Flex/ Advisory
Social Studies	Team Meet	01	02	03	Plan	04	05	Flex/ Advisory
Math	Team Meet	Algebra 01	Algebra 02	Pre-algebra 01	Plan	Pre-algebra 02	Algebra 03	Flex/ Advisory
Science	Team Meet	01	02	03	Plan	04	05	Flex/ Advisory
World Language	Team Meet	Spanish I 01	Spanish I 02	Spanish II 01	Plan	Spanish II 02	Spanish II 03	Flex/ Advisory
Sp. Ed. + Eng. + SS	Team Meet		Inclusion English	Inclusion Social Studies	Resource			Flex/ Advisory
Sp. Ed. + Math + Sci.	Team Meet				Resource	Inclusion Math	Inclusion Science	Flex/ Advisory

time, teachers follow an agenda to discuss student progress, meet with other school personnel such as counselors, meet with parents, plan for team activities, and dedicate one day for professional dialogue that includes looking at student work or testing data and determining strategies to address the findings.

Since Alexander's 1963 proposal to create middle schools that focus on teaming practices of teachers for students, much has been written about the various configurations that best meet the needs of the early adolescent student. Some contend that the transition between elementary and middle school is traumatic and causes student achievement to fall immediately as well as fall later in high school. To alleviate those problems, some advocate a K–8 experience (Sparks, 2011).

Others, such as the National Forum to Accelerate Middle-Grades Reform, present their Schools to Watch program successes. The majority of the schools that have earned the designation of a School to Watch have a Grade 6–8 configuration. In his keynote address at the annual conference of the National School Boards Association's Council of Urban Boards of Education, Hayes Mizell (2004) suggests that the configuration is not as important as what occurs within that configuration and the commitment as well as the level of implementation of middle school philosophy. He encourages the implementation of those factors that are known to support early adolescent achievement in any configuration, including the existence of teams and a common plan time. Interestingly, the parent support for a K–8 configuration mirrors the purpose of the middle school teaming philosophy: Smaller numbers mean more opportunities to develop close ties or personalization with students and parents; smaller classes promote safety because the teachers and other staff closely monitor the student and events at the school (Mizell, 2004).

The team in Table 7.2 is small and has control of time to address issues of transition and instruction, as well as a common plan time in which teachers collaborate. All teachers teach English-language arts as well as their content-area specialty. The middle school team in Table 7.3 controls most of its day. Consequently, the teachers in all three tables have an even greater opportunity for the personalization and support essential for student achievement, elements discussed in their team meetings. Additionally, they have time to develop a rigorous approach to the curriculum, plan interventions, and share strategies that will support student success.

After William Alexander's 1963 observation of student needs and instructional practices, others began to publish studies that called for educational reform. In 1975, Dan Lortie analyzed the culture of school in his book *Schoolteacher: A Sociological Study.* His findings describe school as a segmented structure with isolated working conditions and norms of individualism and conservatism among teachers. Those observations reignited movements to improve teacher collaboration and strong teacher communities (cited in Letgers, 1999, p. 1).

The interactions within a school community are complex and not easily defined. Consequently, the instillation of collaboration within a school produced a variety of forms. While teachers' seclusion from the ideas and collegiality of their peers was bemoaned, a clear solution seemed elusive: Was the result to be collegiality or collaboration, and how did the two ideas relate to the true target—raising student achievement? Letgers (1999, p. 8) discusses Judith Warren Little's (1990) definitions of the differences between collegiality and collaboration. Little identifies four types of interaction: storytelling and scanning, aid and assistance, routine sharing, and joint work. Depending on the need facing the learning community, each form has importance in context and practice. Little (1990), however, encourages movement beyond elongated discussion and advocates action that includes common short-term assessment results as a basis for improvement (Schmoker, 2006, p. 108). In other words, she champions joint work.

Unfortunately, the advent of No Child Left Behind became the basis for a new resistance by the "system-in-place." Armstrong (2006, pp. 7–8) describes NCLB as the cause of a switch from a human development discourse in education to an academic achievement discourse in which the focus is testing and accountability determined by outside factors. In today's political climate, the educational community often succumbs to the pressure of testing demands. Regrettably, the collaboration afforded by teaming or small learning communities (SLCs) dwindles when pressure on teachers to produce high test scores supersedes their discussions on curriculum and strategies to meet the developmental needs of their students. When more intense test preparation comes into practice, advisory programs that provide significant adult contact for the student decline.

Interestingly, the educational and civic community's concern over high school dropouts created interest to adopt some successful and developmental programs that mark the middle school concept of SLCs. Freshman academy and career pathway programs incorporate this feature. Similar to an advisory class, a freshman seminar supports transition needs as well as academic needs of students. Recognizing the power of the SLC, colleges and universities also have incorporated learning communities similar in intent to those in secondary schools that promote smaller size and increased collaboration (Smith, 2001, p. 1).

Table 7.4 is an example of a freshman academy schedule that includes a focus on content with opportunities for personalization for rising ninth-grade students. It enables an interdisciplinary curriculum to be taught. These teachers have control over time for Periods 2, 3, 5, 6, and 7.

Table 7.4 Freshman Academy: Interdisciplinary–Maximum Flexibility

	1	2	3	4	5	6	7	8
English	Plan	9-01	9-02	Team Meet	9-03	9-04	Flex/ Advisory	Yearbook 01
Social Studies	Plan	9-01	9-02	Team Meet	9-03	9-04	Flex/ Advisory	AP Gov. 01
Math	Geometry 05	Algebra II 01	Algebra II 02	Team Meet	Algebra I 01	Algebra I 02	Flex/ Advisory	Plan
Science	AP Biology 01	Biology 01	Biology 02	Team Meet	Biology 03	Biology 04	Flex/ Advisory	Plan
Special Education	In-Class Support	In-Class Support	In-Class Support	Team Meet	In-Class Support	In-Class Support	Flex/ Advisory	Plan

Flex/advisory Period 7 enables academy teachers to meet student needs through a seminar or advisory period, response-to-intervention (RTI) Tier 2 or 3 class, enrichment, or whole team meetings. All five teachers have a common plan period, an essential element for the success of SLCs. During this plan period, teachers share strategies and goals, discuss curriculum integration possibilities, and determine what interventions are necessary and how they will be delivered.

Table 7.5 includes a career pathway house for technology. In this example, students are with the same teachers for core, including the technology teacher who is a part of that core. Team meetings include all teachers. Opportunities exist to integrate and provide real-life applications of the curriculum. Grades 10 and 11 are in this house, making it an example of a vertical organization.

Table 7.5 Career Pathway: Teachers' Schedule

	1	2	3	4	5	6	7	8
English	10-01	10-02	Team Meet	11-01	11-02	11-03	Flex/ Advisory	Plan
Social Studies	10-01	10-02	Team Meet	11-01	11-02	11-03	Flex/ Advisory	Plan
Math	Geometry 01	Pre-calc. 01	Team Meet	Algebra II 01	Algebra II 02	Geometry 02	Flex/ Advisory	Plan
Science	Physical Sci. 01	Physics 01	Team Meet	Physics 02	Physics 03	Physics 04	Flex/ Advisory	Plan
Tech Careers	I-01	II-01	Team Meet	II-02	III-01	I-02	Flex/ Advisory	Plan

As the concept of educational professionals working together in collaboration as well as collegiality takes hold, the premise appears in several forms: co-teaching, interdisciplinary teams, SLCs, and today's emphasis on professional learning communities. Although approached variously, each community embraces goal similarities: personalized teacher-student relationships, curriculum and assessment discussions, and collegiality and collaboration among teachers to improve instruction. Each of these elements leads teachers and students toward the goals identified in their mission/vision statements.

Cotton's (2001) research review identifies multiple forms of SLCs, from teams to houses and magnets. Some are loosely organized and partially implemented while others are highly organized in large environments. Some SLCs mentioned in this book include the following.

- Houses: Students and teachers are assigned to smaller groupings within the larger school. Students take core courses together and share the same teachers. Students and teachers follow the larger school's curriculum, instructional policies, and, often, extracurricular activities. The house organization can be horizontal with one grade level or vertical with two or more levels.

- Magnets: An academic specialization focus in this organization typically draws students from the entire school district such as performing arts or technology. Admission requirements may exist.
- Academies: This school-within-a-school focuses on a broad occupational area, such as engineering, natural resources, or the hospitality industry. Teachers and students are self-selected, and the curriculum includes work-based learning (Cotton, 2001, pp. 8–12). A freshman academy does not focus on an occupational area but is a school-within-a-school.

Cotton (2001) provides a wide range of research and some anecdotal opinion on the merits or failures of SLCs. Her final analysis recognizes that although arguments exist against small schools or SLCs, the majority of research supports them. These structures provide improved educational opportunities for students, professional collaborative experiences for teachers, and connections with parents (Cotton, 2001, pp. 50–54). The caveat remains, however, that like the schedule, the SLC is one part of a larger whole, and if not implemented with prudence and a balanced focus on instruction and personalization, it will fade away as earlier reforms have.

As discussion grows about successful collaboration and SLCs, professional learning communities (PLCs) increase in implementation. Confusion exists between the definition and purpose of each. Brief definitions follow:

- A *small learning community or team* refers to size and is often a subset of a larger group or school. SLCs exist to provide more personalization and closer monitoring of student achievement.
- In its original form, a *professional learning community* consists of a group of teachers who meet to address the learning issues of students. Their focus is on curriculum and its delivery as well as providing small-scale professional development to their members.

Lately, the PLC, too, has been applied in myriad ways, encompassing an increasingly broader definition of groupings. A fear arises that the proliferation of various forms of learning communities, encompassing increasingly large memberships with different purposes, will blur the purpose and intent of the original SLCs and PLCs.

In the 1980s, Richard DuFour became the catalyst for the PLC, the focus of research that sought a champion. His experiences as teacher, principal, and superintendent convinced him of the need for teachers to work together to change the climate and culture of the school. That change could occur only if teachers had time to meet and collaborate about important issues: collective responsibility for student outcomes (Richardson, 2011, p. 29). Perhaps more important, DuFour's emphasis on practice resonates with practitioners. He advocates that PLC meetings are to be filled with discussions about essential curriculum, common assessments, and avoidance of shortcuts in the instruction-learning process (Richardson, 2011, p. 32). His message seems to echo that of his educational forebear, John Dewey: collaboration to deliver an essential curriculum in a manner in which all students can learn.

DuFour (2004) proposes that PLCs espouse three big ideas from which they operate and that set them apart from other collaborative groups:

1. Teachers ensure that students learn the characteristics and practices needed to assure learning at high levels.

2. A culture of collaboration must be nurtured that extends beyond operational procedures and addresses curriculum and instructional practices.

3. The PLC focuses on results and provides ongoing evidence of student success.

These criteria can be met within an SLC during meeting times by identifying a specific day in the agenda for PLC-type collaboration. While several earlier examples show opportunities for team or PLC meetings, Table 7.6 illustrates the use of a Day 1/Day 2 schedule in which the interdisciplinary team meets on Day 1 to discuss operational as well as instructional issues, but on Day 2 the department or data team meets as a PLC to focus on curriculum, common assessments, and intervention-type strategies in its particular discipline.

Table 7.6   Team, Department, Data, or PLC Meetings: Middle School

	Day 1				**Day 2**			
	1	2	3	4	5	6	7	8
English	TM/Plan	01	02	03	DM/Plan PLC Meet.	04	05	06
Social Studies	TM/Plan	01	02	03	04	DM/Plan PLC Meet.	05	06
Math	TM/Plan	01	02	03	04	05	DM/Plan PLC Meet.	06
Science	TM/Plan	01	02	03	04	05	06	DM/Plan PLC Meet.
Special Ed.	TM/Plan							

In order for the PLC to be successful, teachers need to feel they are a part of the process and decision to implement this process. Along with a high level of teacher investment, meeting time is essential for successful implementation. Finding that time within the school day on the high school level requires creativity. A regular meeting time that occurs within the school schedule respects teacher time. The allowance for PLC time legitimizes the strategy and indicates the school or district's seriousness of purpose.

The high school schedule, however, primarily serves students' first choices of courses to the extent possible. Consequently, schedules cannot routinely designate common plan periods for members of a grade-level discipline. To improvise meeting time, schools use early dismissal, late openings, faculty meetings, or professional conference days. The importance of available time necessitates a focused agenda with a targeted goal of action for the meeting. Professional development needs to guide teachers through the expectations and process of a PLC. Linda Darling-Hammond suggests that when teachers share knowledge and expertise, they become successful as individuals and as a team, and that "teaching is a team sport" (Collier, 2011, p. 13).

In this discussion on learning communities, the importance of collaboration emerges along with the need for teacher training, targeted goals for meetings and for students, and a focus on serving student needs and learning. Middle school schedules are more likely to afford opportunities for SLCs and PLCs than high schools. When implemented efficiently, the SLC and PLC formats reinforce Ford's thoughts: *Coming together is a beginning. Keeping together is progress. Working together is success.*

FLEXIBILITY STRATEGIES ■

Teachers are the best judges of time required for learning engagements. When teachers in SLCs have schedules that give them control over time, they are able to flex their classes to meet student and instructional needs. This use of time is beneficial for all students and can be highly beneficial for students in transition from elementary school to the secondary grades. Daniel (2007, p. 1) cites the work of Vars (1993) and Arhar (1992) to support the benefits of flexible time frames for student achievement:

- Less fragmentation
- More engagement possible for problem-based learning engagements and interdisciplinary studies
- Promotion of skill application
- Increased time to build interpersonal relationships
- Additional opportunities for decision-making skills
- Improved student achievement
- Positive social culture

The decisions about when to flex along with why and how to flex are best made by an SLC that has a culture of collaboration. They need clear, articulated plans for implementing each form of flexibility to maximize the results they intend to accomplish. Following are seven strategies for flexing time. Each strategy has an explanation, research support, impact, and a scheduling example that focuses on the implementation of I-MF structural frameworks.

Alter the Sequence of Classes

Students and teachers benefit from altering the sequence of classes. Altering the sequence is a team function. For example, the change can be from Periods 1, 2–3, and 6–7 to Periods 6–7, 1, and 2–3. The different times of the day concur with what is known about the natural biorhythms and chemicals in the body that influence the ability to attend to instruction. In the mid- to late afternoon and at night, the body generally has higher levels of acetylcholine, a neurotransmitter that is associated with drowsiness (Jensen, 1998, p. 44; Sylwester, 1995, p. 81).

Additionally, the body experiences ultradian rhythms that influence the attention cycle. Each cycle lasts about 90–110 minutes. When students are at the bottom of their cycle, they are drowsy and less attentive. Movement helps to counteract the drowsiness (Jensen, 1998, p. 44). The altered schedule provides novelty that assures attention through a change in the tempo of the class day (Jensen, 1998, p. 51).

Teaching students at different times of their attention cycle maximizes their opportunity to master the content and skills of their learning. Sprenger (1999, p. 95) suggests that a rotating schedule is a more brain-compatible approach to teach difficult content; consequently, in the absence of a formal rotational schedule as described in Chapter 4, altering the sequence of classes will accomplish a similar effect as a team function.

Table 7.7 presents a team schedule that is prerequisite to understanding Table 7.8, which illustrates altering the sequence of classes.

Rotation can occur daily, weekly, or monthly. The student sees the teacher at many different times of the day, guaranteeing that some of the times will be at peak times for learning.

Large Group Instruction

At times, a speaker, film, or team meeting is needed. By flexing the time to allow all students on the team to meet, the event can be a one-time

Table 7.7 Altering the Sequence of Classes: Base Schedule for Career Pathway-Technology

	1	2	3	4	5	6	7
English	01	02	03	TM	Plan	H-01	04
Social Studies	H-01	01	02	TM	Plan	03	04
Math	Alg. II 01	Geom. 01	Geom. 02	TM	Plan	Alg. II 02	H. Geom. 01
Science	Chem. 01	H. Chem. 01	Chem. 02	TM	Plan	Chem. 03	Chem. 04
Tech	I-01	II-01	III-01	TM	Plan	I-02	II-02
Sp. Ed.	I-CS	I-CS	I-CS	TM	Plan	I-CS	I-CS

Table 7.8 Altering the Sequence of Classes: Five Rotations

Periods	Rotation 1	Rotation 2	Rotation 3	Rotation 4	Rotation 5
1	1	2	3	6	7
2	2	3	6	7	1
3	3	6	7	1	2
6	6	7	1	2	3
7	7	1	2	3	6

presentation. This process allows all students to have a similar experience and hear similar information, and respects the time of an invited speaker. The instruction can be arranged at any time during the team's assigned class periods.

When planning the large group session or program, students' attention span limits need to be considered. An adult attention span might be 20 minutes; an adolescent's attention span is generally considered to be age plus two. Jensen (1998, p. 45) suggests that highly sustained attention lasts for 10 minutes or less. This phenomenon exists because time is needed to process information. Therefore, if showing a film, it is wise to stop it occasionally to ask students to reflect on the content or to share with a partner how the film supports the stated target learning.

Information and data presented in the large group lays the groundwork for additional discussion in individual classrooms. That form of follow-up provides repetition or rehearsal essential for placing information into long-term memory. The large group can also be a forum for a team meeting in which field trip groundwork is laid or team-building activities are planned.

Tables 7.9 and 7.10 contain the pattern for reallocating time for large group sessions. Table 7.9 contains a regular schedule prior to flexing. Table 7.10 indicates how minutes are redistributed within the blocked time. The original class period length is 45 minutes, including passing time. A speaker will use 30 minutes, so the remaining time for classes is approximately 38 minutes per class.

Table 7.9   Large Group Instruction: Base Schedule for Career Pathway–Health Careers

	1	2	3	4	5	6	7
English	01	02	03	04	Flex/Advisory	TM	Plan
Social Studies	01	02	03	04	Flex/Advisory	TM	Plan
Math	Geom. 01	Pre-calc. 01	Pre-calc. 02	Alg. II 01	Flex/Advisory	TM	Plan
Science	H. Chem. 01	Chem. 01	Chem. 02	Chem. 03	Flex/Advisory	TM	Plan
Sp. Ed.					Flex/Advisory	TM	Plan

Table 7.10   Large Group Instruction

Period	Flexed Period	Minutes
1	Guest Speaker	30
2	Period 1	38
3	Period 2	38
4	Period 3	38
5	Period 4	38
	Period 5	38

Adjust Schedule to Extend Instruction

During the SLC meeting, teachers may decide to adjust the length of classes to extend instruction. Collaboration becomes paramount in the planning of this flex strategy. As noted in the large group schedule, time allocated for the interdisciplinary team can be subdivided into periods of varying lengths. If classes are consecutive, teams can merge minutes to create a longer instructional time and alternate class meetings on a Day 1/Day 2 basis.

Many voices suggest that periods longer than 40–45 minutes enhance the learning process. Marzano (2003, pp. 22–25) suggests that students need time that provides the "opportunity to learn" the intended curriculum. With that opportunity and time, teachers deliver or implement a "guaranteed and viable" curriculum. He cites Walberg's (1997) study that noted a "positive relationship between increased instructional time and learning" (Marzano, 2003, p. 26).

Extended time in and of itself, however, does not guarantee student achievement. Researchers and educational authorities emphasize that only when instructional strategies change to use the time effectively is student achievement increased. Jensen (1998) stresses that adequate time throughout instruction is essential for learning. The brain needs time to process information and to place it into a meaningful context before additional information can take hold. Consequently, the pacing of instruction throughout the entire class period must be carefully planned to include building on prior knowledge, practice or rehearsal, reflection, and formative assessment to determine the student's level of understanding. The time afforded by class periods beyond 40–45 minutes encourages these practices. Hackmann and Valentine (1998, p. 5) suggest that granting teachers the ability to control time increases their sense of empowerment over curriculum. With that power, they are more likely to increase their repertoire of strategies. A detailed explanation of an extended lesson plan appears in Chapter 10.

Within an extended-time period, students should experience a variety of incremental engagements. Rather than passive instruction, they are more likely to be involved in active participation toward the learning targets through a variety of means, including cooperative learning experiences. Time becomes an enhancing factor for learning rather than a limiting one.

The schedule in Table 7.11 is for a health careers pathway. These students have completed the prerequisites for chemistry and are at various stages in meeting the math requirements for graduation. The health careers teacher provides several elective opportunities for students within this pathway. In Periods 7 and 8, students have classes outside of the pathway to meet other required courses and experience electives.

When the cohort of teachers chooses a 90-minute class instead of the 45-minute class, they operate on a Day1/Day 2 basis for Periods 1–6 only. Table 7.12 illustrates this flexible framework.

When Grades 5 and 6 are in the middle school, a three-teacher team as illustrated in Table 7.13 is used. All teachers teach reading/language arts for a double period each day. In Periods 4, 5, and 6, one teacher teaches social studies to all three classes, one teaches math to all three classes, and one teaches science to all three classes. Typically, Periods 4, 5, and 6 are 45-minute classes.

Table 7.11   Adjust Schedule to Extend Instruction: Base Schedule for Health Careers Pathway

	1	2	3	4	5	6	7	8
English	H-01	01	02	03	04	Flex/Advisory	Team Meet	Plan
Social Studies	01	H-01	02	03	04	Flex/Advisory	Team Meet	Plan
Math	Geom. 01	Pre-calc. 01	Pre-calc. 02	Alg. II 01	Alg. II 02	Flex/Advisory	Team Meet	Plan
Chemistry	01	02	03	H-01	04	Flex/Advisory	Team Meet	Plan
Health Careers	Anatomy and Physiology 01	Medical Term. 01	Med. Ethics 01	Anatomy and Physiology 02	Anatomy and Physiology 03	Flex/Advisory	Team Meet	Plan
Sp. Ed.	I-CS Math	I-CS Eng.	I-CS Eng.			Flex/Advisory	Team Meet	Plan

Table 7.12   Adjust Schedule to Extend Instruction: Double Periods in Health Careers Pathway

Period	Minutes	Day 1: Period	Minutes	Day 2: Period	Minutes
1	45	1	90	2	90
2	45				
3	45	3	90	4	90
4	45				
5	45	5	90	6	90
6	45				

Table 7.13   Adjust Schedule to Extend Instruction: Base Schedule for Middle School Grade 5 or 6

	1	2	3	4	5	6	7	8
Reading/Lang. Arts + Social Studies	R/LA 01	Team Meet	Social Studies 01	Social Studies 02	Social Studies 03	Plan	Flex/Advisory
Reading/Lang. Arts + Math	R/LA 02	Team Meet	Math 03	Math 01	Math 02	Plan	Flex/Advisory
Reading/Lang. Arts + Science	R/LA 03	Team Meet	Science 02	Science 03	Science 01	Plan	Flex/Advisory
Sp. Ed.	Replacement R/LA	Team Meet	Replacement Math	I-CS Math	I-CS Math	Plan	Flex/Advisory

Table 7.14   Adjust Schedule to Extend Instruction: Middle School Grade 5 or 6 Adjustment in Periods 4, 5, and 6

Period	Minutes	Day 1	Minutes	Day 2	Minutes	Day 3	Minutes
4	45	4	77	6	77	5	77
5	45	5		4	77	6	77
6	45		77				

In Table 7.14, these teachers can create an extended period for social studies, science, and math using a Day 1/Day 2/Day 3 rotation.

At the high school level, combination teams allow an English and American history teacher to teach the same 50 students for the same two periods of the day. Similarly, a math and science teacher could also share the same 50 students for the same two periods of the day. In addition to making interdisciplinary connections, these teachers can create double or single periods as the need arises according to levels of understanding, formative assessments, or lesson content. When they choose to extend the period, as shown in Table 7.15, they operate on a Day 1/Day 2 basis for those students in those courses.

Table 7.15   Adjust Schedule to Extend Instruction: High School Combination Team

Initial Schedule	1	2	3	4	5	6	7	8
Eng. 11	01	02	TM	03	04	Plan	05	06
Am. Hist.	02	01	TM	04	03	Plan	06	05
Day 1								
Eng. 11	01		TM		03		Plan		05	
Am. Hist.	02		TM		04		Plan		06	
Day 2								
Eng. 11	02		TM		04		Plan		06	
Am. Hist.	01		TM		03		Plan		05	

Group and Regroup Students

On a temporary or fluid basis, teachers may choose to regroup students to improve understanding, to provide an intervention or enrichment, or to change a student's teaching section. Effective regrouping involves short-term placement so that students do not remain in a particular track or level beyond their need. The targeted skill or content-level benefits must be clear. Regrouping also allows students with concept understanding an opportunity to pursue deeper understandings or to put a real-life application into practice. Danielson (2002, pp. 46–47) affirms that "flexibility . . . is the key" to monitor and accommodate student understanding and subsequent achievement.

Regrouping allows teachers to make modifications for students rather than expecting students to modify themselves to fit the curriculum (Tomlinson, 1999). Regrouping also avoids the homogeneity associated with tracking, which has been found by many researchers to be detrimental to student achievement, especially for those in the bottom tracks (Oakes, 2005, cited in Armstrong, 2006, p. 140).

In order to meet students' needs, regrouping overrides the master schedule. When regrouping is done according to student interests, it demonstrates respect for the students as individuals. Occasionally, a student may have to be moved from one teaching section to another to adjust for behavior or peer relationship situations. This smaller version of regrouping illustrates that teachers control time to meet student needs more effectively.

Table 7.16 illustrates regrouping in a single-subject collaboration. Two Algebra I teachers have the same 53 students in the same period of the day. Although the computer randomly places a student in one of two sections, the teachers administer a learning style inventory followed by a pretest on the first unit to determine the first regrouping. For the next 10–12 days of school, the teachers use the data to determine how to teach the unit. Formative assessments provide crucial information for lesson planning. When the unit is completed, teachers administer a unit test and again regroup the students. Some students move into an intervention Tier 2 experience while others complete enrichment engagements associated with that unit. After completing all aspects of Unit 1, the students receive a pretest for Unit 2 and are regrouped accordingly to repeat the cycle.

Table 7.16   Group and Regroup Students: Algebra I Single-Subject Team

Period 1. Initial Placement	Enrollment	
Mr. Bolster	27	
Mrs. Geiss	26	
First regrouping following learning styles inventory and pretest on Unit 1		
	Enrollment	
Mr. Bolster	29	
Mrs. Geiss	24	
Second regrouping following test on Unit 1		
	Enrollment	
Mr. Bolster	18	Intervention Tier 2
Mrs. Geiss	35	Enrichment based on Unit 1
Third regrouping after pretest on Unit 2		
	Enrollment	
Mr. Bolster	31	
Mrs. Geiss	21	

Teachers involved in a three-teacher team use regrouping especially with regard to students with special needs. Table 7.17 reflects the original assignments at the outset of the school year. Table 7.18 exemplifies students moving from the replacement reading/language arts class to the regular program perhaps with a co-teacher or an aide. Some of the students from the replacement math class move into the co-taught math class. Other students change sections to balance the numbers since social studies and science can be grouped on a heterogeneous basis. In Tables 7.17 and 7.18, numbers in parentheses represent enrollment numbers. When regrouping students, teachers alternate between teaching those students who need additional instruction and teaching those who need enrichment. This practice avoids any threat of labeling classes or teachers.

Create Time for Interdisciplinary Connection

An interdisciplinary or cross-curricular unit connects two or more subject areas organized around a particular theme or concept. Use of a theme or concept expands the possibility for more subject areas to become

Table 7.17   Group and Regroup Students: Base Schedule for Three-Teacher Team Showing Student Enrollments

	1	2	3	4	5	6	7	8
Reading/Lang. Arts + Social Studies	R/LA 01 (27)	Team Meet	Social Studies 01 (26)	Social Studies 02 (30)	Social Studies 03 (31)	Plan	Flex/ Advisory
Reading/Lang. Arts + Math	R/LA 02 (25)	Team Meet	Math 03 (26)	Math 01 (27)	Math 02 (25)	Plan	Flex/ Advisory
Reading./Lang. Arts + Science	R/LA 03 (26)	Team Meet	Science 02 (26)	Science 03 (31)	Science 01 (32)	Plan	Flex/ Advisory
Sp. Ed.	Replacement R/LA (10)	Team Meet	Replacement Math (10)	I-CS Math	I-CS Math	Plan	Flex/ Advisory

Table 7.18   Group and Regroup: Midyear Revision of Three-Teacher Team Showing Student Enrollment

	1	2	3	4	5	6	7	8
Reading/Lang. Arts + Social Studies	R/LA 01 (28)	Team Meet	Social Studies 01 (27)	Social Studies 02 (30)	Social Studies 03 (30)	Plan	Flex/ Advisory
Reading/Lang. Arts + Math	R/LA 02 (26)	Team Meet	Math 03 (27)	Math 01 (27)	Math 02 (27)	Plan	Flex/ Advisory
Reading/Lang. Arts + Science	R/LA 03 (27)	Team Meet	Science 02 (27)	Science 03 (31)	Science 01 (31)	Plan	Flex/ Advisory
Sp. Ed.	Replacement R/LA (7)	Team Meet	Replacement Math (7)	I-CS Math	I-CS Math	Plan	Flex/ Advisory

involved. When a topic such as Australia or the Olympics becomes the organizing factor, the scope of involvement and the depth of learning are limited. The use of theme or concept offers students the opportunity to note commonalities and subsequently to integrate content, skills, and knowledge for deep understanding (Tomlinson, 2001, p. 74). Erickson (2001) refers to the research work on higher-level learning instruction published by Hilda Taba in 1966. Taba (1966) found that instruction aligned around concepts, generalizations, and principles caused students to move beyond facts into increasingly complex learning that promoted transfer (cited in Erickson, 2001, p. 23). This approach to instruction allows patterns and relationships among different subject areas to emerge. Most often, the unit exists within a team, an SLC, a career pathway, or a grade level rather than being a whole school experience.

The Common Core State Standards encourage the integration of concepts and subject-area content. The CCSS require literacy strategies to be used in all subject areas. These strategies are to incorporate reading, writing, listening, speaking, and language usage (National Governors Association Center for Best Practices, Council of Chief State School Officers, 2010). The particular focus to be integrated within instruction should be discussed and chosen in an SLC meeting as a skill of the week or month so that students experience rehearsal of the various literacy strategies

Originally, the development of interdisciplinary units or connections by all or some of the teachers on a team promised to make learning more relevant and engaging for students. As the practice became widespread without an understanding of its purpose and integral design, it moved away from focusing on concepts and generalizations that guided depth of understanding. It devolved into an elaborate project with little connection to the curriculum. When the focus becomes the "big event" or hands-on project rather than essential learning defined by each of the participating subject areas, transfer and understanding of the basic concept become muddied in the activity.

Bransford, Brown, and Cocking (2000, p. 48) discuss the importance of pattern recognition to develop expertise in a particular area. When instruction in the interdisciplinary unit focuses on the target learning for the unit, it should also encourage students to see the patterns that evolve from each of the participating disciplines. From the patterns, connections emerge creating a real-world understanding of the unit that can be transferred to new situations. Jensen (1998, p. 96) supports this concept: Interdisciplinary and cross-disciplinary instruction creates relevance and context for students to make meaningful patterns and to understand connections, the relationship of ideas, and how individual subjects and facts relate to a larger context. The unit becomes a vehicle for placing information and skills into long-term memory through elaborative rehearsal that takes place when employing cross-curricular standards in the instruction of the unit. During the learning experiences of an interdisciplinary or cross-curricular unit, information is stored as networks of associations, which in turn allow additional information to connect to that network (Wolfe, 2001, pp. 102–103).

Like other opportunities for making flexible use of time, developing the interdisciplinary or cross-curricular unit requires the SLC or interdisciplinary team of teachers to collaborate on the target or essential learning expected in each subject area. Tables 7.19 and 7.20 show how time in a

Table 7.19   Time for Interdisciplinary Connection: Base Schedule for Freshman Academy

	1	2	3	4	5	6	7
English	Team Meet	01	02	03	04	Flex/Advisory	Plan
Social Studies	Team Meet	01	02	03	04	Flex/Advisory	Plan
Math	Team Meet	Alg. I 01	Geom. 01	Alg. I 02	Geom. 02	Flex/Advisory	Plan
Science	Team Meet	H-01	01	02	03	Flex/Advisory	Plan
Sp. Ed.	Team Meet	I-CS	I-CS	I-CS	I-CS	Flex/Advisory	Plan

Table 7.20   Time for Interdisciplinary Connection: Freshman Academy Modified Schedule

	1	2	3	4	5	6	7
Day 1							
English	Team Meet	Interdisciplinary Engagement: Part 1		01	02	Flex/Advisory	Plan
Social Studies	Team Meet			01	02	Flex/Advisory	Plan
Math	Team Meet			Alg. I 01	Geom. 01	Flex/Advisory	Plan
Science	Team Meet			H-01	01	Flex/Advisory	Plan
Sp. Ed.	Team Meet			I-CS	I-CS	Flex/Advisory	Plan
Day 2							
English	Team Meet	Interdisciplinary Engagement: Part 2		03	04	Flex/Advisory	Plan
Social Studies	Team Meet			03	04	Flex/Advisory	Plan
Math	Team Meet			Alg. I 02	Geom. 02	Flex/Advisory	Plan
Science	Team Meet			02	03	Flex/Advisory	Plan
Sp. Ed.	Team Meet			I-CS	I-CS	Flex/Advisory	Plan

freshman academy maximum-flexibility schedule can be designated for interdisciplinary instruction. Table 7.19 contains the base schedule; Table 7.20 shows the modified schedule in which the interdisciplinary time appears.

Each regularly scheduled class meets for a full period on alternate days. The merged time during Periods 3 and 4 is dedicated to instruction in the interdisciplinary unit. The special education teacher is available for the interdisciplinary time as well as the regular subject classes.

Schedule Project Time

In order to monitor student work and to provide frequent formative assessment, short- and long-term projects require schedule adaptations. By providing time within the school day, students are able to control the depth and pace of their own learning. To motivate students and meet

Maslow's category of self-actualization, Marzano (2003, pp. 150–151) advocates student-designed projects. If the project is to be completed by a group, clearly articulated directions for equal sharing of project completion are needed. Frey, Fisher, and Everlove (2009, p. 60) recommend building individual accountability into the criteria.

Most important, the project needs to enhance understanding of the target learning or skill. Examples abound in which students believed the project to be the target learning. In *Turning Points 2000,* Jackson and Davis (2000) relate Coila Morrow's experience as a standards-based professional development expert in Texas. As she visited Texas schools, she noted a proliferation of "hands-on" activites such as sugar cube Alamos. She discovered that although the students were busily engaged, the topic-based project did not reinforce the fundamental concept being taught (Jackson & Davis, 2000, pp. 51–52). Schmoker (2006) relates a similar anecdote attributed to Elaine McEwan. As a part of whole language experience, students in an elementary school spent 37 hours constructing a papier-mâché dinosaur. The teacher spent over a month of reading instruction time building the dinosaur even though these students could not read well. Schmoker (2006, pp. 91–92) further relates Lucy Calkins's dismay over what she refers to as "literature-based arts and crafts in place of solid reading instruction."

To highlight the problem of the above examples, Wolfe (2001, p. 142) takes the position that projects should be a "means to enhance learning, not an end in themselves." The learning standard guides development of the target learning and the project that will demonstrate understanding of that target. Students need to be able to relate the connection of the target learning to the project assignment and know that assessment of the project arises from those bases.

Table 7.20 can be modified to provide flexible time for projects. Table 7.21 provides a base schedule for an interdisciplinary team in Grade 8. That schedule is modified in Table 7.22 to incorporate project time.

In Table 7.21, the periods are 50 minutes long. Students are in elective or exploratory classes in Periods 1 and 2. The core-team minutes are divided in Table 7.22 to allow project time in Periods 3 and 4 for 70 minutes. Periods 5, 6, and 7 are subdivided into five periods at 36 minutes each. In this way, the team incorporates project time and meeting times for each of the subject-area classes on the team. This alignment will work for

Table 7.21 Project Time: Base Schedule for Grade 8 With 50-Minute Periods

	1	2	3	4	5	6	7
English	TM	Plan	01	02	03	H-01	04
Social Studies	TM	Plan	H-01	01	02	03	04
Math	TM	Plan	Alg. 01	Pre-alg. 01	Alg. 02	Pre-alg. 02	Pre-alg. 03
Science	TM	Plan	01	H-01	02	03	04
Spanish I	TM	Plan	01	02	03	04	05
Sp. Ed.	TM	Plan	ICS	ICS	ICS	ICS	ICS

Table 7.22   Project Time: Grade 8 Modified Schedule

	1	2	3	4	5	6	7
English	TM	Plan					
Social Studies	TM	Plan					
Math	TM	Plan	Project Time 70 minutes		Periods 3–7 Each period 36 minutes for a total of 180 minutes		
Science	TM	Plan					
Spanish I	TM	Plan					
Sp. Ed.	TM	Plan					

freshman academy or some career pathway programs as well. The in-school project time allows for teachers to formatively assess student understanding and progress.

Implement Flex/Advisory Period

The flex/advisory period gives teams and SLCs opportunities to meet a variety of student needs. The time encourages the growth of teacher-student relationships that provides students with a sense of belonging. Many educators and educational organizations such as the Association for Middle Level Education, formerly the National Middle School Association (Bergmann, 2001, p. 108), the Association for Supervision and Curriculum Development, and the National Association of Secondary School Principals (2004, p. 73; 2006, p. 135) promote the importance for students to have an adult who provides academic and personal development support. Through relationship building, teachers are better able to determine student needs. Within the team meeting, the SLC considers the outstanding academic and developmental needs of the students to make decisions about the implementation of the flex/advisory period.

Several schedules in Chapter 4 include a flex/advisory period. When flex/advisory time appears in a fixed-time schedule, the SLC designates how the period will be used. Used as an advisory period, teachers address specific team issues, skill building, study skills, or developmental advisory topics such as conflict resolution and bullying. Besides advisory topics, other uses include RTI Tier 2, enrichment, reading, or project time. Occasionally, an SLC may need extra minutes in the core classes. In that case, the flex/advisory minutes can be incorporated into the core periods. Care needs to be taken, however, that this practice does not become the common use of the flex/advisory time.

If no flex/advisory time exists in the schedule, the SLC can reallocate time so that all periods and an advisory period meet. Uses for the created-time period reflect those listed above.

Table 7.23 sets the stage for teacher control of time through an I-MF schedule for a freshman academy. Each teacher has one class outside of the academy. A common plan time and a personal plan time exist for each teacher. The design of sequential classes in Periods 1–4 indicates the time that is available for the SLC to control. That time is flexed in Table 7.24 so

Table 7.23 Flex/Advisory Period: Base Schedule for Fixed Freshman Academy With No Provision for Flex Period

	1	2	3	4	5	6	7
English	9-01	9-02	9-03	H 9-01	Team Meet	Plan	Yearbook
Social Studies	9-01	9-02	H 9-01	9-03	Team Meet	H. Am. Hist. 02	Plan
Math	H. Geom. 01	Geom. 01	Alg. 01	Alg. 02	Team Meet	Plan	Pre-calc.
Science	Bio. 01	H. Bio. 01	Bio. 02	Bio. 03	Team Meet	AP Bio. 01	Plan
Sp. Ed.	ICS	ICS	ICS	ICS	Team Meet	Plan	

Table 7.24 Flex/Advisory Period: Fixed Freshman Academy Schedule With Modification for Flex/Advisory Period

	1	2	3	4		5	6	7
English	Flex/Advisory Period 40 minutes in length	40-minute period: Period 1 class	40-minute period: Period 2 class	40-minute period: Period 3 class	40-minute period: Period 4 class	Team Meet	Plan	Yearbook
Social Studies						Team Meet	H. Am. Hist. 02	Plan
Math						Team Meet	Plan	Pre-calc.
Science						Team Meet	AP Bio. 01	Plan
Sp. Ed.						Team Meet	Plan	

that the freshman academy can incorporate a flex/advisory period into its schedule on an as-needed basis.

The SLC has 200 minutes of time that can be reallocated. In the modification, a 40-minute flex/advisory period appears at the beginning of the day. The remaining time is redistributed among the four core classes so that each class meets. If desired, the flex/advisory period could be placed at a different time during the 200 minutes.

SUMMARIZING LEARNING COMMUNITIES AND FLEXIBILITY: COMING, KEEPING, AND WORKING TOGETHER

Visionaries in the world of business and education promote the concept and practice of teamwork to address problems and create solutions. In order for teamwork to be successful, purposeful collaboration is essential. From the time of Dewey, both concepts, teamwork and collaboration, have been sporadically implemented in the world of education. Perhaps the simplicity of the concepts belies their perceived potential for success. Perhaps the quest for immediate solutions with immediate results precludes the persistence essential for institutionalizing a reform. Perhaps the rapid movement from Industrial Age to Space Age to Information Age causes information overload. Whatever the reason, the work of those who have investigated the practice of SLCs and PLCs stands strong: When teachers are given the opportunity and the guidelines for collaboration to review student work as well as monitor and create formative or benchmark assessments, instruction and achievement improve.

Flexibility within the schedule contributes another facet for more personalized instruction. The SLC collaboratively determines the level and type of flexibility to meet the instructional need. As noted, when teachers control time, they are more likely to implement different instructional strategies that provide for students' active engagement in their own learning.

Through the provision of time, a schedule empowers teachers to come together, to meet to discuss issues of curriculum and instruction. Then the teachers' task becomes one of maintaining the collaborative culture to meet identified educational goals. When efficiently accomplished, success materializes for all stakeholders.

8

Steps in Building a Middle School Schedule

One step at a time is good walking.

Chinese Proverb

Previous chapters focused on special populations included in secondary schools. To serve the needs of these students and all other groups, the master schedule or organizational plan becomes a challenge. Not only must the pieces fit to create a composite structure, but that structure needs to set the stage for flexibility.

Building the middle school schedule occurs as the result of a nine-step process. Each of these steps is clearly defined to allow smooth, articulated movement from one step to the next. In many middle schools, a scheduling committee that includes a range of stakeholders coordinates these steps. They are responsible for assessing the current schedule, identifying issues and concerns, preparing the first draft of the schedule, obtaining feedback from teachers, and making revisions where necessary.

STEP 1: CONNECT WITH THE MISSION/VISION STATEMENT ■

Initially, members of the scheduling team should review the mission/vision statement to reflect current needs. In all cases, implications of the mission/vision statement affect the schedule to be developed and promote high levels of learning.

■ STEP 2: CHOOSE STRUCTURAL FRAMEWORKS

Chapters 4, 5, and 6 introduced fixed and variable structural frameworks in addition to models for integrating those frameworks into a comprehensive school schedule. Certain frameworks are especially significant for the diverse populations discussed in Chapters 2 and 3. Examples of interchangeability appear in the tables in Chapter 6.

Table 8.1 presents fixed and variable frameworks that are generally used in K–8, 5–8, 6–8, and 7–8 settings.

Table 8.1 Structural Frameworks: Middle School

Choice	Fixed	Choice	Variable
	Double English/Double Math		Interdisciplinary–Maximum Flexibility
	Day 1/Day 2		Interdisciplinary–Limited Flexibility
	Trimester		Interdisciplinary–Encore/ Exploratory
	Rotational		Combination
	Single Subject		
	Traditional: 6-, 7-, 8-Period Day		

As the committee chooses frameworks, it should select at least one from the fixed column in Table 8.1 and at least one from the variable column. Readiness of the faculty to implement a framework influences these choices. A worksheet can plot choices similar to the vertical column in Table 6.3 to identify those frameworks that best fit the school's needs.

■ STEP 3: CREATE BELL AND LUNCH SCHEDULES

Early in the scheduling process, bell and lunch schedules are determined. To gain faculty support, teachers need a concrete example of their workday. In coming steps, the bell and lunch schedule affects the program of studies, the blueprint, and teachers' assignments.

Table 8.2 shows a full period for lunch within available time slots during which recess, intervention, or advisory could be scheduled.

Table 8.3 shows a more typical middle school bell and lunch schedule in which students and teachers have approximately 30 minutes for lunch. No class is interrupted for lunch; each class meets continuously for its allotted time. This schedule is built in modules so that the computer

Table 8.2 Full-Period Lunch Schedule: Middle School

	1	8:00–8:45
	2	8:45–9:30
	3	9:30–10:15
Lunch	**4**	**10:15–11:00**
Lunch	**5**	**11:00–11:45**
Lunch	**6**	**11:45–12:30**
Lunch	**7**	**12:30–1:15**
	8	1:15–2:00
	9	2:00–2:45

Table 8.3 Modular Lunch Schedule: Middle School

		Period and Mod	Time		
		1 (1)	8:00–8:45		
		2 (2)	8:50–9:35		
		3 (3)	9:40–10:25		
A		**B**		**C**	
Lunch (4)	10:25–10:55	4 (4–5)	10:30–11:15	4 (4–5)	10:30–11:15
4 (5–6)	11:00–11:45	Lunch (6)	11:15–11:45	5 (6–7)	11:20–12:05
5 (7–8)	11:50–12:35	5 (7–8)	11:50–12:35	Lunch (8)	12:05–12:35
		6 (9)	12:40–1:25		
		7 (10)	1:30–2:15		
		8 (11)	2:20–3:05		

assigns classes in appropriate time slots. Each class period during the lunch period consists of two modules while lunch consists of one module, both indicated in the parentheses.

For middle schools selecting a Day 1/Day 2 schedule, lunch is a 30-minute module during Period 3 of Day 1 and Period 7 of Day 2. Table 8.4 illustrates that lunch is scheduled at the outset of, during, or at the end of Periods 3 and 7. If scheduled in the middle of Periods 3 and 7, the 90-minute class is interrupted for some students. The lunch slots can be rotated to minimize the negative effects of the interrupted classes.

In many cases, the length of the teachers' lunch period is a contractual issue. The scheduling committee makes bell and lunch decisions to balance contract concerns with the most efficient use of available instructional time.

Table 8.4   Day 1/Day 2 Lunch Schedule: Middle School

Periods	Specific Times:	Number of Class Minutes
1 and 5	8:00–9:30	90 minutes
2 and 6	9:35–11:05	90 minutes
3 and 7	11:10–1:10 (includes lunch)	120 minutes
4 and 8	1:15–2:45	90 minutes

■ STEP 4: FORMULATE PROGRAM OF STUDIES

The term *program of studies* refers to courses a student will take. The scheduling committee cannot create a schedule without this knowledge. The program of studies is typically divided into the core section (English, social studies, math, and science) and the encore/exploratory section (physical education, art, music, health, world language, technology, and family consumer science). In some cases, one or more courses from the encore/exploratory section are moved to the core section to increase the likelihood of interdisciplinary–maximum flexibility (I-MF). To set the stage for I-MF, the number of periods in the core block should not exceed the number of periods a teacher may teach on a daily or weekly basis. Typically, students spend five or six periods of the day in the core block, excluding a flex/advisory or intervention period. Staffing is dependent upon the courses offered to the students and the projected enrollment.

Table 8.5 illustrates a program of studies in which double English/ double math is in the schedule. In this example, core teachers will teach six periods per day.

Table 8.6 introduces five variations of the core program of studies. In some cases, teachers teach 25 periods per week; in other cases, teachers teach 30 periods per week. Each option represents an example of I-MF.

Table 8.5   Program of Studies for Core Team: Middle School

Grade 6		Grade 7		Grade 8	
Course	Periods per Week	Course	Periods per Week	Course	Periods per Week
Reading/ Language Arts	10.0	Reading/ Language Arts	10.0	Reading/ Language Arts	10.0
Social Studies	5.0	Social Studies	5.0	Social Studies	5.0
Mathematics	10.0	Mathematics	10.0	Mathematics	10.0
Science	5.0	Science	5.0	Science	5.0
Total Core	**30**	**Total Core**	**30**	**Total Core**	**30**

Table 8.6   Program of Studies: Other Middle School Core Options

Option 1		Option 2		Option 3		Option 4		Option 5	
Course	Periods	Course	Periods	Course	Periods	Course	Periods	Course	Periods
English	5	English	5	English	5	English	5	English	10
Social Studies	5	Social Studies	5	Social Studies	5	Social Studies	5	Social Studies	5
Math	5	Math	5	Math	5	Math	5	Math	5
Science	5	Science	5	Science	5	Science	5	Science	5
World Language	5	World Language	5	Tech/ Art/ FCS	5	Tech/ Art	5	World Language	5
		Flex/ Advisory	5	Flex/ Advisory	5				
Total	**25**		**30**		**30**		**25**		**30**

Subjects that typically appear in the encore section appear in the core program. The scheduling committee explores numerous core options, recognizing that the options may not be the same from grade level to grade level.

The encore portion of the program of studies generally involves two or three periods of the day. In most middle school situations, the core team has a team or data meeting and personal plan time while students are in the encore portion of the schedule. Table 8.7 illustrates one example of an encore program of studies and will be followed by additional examples in succeeding tables. In the detail of creating the final schedule, X and Y refer

Table 8.7   Program of Studies: Encore/Exploratory Middle School

	Grade 6		Grade 7		Grade 8	
	Course	Periods	Course	Periods	Course	Periods
X	Day 1: Physical Education Day 2: Band, Chorus, or General Music	5.0	Day 1: Physical Education Day 2: Band, Chorus, or General Music	5.0	Day 1: Physical Education Day 2: Band, Chorus, or General Music	5.0
Y	Choose 4: Art, Technology, Family and Consumer Science, World Language, Computers, Health	5.0	Choose 4: Art, Technology, Family and Consumer Science, World Language, Computers, Health	5.0	Choose 4: Art, Technology, Family and Consumer Science, World Language, Computers, Health	5.0
Total Encore		10		10		10

to two different periods in the encore/exploratory program of studies in which a student participates. X, Y, and Z are used when students have three periods per day in the encore/exploratory program of studies.

Three additional examples of an encore/exploratory program of studies in Tables 8.8, 8.9, and 8.10 reflect student choice and required experiences especially where remediation is needed. The number of weeks designated for each course appears parenthetically after the course. If the designation is 20 weeks, the course meets every day for one semester or every other day for the year. A designation of 10 represents every day for a quarter or every other day for a semester. A designation of 40 refers to every day for the year.

Table 8.8   Program of Studies: Encore/Exploratory Program Option 1

Period	Courses With Corresponding Number of Weeks in Course
X	Physical Education (20), Band, Chorus, Orchestra, or General Music (20)
Y	World Language (40)

Table 8.9   Program of Studies: Encore/Exploratory Program Option 2

Period	Course With Corresponding Number of Weeks in Course
X	Physical Education (20), Band, Chorus, Orchestra, General Music (20)
Y	World Language (20), Technology (10), Family Consumer Science (10)
Z	Create a package from the following for a total of 40 weeks: • Special Education Support (20 or 40) • ELL Support (20 or 40) • Tech (10 or 20) • Art Elective (10 or 20) • FCS (10 or 20) • Tier 3 Math (20) • Tier 3 Language Arts (20) • Guitar (10 or 20) • Music Elective (10 or 20) • Computers (10 or 20)

STEP 5: PROJECT ENROLLMENT

Crucial decisions about team structure and full-time-equivalent (FTE) positions needed based upon the program of studies ultimately depend upon the projected enrollment for the school. Sufficient seating is needed in various parts of the schedule for students with special needs. The success of the special education inclusion program depends on the number of standard grade-level classes where co-teaching can occur. Tables 8.11 and 8.12 provide a managerial tool to make these decisions.

Table 8.11 identifies the teaming options available at each grade level. Two-teacher teams facilitate the transition of students from elementary to middle school. In the Grade 7 example, the team model works only if all

Table 8.10 Program of Studies: Encore/Exploratory Program Option 3

Period	Course With Corresponding Number of Weeks in Course
X	Physical Education (40)
Y	World Language (40)
	Create a package from the following for a total of 40 weeks: • Band, Chorus, or Orchestra (20) • Special Education Support (20 or 40) • ELL Support (20 or 40) • Tech (10 or 20) • Art Elective (10 or 20) • FCS (10 or 20) • Tier 2 Math (10 or 20) • Tier 3 Math (20) • Tier 2 Language Arts (10 or 20) • Tier 3 Language Arts (20) • Special Education Math (20) • Special Education Reading (20) • Guitar (10 or 20)

Table 8.11 Projected Enrollment: Teaming Option for Middle School

Grade	Enrollment	Sections	Average Class Size	Teaming Options
5	200	8	25	2,2,2,2
6	200	8	25	4,4; 3,3,2; 2,2,2,2
7	230	9	25.3	4,5
8	245	10	24.5	5,5

teachers on the four-teacher team teach reading in the content areas. In Grade 8, a student generally enrolls in five different subjects; therefore, a pair of five teacher teams is the viable option.

For a more detailed picture of special populations on teams, Table 8.12 provides a worksheet. This table shows additional information about the number of seats needed in encore/exploratory classes as compared to those in core classes.

Analysis of projected enrollment figures sets the stage to identify teaming options that best serve the needs of the total student population.

STEP 6: DECIDE TEAM COMPOSITION

The middle school concept urges a team structure with as much flexibility as possible. The projected enrollment data allow the scheduling committee to closely examine team structures, which differ from grade to grade or school to school. Table 8.13 presents six options. The six-teacher option has two language arts/reading teachers and two mathematics teachers.

Table 8.12   Projected Enrollment: Teaming Option With Special Populations

	Grade 5	Grade 6	Grade 7	Grade 8
Regular education				
Special education: inclusion				
Other (e.g., ELL, gifted)				
Total number of students in regular core sections				
Number of core sections				
Special education: self-contained				
Total number of students				
Number of encore sections based on all students				

Table 8.13   Teaming Configurations: Middle School

Two core teachers plus a special education or ELL teacher: • Language arts, social studies, reading • Mathematics, science, reading • Special education, ELL	Three core teachers plus a special education or ELL teacher: • Language arts/reading + social studies • Language arts/reading + mathematics • Language arts/reading + science • Special education, ELL
Four core teachers plus a special education or ELL teacher: • Language arts • Social studies • Mathematics • Science • Special education, ELL	Four core teachers plus a special education or ELL teacher: • Language arts + flex/advisory • Social studies + flex/advisory • Mathematics + flex/advisory • Science + flex/advisory • Special education, ELL, + flex/advisory
Five core teachers plus a special education or ELL teacher: • Language arts • Social studies • Mathematics • Science • World language • Special education, ELL	Six core teachers plus a special education or ELL teacher: • Language arts/reading 1 • Mathematics 1 • Social studies • Science • Language arts/reading 2 • Mathematics 2 • Special education, ELL

■ STEP 7: DEVELOP A BLUEPRINT

As in an architectural plan, a blueprint guides the construction of the middle school schedule. Data collected in previous steps play a significant role in shaping this blueprint.

A blueprint consists of three parts: when students are in core classes, when students are in encore/exploratory classes, and when students are at lunch. The blueprint is a major factor in setting the stage for flexibility and extended-time instruction. This is accomplished by providing teachers with the greatest number of consecutive classes. The number of encore/ exploratory teachers determines the number of sections or teams that can be in encore at the same time. Core teachers have planning time when students are in encore/exploratory classes; encore/exploratory teachers have common planning time when students are in core classes.

Table 8.14   Blueprint Option 1: All Encore Teachers Full-Time in Building

	Grade 6	Grade 7	Grade 8
1	Core	Core	Encore/exploratory
2	Core	Core	Encore/exploratory
3	Core	Core	Core
4	Core	Encore/exploratory	Core
5	Core	Encore/exploratory	Core
6	Core	Core	Core
7	Encore/exploratory	Core	Core
8	Encore/exploratory	Core	Core
Lunch between:	4 and 5	5 and 6	6 and 7

Table 8.15   Blueprint Option 2: Band and/or Orchestra Teachers Available in Morning or Afternoon

	Grade 6	Grade 7	Grade 8
1	Core	Core	Encore/exploratory
2	Core	Encore/exploratory	Core
3	Encore/exploratory	Core	Core
4	Core	Core	Core
5	Core	Core	Core
6	Encore/exploratory	Core	Core
7	Core	Core	Encore/exploratory
8	Core	Encore/exploratory	Core
Lunch between:	5 and 6	4 and 5	3 and 4

Table 8.16   Blueprint Option 3: Band, Chorus, and Orchestra Scheduled in Flex/ Advisory

Period	Grade 6	Grade 7	Grade 8
1	Core	Encore/exploratory	Core
2	Core	Encore/exploratory	Core
3	Core	Core	Core
4	Core	**Core**	**Core**
5	Encore/exploratory	Core	Core
6	Encore/exploratory	Core	Core
7	Core	Core	Encore/exploratory
8	Core	Core	Encore/exploratory
9	Band, chorus, orchestra, flex/advisory, and interventions		
Lunch between:	4 and 5	5 and 6	3 and 4

Table 8.17   Blueprint Option 4: Day 1/Day 2 Schedule

		Grade 6	Grade 7	Grade 8
Day 1	1	Core	Core	Encore/exploratory
	2	Core	Encore/exploratory	Core
	3	Core	Core	Core
	4	Encore/exploratory	Core	Core
Day 2	5	Core	Core	Encore/exploratory
	6	Core	Encore/exploratory	Core
	7	Core	Core	Core
	8	Encore/exploratory	Core	Core

The four blueprints presented provide different examples of this managerial strategy. The grid of teachers' assignments or actual schedule is based on the blueprint. Therefore, experimentation with the blueprint is essential to provide equity of opportunity for team flexibility and extended-time period instruction.

■ STEP 8: ASSEMBLE GRID OF TEACHERS' ASSIGNMENTS

The working schedule emerges during this step. As demonstrated in Tables 8.18 and 8.19, the specific schedule of each core and encore teacher appears. The grid meticulously follows the blueprint to achieve its objective.

Table 8.18 exemplifies the schedule of one interdisciplinary team. A typical middle school might have as many as six interdisciplinary teams with each team having its own schedule. Table 8.19 shows only a portion of the encore/exploratory teachers' schedules. Art and music meet on an alternate-day basis while physical education meets daily. Students are usually individually scheduled. On the complete schedule, the grid of teachers' assignments will show the exact schedule of each FTE allocated to the school.

In the I-MF framework, all students of a team or of a grade level go to encore-exploratory at the same time. This facilitates interdisciplinary team meetings and, where possible, a data meeting for teachers of the same subject and grade level as they work to address the Common Core State Standards.

Table 8.18 Assemble Grid of Teachers' Assignments: Sample Core Team

Team 7-1	1	2	3	4	5	6	7	8
Miss Brodnick	Reading 01	LA 01	LA 02	Team Meeting	Lunch	Plan	LA 03	LA 04
Miss Ferguson	Reading 02	Social Studies 01	Social Studies 02	Team Meeting	Lunch	Plan	Social Studies 03	Social Studies 04
Mr. Schlesinger	Reading 03	Science 01	Science 02	Team Meeting	Lunch	Plan	Science 03	Science 04
Mrs. Shenk	Reading 04	Math 7 01	Pre-algebra 01	Team Meeting	Lunch	Plan	Math 7 02	Pre-algebra 02
Mr. Miller Special Education	Replacement Reading	In-Class Support	In-Class Support	Team Meeting	Lunch	Plan	In-Class Support	In-Class Support

Table 8.19 Assemble Grid of Teachers' Assignments: Portion of Encore/Exploratory Team

Encore	1	2	3	4	5	6	7	8
Art	8-01/8-02	8-03/8-04	Team Meeting/ Plan	7-01/7-02	7-03/7-04	Team Meeting/ Plan	6-01/6-02	6-03/6-04
Music	8-01/8-02	8-03/8-04	Team Meeting/ Plan	7-01/7-02	7-03/7-04	Team Meeting/ Plan	6-01/6-02	6-03/6-04
Physical Education	8-01	8-03	Team Meeting/ Plan	7-01	7-03	Team Meeting/ Plan	6-01	6-03
Physical Education	8-02	8-04	Team Meeting/ Plan	7-02	7-04	Team Meeting/ Plan	6-02	6-04

■ STEP 9: PLAN PROFESSIONAL DEVELOPMENT

Members of the scheduling committee have a major responsibility to meet the needs of all students who comprise the school family. Consequently, the schedule must enable all of its component parts to function effectively and interdependently.

A professional development program should focus on the details of the change process, the role and function of teams and small learning communities, and effective teaching strategies for variable-length time periods. A focus on flexibility must be an underlying component of that professional development experience. This training is most effective when it occurs as an ongoing process.

■ SUMMARIZING STEPS IN BUILDING A MIDDLE SCHOOL SCHEDULE: STEPS FOR GOOD WALKING

Because the complexity of today's educational climate requires input from many stakeholders, this nine-step schedule-building process relies on a committee effort, not the work of one individual. Throughout the deliberations, a focus on the needs of special populations must mesh with the needs of all students. When the schedule is finalized, professional development becomes the tool with which teachers begin to understand the intent and mechanics of the schedule. At this stage, the steps become good walking when all realize that the schedule is a means to an end and not an end unto itself. No one element improves school culture, climate, or achievement. Those components result from teachers taking responsibility for the teaching and learning process and from all parties taking the necessary steps to begin by creating and implementing a viable, flexible schedule.

9

Steps in Building a High School Schedule

Before anything else, preparation is the key to success.

Alexander Graham Bell

As stated in Chapter 8, previous chapters focused on diverse populations included in secondary schools. To serve the needs of these students and all other groups, the master schedule or organizational plan becomes a challenge. Not only must the pieces fit to create a comprehensive structure, but that structure needs to set the stage for flexibility. Exciting changes are occurring at the high school level. No longer is the schedule a traditional six-, seven-, eight-, or nine-period day. Rather, creative approaches exist to manage time in houses, magnets, and academies.

Ironically, the high school schedule is still based on identifying and spreading singletons, doubletons, and tripletons to maximize the likelihood of students receiving their first choice of courses. Consequently, although change from the traditional is manifested, the comprehensive schedule evolves through individualized course requests by students that reflect their individual needs and aspirations. The high school of today strives to address the needs of all populations, reduce the dropout rate, and facilitate transition to institutions of higher learning and the world of work.

Computer software is a tool for scheduling to achieve the goals, mission/vision statements, and priorities of a high school. The software is, however, subject to the designs and frameworks identified by the scheduling committee.

■ STEP 1: CONNECT WITH THE MISSION/VISION STATEMENT

Initially, members of the scheduling team should review the mission/vision statement to determine that it reflects current needs. In all cases, implications of the mission/vision statement affect the schedule to be developed and promote high levels of learning (Danielson, 2002, p. 118).

■ STEP 2: CHOOSE STRUCTURAL FRAMEWORKS

Chapters 4, 5, and 6 introduced fixed and variable structural frameworks in addition to models for integrating those frameworks into a comprehensive school organization. Certain frameworks are especially significant for diverse populations discussed in Chapters 2 and 3. The examples of interchangeability that appear in the tables in Chapter 6 guide the detail to develop the comprehensive schedule.

Table 9.1 presents fixed and variable frameworks that are generally used in schools that house Grades 9–12.

As the committee chooses frameworks, it should select at least one from the fixed column in Table 9.1 and perhaps one or more from the variable column. The variable frameworks accommodate small learning communities (SLCs), houses, magnets, or academies. Readiness of the faculty to implement a framework influences choices. A worksheet to plot choices similar to the vertical column in Table 6.3 identifies those frameworks that fit the school's needs.

Table 9.1   Structural Frameworks: High School

Choice	Fixed	Choice	Variable
	Semester 1/Semester 2: 4 × 4		Interdisciplinary–Maximum Flexibility
	Semester 1/Semester 2: 5 × 5		Interdisciplinary–Limited Flexibility
	Quarters		Interdisciplinary–Encore/Exploratory
	Day 1/Day 2		Combination
	Trimesters		
	Rotational		
	Single Subject		
	Traditional: 6-, 7-, 8-Period Day		

STEP 3: CREATE BELL AND ■
LUNCH SCHEDULES

Early in the scheduling process, bell and lunch schedules are determined. To gain faculty support, teachers need a concrete example of their work-day. Table 9.2 shows a full period for lunch that maximizes the likelihood of students receiving their first choice of courses. Further, classrooms are available for other teachers to use.

Table 9.2   Full-Period Lunch Schedule: High School

	1	8:00–8:45
	2	8:50–9:35
	3	9:40–10:25
Lunch	**4**	**10:30–11:15**
Lunch	**5**	**11:20–12:05**
Lunch	**6**	**12:10–12:55**
Lunch	**7**	**1:00–1:45**
	8	1:50–2:35
	9	2:40–3:25

Table 9.3 shows a modular lunch in which students and teachers have approximately 30 minutes for lunch. No class is interrupted for lunch; each class meets continuously for its allotted time. This schedule is built in modules so that the computer assigns class time appropriately during the lunch hours. Each class session during the lunch period consists of two modules while lunch consists of one module, both indicated in parentheses. A modular lunch increases instructional time but risks the likelihood of conflicts because the lunch times of teachers and scheduled class times may not be compatible.

For high schools selecting a Semester 1/Semester 2—4 × 4, quarter, or Day 1/Day 2 schedule, lunch is a 30-minute module during Periods 3 and 7. Table 9.4 illustrates how lunch is scheduled at the outset, in the middle, or at the end of Periods 3 and 7. If scheduled in the middle of Periods 3 and 7, the 90-minute class is interrupted. Four lunch periods are possible.

Table 9.5 indicates a bell and lunch schedule when the school operates on a Semester 1/Semester 2—5 × 5 schedule. Lunch occurs in Periods 3 and 8, but is a 40-minute period. A student has either lunch followed by a skinny or a skinny followed by lunch. The skinny classes scheduled in Periods 3 and 7 are not interrupted for lunch.

Schools selecting a rotational schedule must decide on the specifics of the lunch schedule. In the eight-period-day rotating schedule, schools may have a unit lunch preceding the first of the afternoon classes or a

Table 9.3   Modular Lunch Schedule: High School

		Period and Mod	Time		
		1 (1)	8:00–8:45		
		2 (2)	8:50–9:35		
		3 (3)	9:40–10:25		
A		B		C	
Lunch (4)	10:25–10:55	4 (4–5)	10:30–11:15	4 (4–5)	10:30–11:15
4 (5–6)	11:00–11:45	Lunch (6)	11:15–11:45	5 (6–7)	11:20–12:05
5 (7–8)	11:50–12:35	5 (7–8)	11:50–12:35	Lunch (8)	12:05–12:35
		6 (9)	12:40–1:25		
		7 (10)	1:30–2:15		
		8 (11)	2:20–3:05		

Table 9.4   Extended-Time Period Lunch Schedule: High School Option 1

Periods	Specific Times:	Number of Class Minutes
1 and 5	8:00–9:30	90 minutes
2 and 6	9:35–11:05	90 minutes
3 and 7	11:10–1:10 (includes lunch)	120 minutes
4 and 8	1:15–2:45	90 minutes

dual lunch with half of the school eating before and the other half eating after the first of the afternoon classes. Schools selecting the nine-period rotation may use a variation of the modular lunch schedule presented in Table 9.3.

The trimester schedule presents an additional variation for lunch (see Table 9.6). All classes meet for 72 minutes, but Periods 3, 8, and 13 receive an additional 30 minutes for lunch (see Table 9.7). Two thirds of the students will not have an interrupted class period; one third of the students will have a 30-minute instructional module before lunch and a 42-minute instructional module after lunch. The lunch schedule can rotate to allow students to benefit from an uninterrupted instructional period for two thirds of the year.

In many districts, the length of the teachers' lunch period is a contractual issue. The scheduling committee makes bell and lunch decisions to balance contract concerns with the most efficient use of available instructional time.

Table 9.5 Extended-Time Period Lunch Schedule: High School Option 2 English Department

English Department		Semester 1						Semester 2					
		1	2	3 A	3 B	4	5	6	7	8A	8B	9	10
1	Mrs. Jabar	10-01	10-02	Lunch	Tutorial	Plan	Journalism 1-01	10-03	Honors 11-01	Lunch	Tutorial	Honors 11-02	Plan
2	Mr. Toor	AP 12-01	Plan	Yearbook	Lunch	AP 12-02	11-01	11-02	Plan	Yearbook	Lunch	11-03	11-04
3	Mr. Lipsitz	9-01	9-02	Lunch	SAT Prep	9-03	Plan	Drama 1-01	Plan	Lunch	SAT Prep	Honors 9-02	9-04
4	Mrs. Jackson	Honors 11-01	Honors 11-02	AP Tutorial	Lunch	12-01	Plan	Plan	AP 12-02	Tier 3	Lunch	Speech 01	Speech 02

Table 9.6   Trimester Lunch Schedule: High School

Minutes	Trimester 1	Trimester 2	Trimester 3
	Period	Period	Period
72	1	6	11
72	2	7	12
72 + 30	3	8	13
72	4	9	14
72	5	10	15

Table 9.7   Trimester Lunch Schedule: Periods 3, 8, and 13

Distribution of 102 minutes					
Lunch	30	Class	30	Class	72
Class	72	Lunch	30	Lunch	30
		Class	42		

■ STEP 4: FORMULATE PROGRAM OF STUDIES

Each year the principal coordinates the publication of a curriculum booklet for the following school year. In some cases, courses are added, and in others, courses are deleted from the booklet. Two of the important pieces for students are the graduation requirements and the elective courses available. When schools offer magnet experiences, it is important to identify essential courses for each magnet.

Table 9.8 illustrates the program of studies for a freshman academy. If the school schedule includes eight periods, four of the periods are in the freshman academy while the other four periods are in other required courses and electives outside of the freshman academy.

Table 9.8   Freshman Academy: Required Courses

Course	Periods
English 9	5
Social Studies	5
Algebra I, Algebra II, or Geometry	5
Biology	5
Total	20

Table 9.9 Technology Career Pathway: Program of Studies

Course	Periods
English	5
Social Studies	5
Math	5
Science	5
Applied Technology	5
Total	25

Table 9.9 shows the program of studies for a career pathway focusing on technology. The example includes five required experiences, allowing three periods for electives or other courses required for graduation. The Applied Technology course may be an introduction to that particular career pathway or a next course in sequence for students interested in careers related to technology.

STEP 5: DEVELOP STUDENT REGISTRATION MATERIALS ■

As a companion to the curriculum booklet, schools create a packet of registration materials. These materials reflect the structural frameworks selected. For example, a school with a traditional seven-period day asks students to register for seven yearlong courses or a sufficient number of yearlong and semester courses to complete the seven periods of the schedule. For a trimester schedule, students register for 15 courses. Requirements of specific houses, magnets, or academies will have an impact on course selection.

STEP 6: ESTABLISH STUDENT DATABASE ■

The student database emerges from the registration process and the careful numbering of all courses. A course number typically consists of digits that reflect the department, specific course, and academic level. In some cases, an additional digit reflects the house, magnet, or academy.

The student database must be initiated in January, February, or March for the most efficient decisions about full-time-equivalent (FTE) distribution and the provision for sufficient sections for each course. This database must be revised at the end of the school year and periodically during the summer to accommodate new entrants, withdrawals, retentions, summer school attendance, and students who alter their requests. Table 9.10 illustrates a student's course requests based on the Semester 1/Semester 2—4 × 4, Day 1/Day 2, quarter, rotational, single-subject, or traditional structural frameworks.

Table 9.10   Course Requests: Eight-Period Day

Course	Course Number
English 9	1010
Social Studies 9	2020
Algebra I	3031
Biology	4051
French II	6042
Physical Education and Health	8060
Band	5306
Animation	8092

Table 9.11   Course Requests: Semester 1/Semester 2—5 × 5

Course	Course Number
English 9	1010
Social Studies 9	2020
Algebra I	3031
Biology	4051
French II	6042
Physical Education and Health	8060
Band	5306
Animation	8092
Semester 1 Skinny: Tier 3 Reading and Math	1525
Semester 2 Skinny: Art Elective	8097

As shown in Table 9.11, a skinny must be indicated for each semester.

Table 9.12 is an example of a student's course requests for a trimester schedule. The columns in Table 9.12 indicate not a particular trimester but the listing of 15 courses requested.

Table 9.12   Student Requests: Trimesters

Course	Course	Course
Credit Recovery: English 9 B	Geometry B	Physical Education A
English 10 A	World Cultures A	Physical Education B
English 10 B	World Cultures B	Art I A
Credit Recovery: Algebra I B	Biology A	Art I B
Geometry A	Biology B	Art II A

Table 9.13 shows an example of an alphabetized student course file. This file is typically maintained by the school counselors but is accessed by school administrators as needed. These entries become the basis of the overall tally and the department summaries to be discussed later in the chapter. The example provided does not reflect the 15 requests of a trimester schedule.

The student database step is critical. As a result of the compilation and analysis of data, a comprehensive schedule emerges that addresses the needs of school populations and is based on student course requests.

Table 9.13   Student Alphabetical Course Request File

Student	Student ID	1	2	3	4	5	6	7	8	9
Howard, Joshua	0798641	1010	2010	3010	4010	5010	7326	7816	8604	8605
Kazeer, Orlando	1384016	1011	2010	3111	4010	5111	5174	6151	X	X
Oskar, Josea	2374161	1411	2407	3411	5611	5111	6203	6205	7118	7119

STEP 7: PROJECT ENROLLMENT   ■

In addition to the collection of individual student course requests, the scheduling committee must have knowledge of the total school enrollment, grade-level enrollment, and number of students enrolled in courses by department. Consideration must be given to anticipated retentions, trends of increasing or decreasing enrollment, and the impact of credit recovery programs.

Generally, the superintendent assigns a total number of FTEs to a school. With that information, the principal with the help of the scheduling committee distributes those positions by department, using the department summary managerial tool. The specifics of this process appear in Step 9.

STEP 8: DECIDE COMPOSITION   ■
OF HOUSES, MAGNETS,
OR ACADEMIES

Prior to the course request analysis by department, decisions are made on the composition of houses, magnets, and academies, hereafter referred to as SLCs. Once confirmed, these configurations will be entered into the schedule prior to the placement of singletons, doubletons, or tripletons on the grid. In many cases, SLC teachers appear on the schedule as a cohort, not as members of a department. The scheduling committee identifies teachers for these assignments prior to department summaries, the FTE distribution chart, and teacher assignment charts.

Examples of SLCs in Grades 9–12 include a traditional freshman academy, a freshman academy based on combination teaming, and a communications career pathway. The traditional freshman academy in Table 9.14

Table 9.14   Freshman Academy: Maximum Flexibility

	1	2	3	4	5	6	7	8
English	Plan	H 9-01	9-01	Team Meet	9-02	9-03	Flex/ Advisory	Yearbook 01
Social Studies	Plan	9-01	9-02	Team Meet	9-03	9-04	Flex/ Advisory	AP Government 02
Math	Pre-calculus 04	Alg. I 01	Alg. I 02	Team Meet	Geometry 01	H Geometry 01	Flex/ Advisory	Plan
Science	AP Biology 01	Biology 01	H Bio. 01	Team Meet	Biology 02	Biology 03	Flex/ Advisory	Plan
Special Ed.	Other	In-Class support	In-Class support	Team Meet	In-Class support	In-Class support	Flex/ Advisory	Plan

includes five teachers who teach the same students for the same five periods of the day. Each student has the same teacher for English, social studies, math, and science. The special education teacher is available for in-class support in Periods 2, 3, 5, and 6 as well as the flex/advisory period. Although the students in the freshman academy have the same teachers, they do not travel as a group from class to class. Students enroll in three additional courses outside of the academy.

Teachers have common plan time and teach one course outside of the freshman academy. They have full control over instructional time in Periods 2, 3, 5, 6, and 7. Period 7 is a flex/advisory period in which teachers address guidance and intervention needs.

A variation of the freshman academy model appears in Table 9.15 as a combination team. Although the cohort of teachers remains the same, the SLC occurs through the pairing of English and social studies and, separately, math and science. Curriculum integration and connections to the Common Core State Standards between the paired courses provide the emphasis for this team format. Opportunities for variable-length time periods exist within each pairing.

Table 9.15   Freshman Academy: Combination Team Pairings

	1	2	3	4	5	6	7
English	9-01	9-02	Team Meet	9-03	9-04	Plan	H 11-01
Social Studies	9-02	9-01	Team Meet	9-04	9-03	Plan	SS 10-03
Special Ed.	Co-T	Co-T	Team Meet				
Math	9-03	9-04	Team Meet	Plan	Pre-calculus 02	9-01	9-02
Science	9-04	9-03	Team Meet	AP Biology 01	Plan	9-02	9-01
Special Ed.			Team Meet			Co-T	Co-T

Unlike the previous examples, the following career pathway example does not have flexibility. Table 9.16 shows a high school communications career pathway. Students in this pathway focus on broadcasting, journalism, or TV and film. Each day during Period 1, all teachers assigned to the pathway attend a common planning time that focuses on student needs but emphasizes curriculum integration and real-life applications of content and skills. For example, the English teacher offers a differentiated assignment that coincides with each of the communication majors. Conversely, each of the three communication teachers makes curriculum connections with the four core subjects on a regular basis.

Sections away refers to the availability of courses students have chosen outside of the cohort. A conflict matrix is used to place these courses on the grid.

Table 9.16   Career Pathway: Communications

	1	2	3	4	5	6	7
English	Team Meet	H 01	01	02	Plan	03	04
American History	Team Meet	01	H 01	02	Plan	03	04
Chemistry	Team Meet	01	02	H 01	Plan	03	04
Math	Team Meet	Algebra II 01	Algebra II 02	Algebra II 03	Plan	Pre-calculus 01	Algebra II 04
Broadcasting	Team Meet	01				02	
Journalism	Team Meet		01		02		
TV and Film	Team Meet			01			02
Sections Away	5	0	0	0	4	0	0

This pathway consists of five teaching sections or approximately 130–140 students. Students have an individual schedule based upon the honors placements and the choice of broadcasting, journalism, or TV and film. To facilitate the team meeting in Period 1, all students (five sections) are scheduled in other required courses or electives. In Periods 2, 3, 4, 6, and 7, all students are in one of the pathway classes. In Period 5, those students not in Journalism Section 02 are in another required course or elective. Occasionally, a student may leave the career pathway for a special placement in a core subject such as replacing chemistry with physics that is offered in another pathway.

STEP 9: CREATE DEPARTMENT SUMMARIES ■

Creating department summaries, a major managerial strategy, aligns staff assignments to student course requests. Table 9.17 introduces a departmental overview based upon enrollment, number of sections, average class size per section, and the aggregate periods of instruction per week based upon weighting. Each department of instruction completes this analysis.

Table 9.17 Mathematics Department Summary: Nontrimester Schedule

Department: Mathematics	Enrollment	Sections	Average Class Size	Weighting	Aggregate Periods
Tier 3 Math	18	4	4.5	2.5	10
Algebra I	150	7	21.4	5	35
Honors Algebra I	58	2	29.0	5	10
Geometry	150	6	25.0	5	30
Honors Geometry	58	2	29.0	5	10
Algebra II	150	6	25.0	5	30
Honors Algebra II	58	2	29.0	5	10
Pre-calculus	130	5	26.0	5	25
Probability and Statistics	74	3	24.6	5	15
Calculus	75	3	25.0	5	15
AP Calculus	42	2	21.0	5	10
Total	963	42			200
FTEs Needed Based on Teachers' Contract					30-6.6; 25-8.0

The completion of this chart occurs in a series of stages.

- Stage 1: Enrollment. From the student request tally, enter the enrollment for each course in that department.
- Stage 2: Sections. Based upon a desired class size for each course, determine the number of sections to be offered.
- Stage 3: Weighting. A course that meets the equivalent of 5 periods per week for the year receives a weighting of 5 in the weighting column. Courses that meet every other day for the year or every day for one semester receive a weighting of 2.5. Courses that meet the equivalent of 2 periods per day for the year have a weighting of 10.
- Stage 4: Aggregate periods per course. Multiply the number of sections times the weighting of that course to arrive at the aggregate total. For example, if 7 sections of Algebra I are offered the equivalent of 5 times a week for the year, the aggregate number for that course is 35.
- Stage 5: FTEs needed. A direct correlation exists between the number of courses a teacher can teach per week, the total aggregate periods in a department, and the number of FTEs needed for that department. In Table 9.17, the mathematics department has 200 aggregate periods. If teachers can teach the equivalent of 30 periods per week, 6.6 FTEs are needed in that department. If teachers can teach 25 periods per week, the number of FTEs needed in that department is 8.

In the trimester schedule, the department summary is modified. The number of sections becomes the key factor. To calculate the number of

Table 9.18   Mathematics Department Summary: Trimester Schedule

Department: Mathematics	Enrollment	Sections	Average Class Size
Tier 3 Math	18	4	4.5
Algebra I A	150	7	21.4
Algebra I B	150	7	21.4
Honors Algebra I A	58	3	19.3
Honors Algebra I B	58	3	19.3
Geometry A	150	6	25.0
Geometry B	150	6	25.0
Honors Geometry A	58	2	29.0
Honors Geometry B	58	2	29.0
Algebra II A	150	6	25.0
Algebra II B	150	6	25.0
Honors Algebra II A	58	2	29.0
Honors Algebra II B	58	2	29.0
Pre-calculus A	130	5	26.0
Pre-calculus B	130	5	26.0
Probability and Statistics A	74	3	24.6
Probability and Statistics B	74	3	24.6
Calculus A	75	3	25.0
Calculus B	75	3	25.0
AP Calculus A	42	2	21.0
AP Calculus B	42	2	21.0
AP Calculus C	42	2	21.0
Total	1,950	84	
FTEs Needed Based on Number of Sections		7.0	

FTEs needed, divide the number of sections by 12, which is the number of periods taught by a full-time teacher. In Table 9.18, the number of sections is 84; therefore, the number of FTEs needed is 7.

STEP 10: DISTRIBUTE AVAILABLE FTES   ■

Once the FTEs for each department are determined, a chart that summarizes the available FTEs is created. The aggregate period column in Table 9.17 indicates the number of FTEs. In the trimester summary in Table 9.19, the number of sections determines the FTEs needed.

Table 9.19   FTE Distribution Chart

Department	FTE Allocation
English	9.0
Social Studies	8.0
Mathematics	9.0
Science	8.0
World Language	4.0
Special Education	5.0
ELL	2.0
Art	2.5
Music	3.0
Career and Technical Education	4.0
Physical Education	6.0
Technology	2.5
Family Consumer Science	2.0
ROTC	2.0
Agricultural Science	2.0
Total	69

If the number of FTEs in the preliminary calculation for allocation exceeds the number of FTEs provided by the superintendent, reductions must be made. Reduction accomplished by decreasing the number of sections in a given course increases average class size. Some courses with low enrollment may need to be eliminated. This department allocation becomes the basis of teachers' assignments in that department.

■ STEP 11: CATEGORIZE TEACHER ASSIGNMENTS

Until this step is complete, the schedule-building process cannot be initiated. Based on department summaries and adhering to the allocation for each department, the exact assignment of each teacher is created. In many schools, this responsibility rests with the department head. Because SLCs are placed in the master schedule first, teachers with SLC responsibilities must be identified first.

Table 9.20 illustrates a teacher assignment chart for all structural frameworks with the exception of trimesters. Average daily pupil load and number of lesson preparations must be monitored for equity.

Table 9.21 is an example of a teacher assignment chart based on the trimester schedule. Each teacher teaches 12 sections.

Table 9.20   Mathematics Teacher Assignment Chart

Teacher	Assignment	Aggregate Periods	Full-Time Equivalent	Average Daily Student Load
Ms. Carla Estrada	4 Algebra I (20) 2 Algebra II (10)	30	1.0	165
Mr. James Corwin	2 Algebra II (10) 2 H Algebra I (10) 1 Algebra II (5)	25	1.0	145
Mrs. Penelope Booth	4 Geometry (20) 1 H Geometry (5)	25	1.0	150

Table 9.21   Teacher Assignment Chart: Trimesters

Mrs. Britton	6 English 9 A 6 English 9 B = 12 (Freshman Academy)
Mr. Watkins	4 Algebra I A 4 Algebra I B 2 Geometry A 2 Geometry B = 12 (Freshman Academy)
Mr. Williams	3 Spanish II A 3 Spanish II B 3 Spanish III A 3 Spanish III B = 12 (Career Pathway–International Studies)
Mrs. Thomas	3 FCS I A 3 FCS I B 3 FCS II A 3 FCS III A = 12 (Human Growth and Development Academy)
Mrs. Rohr	6 Art I A 6 Art I B = 12

The sequence of the department summary, FTE distribution chart, and teacher assignment chart is one of the most crucial aspects of building a high school schedule. Every position must be justified and clearly defined.

STEP 12: DEVELOP A BLUEPRINT FOR SMALL LEARNING COMMUNITIES ■

Once teachers are assigned to their responsibilities in SLCs, a master plan indicates when students are in the academy and when they are available for electives and other required courses. Table 9.22 provides a sample based upon a high school with four freshman academy cohorts. The objective is to avoid tracking one of the academies based upon the placement of singleton electives.

Period 5 allows students in band, chorus, or orchestra to be equally distributed among all the academies.

Table 9.22   Blueprint for Freshman Academies

Period	Team 9 A	Team 9 B	Team 9 C	Team 9 D
1	Core		Core	
2	Core		Core	
3		Core	Core	Core
4		Core	Core	Core
5				
6		Core		Core
7	Core	Core		Core
8	Core			

■ STEP 13: LIST SINGLETONS, DOUBLETONS, AND TRIPLETONS

Based upon a critical review of the department summary, a crucial step in building a high school schedule occurs: the listing of singletons, doubletons, and tripletons. A singleton is a course with only one section; a doubleton, a course with only two sections; and a tripleton, a course with only three sections. Tripletons are mainly evident in a large high school. Following the listing, the singletons, doubletons, and tripletons are distributed over the school day to maximize the likelihood of students receiving their first choice of courses.

■ STEP 14: FORMULATE CONFLICT MATRIX FOR SINGLETONS, DOUBLETONS, AND TRIPLETONS

The objective of this step is to identify patterns of student requests. These patterns dictate the placement of courses on the grid of teachers' assignments. Table 9.23 provides the matrix that guides the scheduling committee in placing singleton courses in the master schedule. In this matrix, the focus is on the position of Advanced Placement (AP) English 12 with an enrollment of 23 students. To complete the "number of sections available" column, refer to the department summary.

The chart demonstrates what other courses students in AP English 12 have chosen. For example, of the 23 students in AP English 12, 20 are also

Table 9.23   Matrix for Singleton Course: AP English 12

Course Number	Course Name	Corresponding Enrollment	Number of Sections Available
1089	AP English 12	23	1
2095	AP U.S. Government and Economics	20	2
2090	U.S. Government and Economics	3	8
3195	AP Calculus	18	2
3193	Pre-calculus	5	4
3185	Probability and Statistics	7	4
4195	AP Biology	12	1
4185	AP Chemistry	11	1
5192	French V	10	2
5142	Spanish V	13	2

enrolled in AP U.S. Government and Economics. The placement of these courses is critical so that students can be involved in both experiences. Consequently, the critical placements are AP English 12, AP Biology, and AP Chemistry since all are singleton courses.

In the Table 9.24 trimester schedule, most courses will be a double or triple entry. For example, English 11 becomes English 11 A and English 11 B. Calculus becomes Calculus A, Calculus B, and Calculus C.

Table 9.24   Matrix for Singleton Course in Trimesters: AP English 12 A

Course Number	Course Name	Corresponding Enrollment	Number of Sections Available
1089 A	AP English 12 A	23	1
1089 B	AP English 12 B	23	1
2095 A	AP U.S. Government and Economics A	20	2
2095 B	AP U.S. Government and Economics B	20	2
2090 A	U.S. Government and Economics A	3	8
2090 B	U.S. Government and Economics B	3	8
3195 A	Calculus A	18	2
3195 B	Calculus B	18	2
3195 C	Calculus C	18	2
3193 A	Pre-calculus A	5	4
3193 B	Pre-calculus B	5	4

Because the AP English 12 and AP U.S. Government and Economics courses are only scheduled for two trimesters, a decision is needed to determine if they should be offered in Trimesters 1 and 2 or Trimesters 2 and 3. The AP Calculus course is scheduled for three trimesters; therefore, A must be in Trimester 1, B in Trimester 2, and C in Trimester 3.

At this point, members of the scheduling committee are ready to build the master schedule. SLCs are entered first, followed by singletons, then doubletons, then tripletons.

■ STEP 15: PLACE SINGLETONS, DOUBLETONS, AND TRIPLETONS ON MASTER SCHEDULE BY TEACHER AND BY PERIOD

Tables 9.25, 9.26, and 9.27 provide three examples of placing singletons, doubletons, and tripletons on the grid of teachers' assignments. Table 9.25 is a typical nine-period day in which lunch is a full period. As demonstrated, a course can be scheduled in any of the nine periods.

Table 9.26 provides the model for a Day 1/Day 2 or Semester 1/Semester 2—4 × 4 schedule. Teachers will teach three of the four periods on Day 1 or in Semester 1 and three of the four periods on Day 2 or in Semester 2. Lunch occurs at the beginning of A-3 and B-3, during A-3 or B-3, or at the end of A-3 and B-3.

Schools selecting Semester 1/Semester 2—5 × 5 modify Table 9.26 and schedule A-1 through A-5 and B-1 through B-5. Lunch is scheduled during

Table 9.25 Place Singletons, Doubletons, and Tripletons: Nine-Period Schedule

	1	2	3	4	5	6	7	8	9
Mrs. Salazar	S 1015 01	S 1900 01							
Mr. Unitas				S 2105 01	S 2107 01				
Mr. Donovan						S 4617 01			
Mr. Pricer		D 6262 01		D 6365 01			D 6365 02	D 6262 02	
Mr. Suggs	D 7902 01		D 7901 01			D 7902 02			D 7901 02
Dr. Owings		T 1217 01			T 1217 02			T 1217 03	
Mr. Hester	T 2345 01				T 2345 02		T 2345 03		

Table 9.26 Place Singletons, Doubletons, and Tripletons: Day 1/Day 2 or Semester 1/ Semester 2—4 × 4

	A-1	A-2	A-3	A-4	B-1	B-2	B-3	B-4
Mrs. Salazar	S 1015 01	S 1900 01						
Mr. Unitas				S 2105 01	S 2107 01			
Mr. Donovan						S 4617 01		
Mr. Pricer		D 6262 01		D 6365 01		D 6365 02	D 6262 02	
Mr. Suggs	D 7902 01		D 7901 01		D 7902 02			D 7901 02
Dr. Owings		T 1217 01			T 1217 02			T 1217 03
Mr. Hester	T 2345 01		T 2345 02		T 2345 03			

the first half of A-3 and B-3 or the second half of A-3 and B-3. Students have a skinny course in the remaining portions of A-3 and B-3. Table 9.27 illustrates the double entries needed and the different format for a trimester schedule.

STEP 16: ENTER REMAINDER OF COURSES ■

Once the SLC courses, singletons, doubletons, and tripletons have been placed on the grid of teachers' assignments, the remaining sections are entered. Three important checks emerge in this step: (1) Each teacher's required number of planning periods appears on the grid; (2) the same number of sections or seats is available each period to distribute students equally; (3) the same number of sections or seats is available for each grade level each period. These checks will enhance the likelihood of a successful first run of the master schedule. Tables 9.28, 9.29, and 9.30 demonstrate this process.

STEP 17: INITIAL AND SUBSEQUENT ■ COMPUTER RUNS

At this point, the scheduling committee is ready for its first computer run. Those students with the greatest number of singletons or diverse education needs should be weighted and run through the computer before the students in standard classes who may have fewer conflicts. The

Table 9.27 Place Singletons, Doubletons, and Tripletons: Trimester Schedule

	Trimester 1					Trimester 2					Trimester 3				
	1	2	3	4	5	6	7	8	9	10	11	12	13	14	15
Eng.	AP Eng. 12 A 01				H Eng. 11 A 01	AP Eng. 12 B 01		H Eng. 10 A 01		H Eng. 11 B 01			H Eng. 10 B 01		
Soc. Stu.			AP U.S. A 01			H SS 11 A 01		AP U.S. B 01			H SS 11 B 01				
Math					Alg. I A 01	H Alg. I A 01			H Geo. A 01	Alg. I B 01	H Alg. I B 01			H Geo. B 01	Alg. I C 01
Sci.	H Bio. A 01			H Phy. A 01				H Phy. B 01					H Bio. B 01		
Band		A 01					B 01					C 01			
Chorus		A 01					B 01					C 01			

Table 9.28 Enter Remainder of Courses: Nine-Period Schedule

	1	2	3	4	5	6	7	8	9
Mrs. Salazar	S 1015 01	S 1900 01		1013 04	Lunch		1013 05		1013 06
Mr. Unitas		2100 05		S 2105 01	S 2107 01	Lunch	2100 06		2100 07
Mr. Donovan	4100 08	4100 09			Lunch	S 4617 01		4811 06	4811 07
Mr. Pricer	6800 06	D 6262 01		D 6365 01		Lunch	D 6365 02	D 6262 02	
Mr. Suggs	D 7902 01		D 7901 01		Lunch	D 7902 02	7476 05		D 7901 02
Dr. Owings		T 1217 01		1219 09	T 1217 02	Lunch		T 1217 03	1219 10
Mr. Hester	T 2345 01				T 2345 02	Lunch	T 2345 03	2346 04	2347 05

Table 9.29 Enter Remainder of Courses: Day 1/Day 2 or Semester 1/Semester 2—4 × 4

	A-1	A-2	A-3	A-4	B-1	B-2	B-3	B-4
Mrs. Salazar	S 1015 01	S 1900 01		1013 04		1013 05	1013 06	1013 07
Mr. Unitas	2100 05	2100 06		S 2105 01	S 2107 01		2100 07	2100 08
Mr. Donovan		4100 08	4100 09	4811 06	4100 10	S 4617 01		4811 07
Mr. Pricer	6800 06	D 6262 01		D 6365 01	6800 07	D 6365 02	D 6262 02	
Mr. Suggs	D 7902 01		D 7901 01	7476 07	D 7902 02		7476 08	D 7901 02
Dr. Owings	1219 07	T 1217 01	1219 08		T 1217 02		1219 10	T 1217 03
Mr. Hester	T 2345 01		T 2345 02	2346 03	T 2345 03	2346 04	2347 05	

Table 9.30 Enter Remainder of Courses: Trimester Schedule

	Trimester 1					Trimester 2					Trimester 3				
	1	2	3	4	5	6	7	8	9	10	11	12	13	14	15
Eng.	AP Eng. 12 A 01	Eng. 11 A 06	Eng. 11 A 07		H Eng. 11 A 01	AP Eng. 12 B 01	Eng. 11 A 09	H Eng. 10 A 01		H Eng. 11 B 01	Eng. 11 B 06	Eng. 11 B 07	H Eng. 10 B 01	Eng. 11 B 10	
Soc. Stu.	U.S. A 01	U.S. A 02	AP U.S. A 01	U.S. A 03		H SS 11 A 01	U.S. A 07	AP U.S. B 01	U.S. B 01		H SS 11 B 01		U.S. B 08	U.S. B 09	U.S. B 10
Math	Alg. I A 05	Alg. I A 06		Alg. I A 07	Alg. I A 01	H Alg. I A 01		Alg. I B 05	H Geo. A 01	Alg. I B 01	H Alg. I B 01	Alg. I B 06		H Geo. B 01	Alg. I C 01
Sci.	H Bio. A 01	Bio. A 05	Bio. A 06	H Phy. A 01		Bio. A 07	Bio. A 08	H Phy. B 01	Bio. B 06		Bio. B 07	Bio. B 08	H Bio. B 01	Bio. B 09	
Band		A 01					B 01					C 01			
Chorus		A 01					B 01					C 01			

computer will report the names of students with complete schedules, the names of students with incomplete schedules and the conflicts, as well as the number of sections that loaded and those that did not load fully. The scheduling committee is then charged with the responsibility of analyzing these data and adjusting the master schedule.

Once the revision is complete, a second computer run takes place. This process is repeated as many times as necessary to reach the conclusion that the greatest number of students can receive their first choice of courses. At this point, the school counselor should be involved in meeting with students and helping them to alter their course requests in light of the final version of the schedule.

STEP 18: IMPLEMENT ■
PROFESSIONAL DEVELOPMENT

The schedule is a means to an end, not an end unto itself. The schedule must enable all component parts to function effectively and interdependently. At this point, the energy of the scheduling committee is to assist those who coordinate the staff development program to focus on implementing the schedule.

A professional development program should focus on the details of the change process, the role and function of SLCs, and effective teaching strategies for variable-length time periods. A focus on flexibility must be an underlying component of that professional development experience. This training is most effective when it occurs as an ongoing process.

SUMMARIZING STEPS IN BUILDING ■
A HIGH SCHOOL SCHEDULE

Throughout this chapter, the importance of various forms of communication with interested parties emerges as well as the need for adequate preparation. Appropriately, our epigram cites Alexander Graham Bell who may be the great-great-grandfather of our smartphones and who initiated an era of increased communication. His words bring to mind that success in all endeavors depends on adequate preparation: "Before anything else, preparation is the key to success."

Several steps in building a high school schedule emerge as essential in preparing all of the pieces to fit into a workable whole. The careful consideration and selection of structural frameworks impacts the number of courses a student takes. Therefore, the scheduling committee's recognition of the school's pressing needs impacts the committee's choice or choices. Guidance toward that end appears in the school's mission/vision statement with a clear understanding of the community the school serves.

After student requests are tabulated, attention shifts to the department summaries, FTE distribution, and teacher assignment charts. These steps prove to be vital managerial tools. Following those steps, the actual creation of the schedule begins. The order of the steps guarantees the intended outcome. SLC assignments are placed on the grid of teacher assignments prior to listing each department. Placing the singletons, doubletons, and tripletons increases the likelihood of students receiving their first choice of courses. The community may judge the schedule based on the number of students receiving their first choice of courses.

Finally, key to the preparation for creating and implementing the schedule successfully involves open communication with the faculty and consideration of their ability to adapt to the changes presented in the schedule. Because the schedule is but a vital catalyst within which effective instruction takes place, the faculty's role becomes paramount in this process.

10

Using the Schedule for Effective Instruction

You got to be careful if you don't know where you're going,
because you might not get there.

Yogi Berra

Improved student achievement ignites the quest for educational reform. To know where it is going, each school district seeks a path to the end that fits its community. Signposts for those paths vary but include the school schedule. As stated in earlier chapters, the schedule itself does not improve student achievement (National Association of Secondary School Principals, 1996). Instruction does. The schedule provides a framework within which effective instruction, the target destination for essential learning, occurs. This chapter focuses on a research-based lesson plan to deliver instruction in a student-centered classroom that addresses the needs of diverse populations as well as other students.

A BRIEF HISTORY OF INSTRUCTIONAL INFLUENCE

The implementation of student-centered instructional techniques in the classroom has a sporadic history, beginning with the efforts of Meiklejohn and Dewey discussed in Chapter 7. In the early 20th century, they brought the focus in education from dispensing content to that of instruction to facilitate learning. They, with other like-minded individuals, developed what became known as progressive education. Marzano (2000) traces the effects of this movement from the early part of the 20th century. He begins by citing Schaefer's (1971) list of principles of the Progressive Education Association, established in 1919:

- Instruction must address the learner's developmental needs.
- Knowledge cannot be imposed but must be constructed by the learner.
- Social participation is central to learning.
- The scientific method is a primary tool for learning.
- The development of the individual is a primary purpose of education. (Marzano, 2000, p. 69)

Although programs using progressive education strategies proved successful, the impetus was lost when World War II crashed onto the scene, creating a distraction in public interest. Today, these principles ring familiar through the work of educational researchers, experts, studies, and practitioners.

In his presentation, Marzano (2000, pp. 70–78) identifies some of the mid-20th-century educators who reinvigorated the focus on instruction, the "how to teach" combined with the "what to teach":

- Ralph Tyler (1930–1970): Identified the importance of specific learning outcomes and the need for varied forms of instruction to impact different types of knowledge
- Jerome Bruner (1960): Summarized the groundbreaking 1959 Woods Hole Conference in his report through the idea that "the act of teaching profoundly affects what and how students learn"
- Hilda Taba (1962): Echoed Tyler's work by emphasizing that different types of knowledge require different instructional techniques
- Benjamin Bloom (1976): Believed that testing needs to determine levels of mastery and the need for reteaching or enrichment
- Madeline Hunter (1967–1976): Advocated a lesson design geared toward mastery teaching
- Roger T. Johnson and David W. Johnson (1995): Introduced a comprehensive form of cooperative learning

As the 1970s saw an increased interest in instruction, the 1990s ushered in a renewed interest in cognitive psychology that started in the 1950s. Marzano (2000) presents two cognitive psychology principles that impact teaching and learning: (1) Learners construct their own meaning, and (2) learning and thinking involve interactive systems. During the same time frame, brain research brought to light the brain's effect on learning, becoming another influence on instruction (Marzano, 2000, pp. 81–83).

The science of meta-analysis as practiced by Marzano and Hattie reveals the research on those strategies and programs that influence student achievement. Hattie has an extensive list of these efforts in his 2008 work *Visible Learning: A Synthesis of Over 800 Meta-analyses Relating to Achievement.* He expands and reinforces the impact of these listed efforts in speeches (Hattie, 2009) and books for teachers (Hattie, 2012). In the delivery of his inaugural address at the University of New Zealand in 1999, he indicated some strategies that informed his thinking and subsequent published work:

1. Critical innovations are an underlying theme. Through reflection on teaching and the determination of the effect of methods being used, teachers can improve the quality of learning, which is a prerequisite for excellence.

2. The single most powerful tool to enhance achievement is feedback. Hattie listed five forms of positive feedback and suggested three forms that demonstrate negative impact.

   Positive:

   a. Reinforcement that provides a student with information and motivation

   b. Corrective feedback

   c. Remediation and feedback

   d. Diagnosis feedback

   e. Mastery learning based on feedback

   Negative:

   a. Extrinsic rewards

   b. Delayed feedback

   c. Punishment

3. The setting of appropriate, specific, challenging goals is critical.

4. What teachers do makes a difference.

5. Introduction of teaching and school influences only impacts the probability of positive effects being used, not the actuality.

Close reading of Hattie's (1999, 2008, 2009, 2012) lists and rationale for each item aids our understanding of the need to move from those entrenched practices that have not produced positive results and toward the type of critical innovation he promotes.

The lesson plan featured in this chapter integrates the above findings. It is a plan for student learning and coincides with Marzano's (2000, p. 84) belief that teaching and learning in the 21st century must become more of a science, using all the resources and data available. While the process of the lesson plan can and should be implemented in all time frames for class periods, it is especially effective in extended-time periods. The format encourages the use of each instructional minute to enable bell-to-bell teaching and learning.

PACING THE CURRICULUM

A lesson emerges from a well-planned, intended curriculum that includes "essential standards" (Marzano, 2003, p. 27; Reeves, 2006, p. 106; Schmoker, 2006, p. 129). Developing a viable curriculum necessitates careful consideration of the standards by the faculty in order to avoid the "inch deep and mile wide" syndrome. Rather, the focus must be on incorporating the essential learning for each subject area. A caution arises for curriculum writers to be certain that the "what," meaning the facts in the curriculum, does not overshadow the "why," or the deeper understandings (Erickson, 2001; Marzano, 2003; Wiggins & McTighe, 1998). Materials to facilitate the decisions about essential standards to be taught can be gained through a review of testing materials and sample tests provided by testing agencies and states. When the curriculum is complete, a written and agreed-upon pacing guide or timetable for the designated units provides a vehicle for commitment by all teachers to deliver the intended curriculum (Hayes-Jacobs, 1997, p. 4; Schmoker, 2011, p. 10). Without a written source, elements of the curriculum may be lost to "love units," those favorite units of teachers brought from outside the intended curriculum for a particular subject or grade level. To indicate the developmental process, Figure 10.1 presents a nesting graphic in which instruction moves from the macrocosm to the microcosm, the curriculum map to the daily lesson plan.

In Figure 10.1, the curriculum map represents the yearlong vision of a given course written with the end in mind (Wiggins & McTighe, 1998, p. 8). It gives rise to the pacing guide that contains what is to be taught by all teachers to ensure a "guaranteed and viable curriculum" (Marzano, 2003, p. 22). The written pacing guide lists the various units that encompass the essential learning and standards to be taught. Originating from the unit,

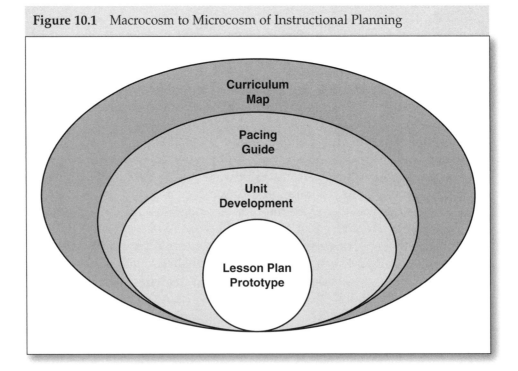

Figure 10.1   Macrocosm to Microcosm of Instructional Planning

Curriculum
Map

Pacing
Guide

Unit
Development

Lesson Plan
Prototype

the daily lesson becomes an incremental stepping-stone for purposeful student learning that guides the student toward successful mastery of the target learning.

LESSON PLAN FOUNDATIONS: CONCEPTUAL LENS, TARGET LEARNING, AND ESSENTIAL QUESTIONS ■

Similar to the unit, each lesson contains its own target learning and essential question(s) to guide student learning around a conceptual lens. The conceptual lens or concept serves as a broad or integrating idea for learning that allows students to see patterns or connections and promotes transfer (Erickson, 2001; Tomlinson, 1999). The inclusion of a conceptual lens provides the student with a basis for clustering, the organization of information into chunks that make sense to the learner (Bransford, Brown, & Cocking, 2000). It further gives rise to the "big ideas" of learning (Wiggins & McTighe, 1998). Examples of concepts that can be applied to lessons or units appear in Table 10.1.

Table 10.1 Conceptual Lens Options

adaptation	creativity	futures	power
balance	cultures	heroism	progress
beginnings	cycles	independence	relationships
changes	energy	influences	structures
communication	equality	justice	survival
community	exploration	matter	systems
conflict	forces	migration	time
cooperation	freedom	order	traditions
courage	frontiers	patterns	truth

Source: Adapted from Martin and Morrow, 1997.

This chapter models the conceptual lens of adaptation. Activating Piaget's (1971; cited in Marzano, 2003, p. 112) description of learning as comprising the acts of assimilation and accommodation, the educator engaged in reading this chapter assimilates a new or different way of planning for student learning and accommodates that learning to what is being practiced. Applied to the chapter's conceptual lens of adaptation are generalizations that fit a variety of experiences, provide opportunites to form connections to other practices, and make the learning valid:

- Adaptations can be immediate or long term.
- Adaptation is a process.
- Adaptation allows change to occur.
- Adaptation cultivates a "fit" to circumstance or context.

Once the conceptual lens is established, the day's target learning is identified. Target learning consists of a broad statement that represents the enduring understandings to be learned, retained, and transferred to new situations (Wiggins & McTighe, 1998). It provides a clear learning goal that moves beyond facts to a broader understanding of an idea. Encouraging the broad application of target learning, Erickson (2001, p. 20) cautions against a lesson becoming a form of "trivial pursuit" in which facts overwhelm depth of understanding. Others echo her concerns and promote the inclusion of content, skills, and life applications in the target or essential learning in the lesson (George & Alexander, 1993; Hayes-Jacobs, 1997; Wiggins & McTighe, 1998). Wolfe (2001, p. 132) suggests asking three questions to determine the relevance of the curriculum's target learning: "What are the big ideas or concepts?" "What is the lifelong benefit of what I am teaching?" and "How will students be able to use what they are learning today in their adult lives?" Her questions emulate George and Alexander's (1993) focus on content, skills, and life applications.

To develop target learnings, Marzano (2003, p. 114) emphasizes the importance of both declarative and procedural knowledge in instruction. *Declarative* refers to the information presented and learned; *procedural* refers to the skill or process essential to apply the information. Glatthorn and Jailall (2000) reinforce the importance of learning skills and content by citing the 1993 work of Brooks and Brooks that urges the formation of generative knowledge. The generative form of knowledge provides students with the skills to solve "meaningful problems" (Glatthorn & Jailall, 2000, p. 109). Increasingly, as noted above, studies indicate the importance of providing students with the necessary skills for learning as well as the knowledge or content. From these sources and others, the importance of developing broad target learning to promote depth of understanding rather than superficial coverage becomes apparent.

Depth of understanding promotes student ownership of learning. The student's working memory applies skills and previously learned content to new content in a self-created schema. Fisher and Frey (2008) recognize that identifying and posting the target learning in the classroom gives the student a clear goal for learning and encourages the student to assume responsibility for learning. Mere posting, however, will not motivate. Consistent connections made by the teacher between the posted target and the delivered instruction aid the student in assimilating the desired learning. The target learning for this chapter follows: Research aids the development of purposeful lessons and learning engagements to guide instruction.

Essential questions set the tone for each lesson plan and offer an instructional guide toward an understanding of the target learning. The questions should not be able to be answered in a word or sentence, but should be open-ended, provoke inquiry, and be written in student-friendly language. Wiggins and McTighe (2002) describe three types of essential questions: overarching questions, which transcend a topic; topical questions, which lead to specific ideas or issues of the unit or lesson; and convergent and divergent questions. Convergent questions promote desired understanding, and divergent questions arouse additional questions and inquiry. Beyond those types, they further identify five categories: definitional questions, which require explanation or clarification; personal questions; practical questions; epistemological questions, which address nature, the structure of knowledge, and processes of knowing; and philosophical questions, dealing with beliefs, values, and the metaphysical (Wiggins & McTighe, 2002, pp. 94–95). Depending on the desired learning of the lesson or unit, the questions may vary from global and abstract to specific, which more closely guide immediate instruction.

Erickson (2001, p. 91) refers to essential questions as guide questions because they guide students to discover patterns, meaning, and complexity and engage their individual intellects. She further suggests that while a few questions are necessary to set foundational understanding through the use of "what" constructs, most of the questions should be "why" or "how" questions to extend thinking. The overuse of "what" questions keeps instruction at the factual level rather than moving into a depth of understanding. As an integral part of lesson design to promote student engagement, essential questions provide a basis for the incremental advance toward understanding the target learning. Additionally, they serve as a basis for formative and summative assessment of the target learning. At the end of class, students should be able to answer the essential question(s) of the day.

Each day the concept is posted with the target learning and essential questions. In doing so, students have a clear understanding of their learning goals and the connections necessary for depth of understanding. The posting of these elements of the lesson format encourages students to become participants rather than passive recipients of the instruction. It is essential that the teacher make frequent connections between the ongoing instruction and these guiding elements throughout the lesson to emphasize the importance of the conceptual lens, target learning, and essential questions.

As with conceptual lens and target learning, essential questions exist for this chapter. These essential questions guide the reader to the target learning of the chapter:

- How does an articulated-engagement approach to instruction enhance learning?
- How does research support the articulated-engagement lesson plan model?
- In what ways do recall, rehearsal, and reflection enhance the learning process?
- How do formative assessment and feedback influence instruction?
- How does this lesson plan meet the needs of diverse populations as well as mainstreamed students?

Using the above examples for conceptual lens, target learning, and essential questions, the lesson plan prototype appears in Table 10.2.

THE LESSON PLAN AND LEARNING ENGAGEMENTS

Engagement Length, Number, and Sequence

The lesson plan provides an incrementally sequenced approach to instruction based on research and the use of varied time, strategy, and modality engagements. The engagement process takes into consideration

Table 10.2   Lesson Plan Prototype With Conceptual Lens, Target Learning, and Essential Questions

Course: Effective Instruction	**Unit:** Lesson Plan Prototype
Grade: Faculty	

Conceptual Lens:	Adaptation
	Adaptation can be immediate or long term.
	Adaptation is a process.
	Adaptation allows change to occur.
	Adaptation cultivates a "fit" to circumstances or context.
Target Learning:	Research aids the development of purposeful lessons and learning engagements to guide instruction.
Essential Questions:	How does the articulated-engagement approach to instruction enhance learning?
	How does research support the articulated-engagement lesson plan model?
	In what ways do recall, rehearsal, and reflection enhance the learning process?
	How do formative assessment and feedback influence instruction?
	How does this lesson plan meet the needs of diverse populations as well as mainstreamed students?

the amount of time that people stay focused on one activity or engagement. As many studies and experts recommend, instruction needs to be delivered incrementally in short segments to allow for adequate processing and to retain attention. Schmoker (2011) emphasizes this point: "Good lessons respect the limits of memory and the average attention span." Marzano (2009) refers to short learning experiences as chunking the instruction. He highlights the need for students to have frequent opportunities for interaction with one another to process the new information (Marzano, 2009, p. 86).

Sousa (2001, p. 92) notes that a 20-minute engagement allows the learner time to assimilate the information. Beyond 20 minutes, the learner's attention drifts. Sousa concludes that shorter engagements promote greater retention. In part, this effect compensates for today's fast pace in which learners in their daily lives experience quick change and novelty. Jensen (1998, p. 46) counsels that constant attention or lengthy engagements are counterproductive for three reasons: (1) Learners need time to process information; (2) reflection on the information requires internal time to create meaning by the learner; and (3) new learning needs time to be assimilated. With these findings in mind, the following lesson plan prototype implements sequential and incremental uses of varied engagements to promote student involvement and the ability to answer the essential question(s) for the lesson.

The lesson plan illustrated in Figure 10.2 divides available class time into separate learning engagements. Each engagement consists of six elements that give direction or sequence for building instruction from concrete to abstract understanding: purpose, motivation, recall, engagement, assessment, and connection. In this form of scaffolding, student participation

Figure 10.2 Sequence of Learning Engagements

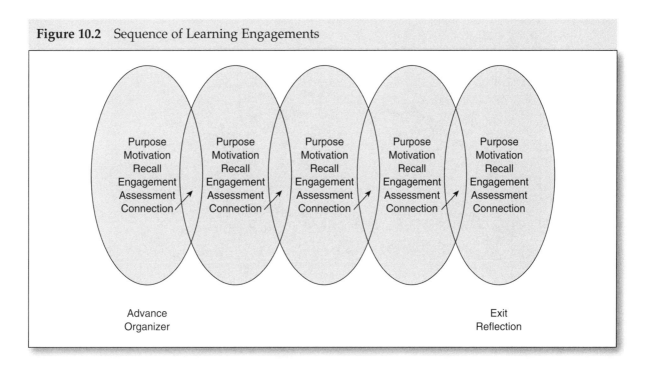

varies in format but remains essential to maintain active student involvement. The length of each engagement varies as well according to its intent or purpose. Boykin and Noguera (2011) stress that active engagement and length of instructional time are not comparable in raising student achievement. They maintain that active, focused engagements are essential to the goal of increased student achievement, not the amount of time allocated in the schedule (Boykin & Noguera, 2011, p. 45). When time frames within the schedule are not filled with high-quality instruction and do not involve students from bell to bell, schools and districts may abandon creative schedules, denying students extended opportunities to learn (Elliot Merenbloom, 2012, personal observation). Rather than abandoning the schedule, schools need to take measures to ensure effective bell-to-bell teaching by providing professional development and support to teachers.

Although Figure 10.2 indicates the presence of five learning engagements, the lesson plan can be adapted to fit any length of time. For instance, a 40-minute class period should include no fewer than three learning engagements while a longer class period can have more than five.

Springing from the conceptual lens, target learning, and essential questions, two dimensions of the lesson plan process appear in Figure 10.3 and Table 10.3. The flowchart in Figure 10.3 indicates how the conceptual lens influences each of the engagement elements. Each element emerges from and moves toward the end goals contained in the target learning and essential questions. This process coincides with Schmoker's (2011, p. 21) premise that successful instruction occurs when three elements exist: a clear learning objective, short instructional chunks or segments, and multiple cycles of guided practice and formative assessment.

Table 10.3 presents a narrative sequential format for lesson development. The conceptual lens is the earlier example of adaptation.

Figure 10.3   Lesson Plan Flowchart

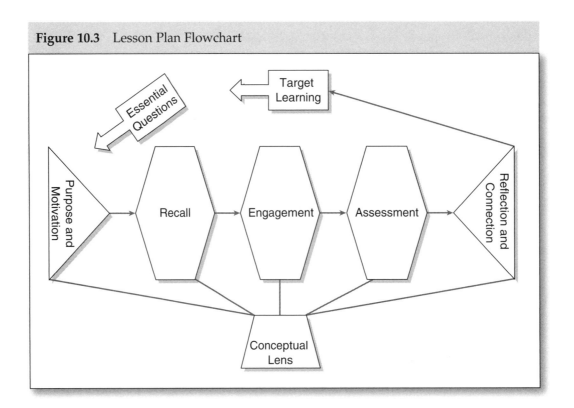

Purpose

Purpose establishes reasoning for the engagement. It is the answer given to students when they question the importance of the actual engagement. In the teacher's plan, it sets the stage for a focus on the content, skills, or real-life applications that make up the engagement. While not always a part of the voiced lesson, the purpose of each engagement must be clear in the teacher's mind to allow seamless connections from one engagement to the next. The purpose connects with the ongoing learning and not something that will take place at a future time. Ultimately, the purpose of the engagement seeks to connect the curriculum to life outside of the classroom when students apply what they have learned.

Motivation

Motivation aids students to acquire or increase interest in the engagement. It supplies the reason for a behavior and explains why certain actions are taken. A carefully planned engagement captures students' attention and assists the process for students to connect with the lesson. Tomlinson and Imbeau (2010, p. 17) remind us that when the interests of students are tapped, the "motivation to learn is heightened, and learning is enhanced." In this vein, the teacher needs to know the students' interests by considering strengths, culture, personal experiences, and developmental needs. At this level, motivation refers to inspiring interest in the engagement.

A broader application of motivation arises from a student's attitude toward being competent and able to master the learning at hand. This broader application placed in a positive light is a desirable goal for all teaching. Students generally come to the classroom with one of two mind-sets: a

Table 10.3   Lesson Plan Sequential List

Conceptual Lens: Adaptation
Target Learning
Essential Question(s)

Learning Engagement #1
   Purpose
   Motivation
   Recall
   Engagement
   Assessment
   Connection

Learning Engagement #2
   Purpose
   Motivation
   Recall
   Engagement
   Assessment
   Connection

Learning Engagement #3
   Purpose
   Motivation
   Recall
   Engagement
   Assessment
   Connection

Learning Engagement #4
   Purpose
   Motivation
   Recall
   Engagement
   Assessment
   Connection

Learning Engagement #5
   Purpose
   Motivation
   Recall
   Engagement
   Assessment
   Connection

growth attitude toward learning, meaning that they believe they can learn, or a fixed attitude, believing that they do not have the ability to learn (Dean, Hubbell, Pitler, & Stone, 2012; Tomlinson & Imbeau, 2010).

Carol Dweck, a well-known research psychologist at Stanford University, advocates praise to improve motivation for work and persistence (Glenn, 2010). When Dwek conducted a research study on the effects of praise for talent and praise for effort, the results indicated that when students are praised for talent, they enter into a fixed mind-set and actually begin to perform less well than when they began. They become afraid that their talent will not carry them through to success (Dwek, 2006, pp. 72–73). When teachers emphasize the effort put forward by students, they build a positive relationship that carries over to the application of motivation in the lesson plan. Students are more likely to be motivated for an engagement-level experience when they have a sense of being assessed on effort rather than competitive grading.

Enduring motivation for engagements arises best from intrinsic motivation rather than the extrinsic motivation of rewards. MacIver and Plank (1996, p. 1) reinforce the importance of the teacher-student relationship on motivation: "One of the most potent sources of motivation is to have teachers and peers who are rooting for them to do well."

By knowing student interests and needs, teachers determine types of motivators. Successful motivators can be as simple as having students work in pairs or small groups, serving the human and learning need for socialization. Because movement aids attention, providing an engagement that includes movement satisfies that physical need. Movement also furnishes novelty from the usual sitting during instruction. Again, the probability of success motivates students as do engagements that are relevant to their lives and authentic in nature (Brough, Bergmann, & Holt, 2006).

Recall

The recall element of the lesson plan addresses two important aspects of instruction and learning: retrieval of skills or knowledge from long-term memory or prior knowledge and rehearsal of information. The recall process establishes connections between what the student knows and what will be learned. While a question about previously learned content or skills provides an impetus for recall, cues and visuals are also effective. Both content and skills are gleaned from either a vertical source, such as a previous lesson from the same class or from another year, or a horizontal source, such as another content area in the same grade level. In some cases, the prior knowledge may arise from everyday experiences as well as that learned in school. Jensen (1998, p. 102) cites the memory study by Calvin (1996) in which he identifies the retrieval process of memory: Association best avails memories to be recalled from their multiple storage areas. In other words, making connections between what is known and what is to be learned encourages the working memory to pull information from a variety of storage areas in the brain.

Because the lesson plan process employs an incremental approach, it encourages scaffolding, an essential approach to fortify learning. The choice of recalling content or skills as a focus at this stage depends on what the actual engagement will be. It is necessary to build sometimes on previous knowledge of content and other times on the correct understanding or application of skills. Cooperative learning roles, note taking, mathematical processes, use of the scientific method, and inferencing exemplify some skills to be recalled prior to their direct application. Taking time to determine the students' level of understanding catches student misunderstandings and enhances the level and accuracy of the engagement.

According to Sousa (2001), rehearsal of information appears in two main forms: rote and elaborative, both of which are influenced by time factors. In the introduction of new content or skills, sufficient time for processing is essential to make meaning and to place the information or skill into working memory (Sousa, 2001, p. 86). Recall provides quick opportunities to rehearse what has been previously learned.

Sousa's (2001, p. 81) description coincides with Marzano's premise that practice is essential for the mastery of a skill, a form he refers to as developing procedural knowledge. The amount of time devoted to particular skill development depends on the level of automaticity required for the skill. Within the lesson plan model, the recall element provides an additional opportunity to solidify automaticity through incremental and periodic practice.

The recall segment of the lesson plan does not demand large allotments of time. It simply focuses on previously learned information or skills so the student is clear about what to apply in the upcoming engagement. When carefully framed, recall reinforces the clear target for learning expected of the student. Later in the engagement element of the lesson plan, more elaborate and extensive forms of rehearsal appear.

Engagement

The actual engagement element of the lesson plan defines the strategies, processes, and experiences open to the learner. Each engagement in the sequential lesson plan should lead the student to answer successfully the essential questions posted for the day. Lessons are sometimes direct and scaffolded and other times designed for more inductive learning. Whatever the choice, strategies need to vary from day to day and within the day. Although students appreciate the comfort that comes with structure, they also respond to novelty and challenge. The teaching challenge is to provide a comfort level with motivation.

Increasingly, the value of students' active engagement in their learning is noted to be a factor, especially for minority and at-risk students (Boykin & Noguera, 2011, p. 42). Within an engagement, a student should be expected to construct meaning, an endeavor that is embedded in the Common Core State Standards (CCSS). Academic researchers identify three forms of engagement that affect student participation and interest: behaviorial, cognitive, and affective (Boykin & Noguera, 2011; Fredricks et al., 2011). Behavioral strategies require students to be on task. They involve effort and persistence and are measured by students' attentiveness, questioning, requests for help, and participation in discussion. Cognitive strategies provoke student investment in complex concepts and issues. Through these strategies, students acquire difficult skills, process a depth of information, and solve challenging problems. Affective strategies involve the level of interest the engagement has for the student. They provide an emotional attachment that reflects positive affect and attitude and encourages curiosity leading to task absorption (Boykin & Noguera, 2011, pp. 42–43).

Many factors form a successful engagement. Varying intensity is one. Williams and Dunn (2000) cite the study of Ron Fitzgerald (1996) that emphasizes the importance of alternating intense and reflective engagements. An intense or highly active engagement should be followed by one that requires more reflection; an engagement that includes several students in a cooperative learning venture should be followed by a more individualized one. Sousa (2001) supports this need: Working memory can only handle a few items at once. Therefore, shifts in types of engagements are needed to maintain interest and focus as well as provide time for rehearsal or reflection. This process conincides with the earlier discussion on attention span as well as prime-time 1 and 2 (described later in this chapter). Reaffirming what effective teachers inately know, Sousa (2001, pp. 45–46) cites Russell's (1979) study on focus time: adults, 10–20 minutes; pre- and early adolescents, 5–10 minutes. Without an understanding of students' ability to focus, teachers may deliver a curriculum, but it is not necessarily learned.

Moving from concrete to abstract engagements aids understanding. The use of prior knowledge and real-world examples give students a concrete foundation to comprehend representational or abstract concepts. Without the concrete experience on which to build, no amount of explanation will make the abstraction meaningful (Wolfe, 2001).

When planning engagements for the lesson, it is important to include procedural knowledge (Marzano, 2010), the actual teaching and practicing of skills. Foster (2012) encourages preparation for life with transferable skills to be able to apply knowledge. His research on college graduates' attitudes toward their future reveals that many of them are unprepared for the work or career world. While Foster's (2012) identified skills focus on those necessary for the workplace such as communication, networking, and people skills, the importance of this type of skill building resonates with students who report that school and its curriculum are not relevant to life. The skill instruction, however, must be embedded in lessons with context in order to provide students with transferable understanding of application.

The importance of integrating real-life experiences is not new. As a focus on the delivery of curriculum grew, William Alexander presented this argument in the 1960s. Later he and Paul George reaffirmed the importance of melding content, skills, and real-life experiences into instruction (George & Alexander, 1993). Today's authorities reinforce George and Alexander's (1993) position. Schmoker (2011, p. 31) cites Hirsch (2008) to reinforce his argument about linking content, critical thinking, and higher-level skills in context: "being able to argue, evaluate, and reason are 'attained by studying a rich curriculum . . . and learning higher-level skills in context.'" Schmoker (2011) emphasizes the vital nature of literacy skills in all areas of the curriculum.

Other skills to be addressed and taught vary as the need arises: listening, inferencing, separating fact from fiction, cause and effect, predicting, generalizing, and other essential basic and learning skills pertinent to subject areas. Some of these skills can be presented across curricular areas as skill of the week or month, another method for rehearsal or practice. As the CCSS are adopted, some concern arises that procedural skills will be overshadowed by a preponderant focus on content. Hersh (2009, p. 51) argues the point: "This issue of either content or skills is a false dichotomy, one that we need to transcend if we are going to make significant progress."

Schmoker (2011) offers guidance on what constitutes essential instruction, a focus on what he considers a return to simplicity: Teachers need to focus on what is being taught and how it is being taught, and to use authentic literacy in the instruction. The "how" aspect of his recommendation reflects the importance of the entire learning engagement as well as the specific engagement segment. His admonition is echoed in Boykin and Noguera's (2011, p. 174) strong endorsement of high-quality teaching that includes purposeful, active engagements to provide measureable student achievement.

Target learning and the ability to answer the essential questions are motivators for each engagement. Moving incrementally toward these goals requires a repertoire of effective and proven strategies. Contributors to educational research offer guidelines and suggestions for effective, strategic instruction. Marzano (2003, p. 80) identifies nine strategies that are fundamental to student achievement and should be considered during the engagement planning stage:

- Identifying similarities and differences
- Summarizing and note taking
- Reinforcing effort and providing recognition
- Homework and practice
- Nonlinguistic representations
- Cooperative learning
- Setting objectives and providing feedback
- Generating and testing hypotheses
- Questions, cues, and advance organizers

Each element presents opportunities for multiple applications and reinforcement of content and skills, but teachers need to understand the component parts of each and the anticipated results in order for the strategies to be effective (Dean et al., 2012, p. xiii).

Instructional Strategies for Effective Engagements

A host of strategies exist to implement Marzano's (2003) fundamental strategies or Schmoker's (2011) and Boykin and Noguera's (2011) urgency for high-quality instruction. Delivered in small, incremental steps, each engagement strategy augments the process toward the target learning. Each engagement varies in modality or context of instruction to promote flexible transfer and understanding. Changing the modality also provides novelty to keep students focused and the brain attentive.

Reading, both guided and authentic, to provide context for enthusiastic discussion and analysis is essential for success in all content areas. Schmoker (2011) and Gallagher (2010) argue that students need authentic literacy experiences by reading texts of all types and learning to interact with them. Some authentic reading experiences include those that people outside of school actually use: nonfiction articles, data for specific purposes, spreadsheets, novels, online forums, and other rich sources of information (Wilhelm, 2009, p. 13).

Teacher modeling conveys to all students strategies that help them make meaning from text. Modeling a reading strategy such as "Think Aloud" makes the experience authentic for the student, reinforcing strategies already in place for good readers and providing strategies for struggling readers.

In any content area, planning successive engagements for reading, discussion, reflection, and writing allows students to build knowledge as well as skills. Authentic vocabulary instruction when embedded within the reading experience is more effective than a fragmented experience relegated to language arts only (Allen, 2004; Beers, 2003; National Council of Teachers of English, 2005).

Authentic *writing* evolves from the context of the lesson and content area. Students need the opportunity to write papers of varying lengths for different purposes. Short summaries, extended analysis, arguments, narratives, and research papers both long and short are examples of academic writing to engage stduents. Additionally, students' writing experiences should incorporate 21st-century forms of writing such as blogs and the protocols that form social media. Purposeful writing conveys student-generated thought, analysis, and understanding of procedural writing skills. Further, students gain in competence when writing is rehearsed as a part of each department's curriculum (Gere, 2010; Schmoker, 2011).

Graphic organizers provide visual contexts for focused learning. A non-linguistic strategy, graphic organizers allow students to see patterns and relationships of information. A variety of formats are available or can be created for each of the six types: descriptive, time sequence, process/cause-effect, episode, generalization/principle, and concept (Dean et al., 2012, p. 67). They are effective for identifying similarities and differences as well as the beginning step in creating a summary of a movie, lecture, or reading. Because memories are stored not in a single place but within networks, the addition of a visual, nonlinguistic form acts as a type of rehearsal and aids recall. In order to maximize the effectiveness of the graphics, students need to understand the purpose and use of the organizers prior to using them.

In some engagements, *note taking* is required, focusing on the big ideas of a film, discussion, reading, or lecture. This skill needs to be taught so that students understand how to identify main points and that note taking is a work in progress. One type of note taking exists under several names but is essentially similar in style: T-notes, double-entry data (DED) notes, Cornell notes, or combination notes. Each of these formats uses a vertical line that divides the page into two parts. Marzano, Pickering, and Pollock (2001) use a combination notes model with a horizontal line drawn at the bottom. On the left side of the combination notes, an informal outline of main points is written. Visualizations of the information are drawn on the right side. Under the horizontal line, summary ideas are placed. The other note-taking forms record big ideas on the left, details on the right. Ideas rather than complete sentences are entered.

These forms can be expanded into three columns much like a "know, want to know, learn" activity. The TED or triple-entry data notes encourage thought beyond the text or lecture from which the notes are taken. In the third column, students write questions or connections of their own based on the information in the first two columns. This reflective engagement allows the student to make meaning of information. The metacognitive notes or questions written in the third column provide points for discussion or further investigation (Tomlinson, 1999). When schools adopt a specific format of note taking, the process becomes automatic for students who can easily transfer the skill to other arenas. When a common form of note taking is adopted by a school or district, instruction rather than each teacher's varied protocols becomes the student's focus.

Group work and cooperative learning appeal to students' social needs as well as shared learning goals. They provide a fertile ground for students to develop some of the workplace skills identified by Foster (2012). Cooperative learning advances the function of group work by providing specific roles for each participating student. Expectations for each role require clear definition to provide an equitable learning experience for each group member.

During and after the cooperative group experience, students should have opportunities to reflect on the task. Provided with a rubric, they self-evaluate their work to determine their level of success and what has been learned. Through this process they again experience a rehearsal of the content or skill and make accommodations to their knowledge repertoire. Further, the students have gained in responsibility for their own learning but have had the support of peers throughout the experience. Accountability for the task rests on the entire group and the individuals who make up the group. Consequently, tasks must be designed to allow for this type of collaboration (Fisher & Frey, 2008, p. 36).

Similar outcomes but different cooperative learning tasks within the same classroom allow for differentiation to occur. When alternated with individualized formats, group and cooperative work enhance interest in the lesson and reinforce multiple ways of learning.

Dramatization appears in the form of simulations, demonstrations, and skits. In a meta-analysis of learning research, Marzano et al. (2001, p. 131) find that dramatization has a stronger effect on learning and memory than verbal or visual presentations. The dramatization experience can be the viewing of a dramatic scene or creating a dramatic event. Although often thought to be the domain of elementary teachers, the process holds firm in secondary instruction as well.

Projects allow students to apply their learning to new situations, demonstrating their level of transfer. A well-designed project presents possibilities for answering essential questions in a creative way. Successful projects are thoughtfully developed in line with the target learning and assigned when students have sufficient understanding of the content and skills of the unit for independent practice.

The time required to complete a project should be commensurate with its value to the learning involved. Wolfe (2001, p. 142) cautions against projects that depart from the intended learning: "Projects and activities should be a means to enhance learning, not an end in themselves." One young mother reported that her fifth-grade daughter's class had constructed exquisite famous pieces of architecture that were completed at home for an architectural unit. She questioned, however, the degree of understanding of measurement and proportion that students assimilated during their at-home project completion (Susan Kalina, personal communication, February 8, 2012). For younger students, projects are best completed during designated parts of class or team time so that effective formative assessment occurs during the process.

The advance of *technology* into the classroom changes the delivery of instruction and the face of learning. Classroom technology needs to be interactive and purposeful and exists in multiple formats. Computers and electronic tablets open editing and research possibilities for students. Use of the Internet reflects real-world experiences and establishes new opportunities for communication beyond the classroom. Classroom blogs encourage precise communication as students become aware of the importance of word choice, grammar, and punctuation to expedite their messages. The ready access of information causes students to develop discrimination skills, to distinguish valid information from invalid information and valid sources from invalid sources. An increasing amount of students belong to social networks and use texting as a major form of communication. The protocols for those media forms need to be a part of students' repertoires. Elective programs use robots that can be programmed and CAD/CAM programs applied for design projects, reinforcing math concepts and rehearsing thinking skills. Rather than hand out "how-to-do" sheets, teachers can post links on their websites for student use such as bibliography maker sites.

When teachers embrace and use technology, caveats exist. Students must be kept safe when working on the Internet and on social networks. PowerPoint projects require rubrics that expect informational slides and discourage an abundance of glitz and flying letters. A whiteboard or LCD projector opens opportunities for student involvement and should be used by the teacher for more than projecting notes. Like all class engagements, technology engagements need to make clear connections to the conceptual lens, target learning, and essential questions of the lesson or unit.

The sequencing of engagements takes the student from an introduction to the day's learning to the ability to answer the essential questions. Careful planning of these engagements fills the class period from bell to bell, which in turn often alleviates behaviorial problems. Generally, the first engagement in the sequence is an advance organizer.

Advance Organizer

As noted earlier in Figure 10.2, an advance organizer sets the stage for the day's learning. It provides an expanded opportunity for recall. By building on prior knowledge, an essential element to construct a personal understanding of new content, students are immediately involved in the day's lesson. Marzano et al. (2001) champion the advance organizer to begin a lesson and to connect what is known with what is to be learned. David Ausubel (1968) originally introduced and defined advance organizers:

> Appropriately relevant and inclusive introductory materials . . . introduced in advance of learning . . . and presented at a higher level of abstraction, generality, and inclusiveness than the information presented after it. . . . [They are] designed to bridge the gap between what the learner already knows and what he needs to know before he can successfully learn the task at hand. (Marzano et al., 2001, p. 117)

As Ausubel (1968) implies, an advance organizer encourages thinking about new knowledge before experiencing it. It further identifies any misunderstandings students may hold.

An advance organizer takes various forms: Expository, narrative, skimming, cueing or questioning, and illustrative formats such as graphic organizers are examples. The intention of the format choice is to frame the direction of the sequenced learning engagements toward the target learning. For instance, the engagement could be the beginning of a K-W-L chart: what is known, wanted to be known, and learned. The choice of strategy should promote thinking but not frustrate students. As its label implies, the advance organizer organizes thinking in advance of instruction and is not to be graded.

Using an advance organizer at the beginning of a lesson not only stimulates prior knowledge but also effectively uses the first minutes of class. Sousa (2001) emphasizes the importance of this time in his discussion of the primacy-recency effect on retention. Although this effect has long been in learning repertoire, it lacked explanation until contemporary studies in neuroscience emerged. In the primacy-recency effect, learners best remember information that comes first, the primacy effect referred to as prime-time 1. The second best time for remembering occurs in the last part of instruction, the recency effect, or prime-time 2 (Sousa, 2001, p. 88). Consequently, instruction needs to begin immediately in the first minutes of the class period as the first engagement of the lesson plan model.

The primacy-recency effect appears in Figure 10.2 in which the lesson plan prototype includes several engagements. By changing the modality of each engagement, the instruction assumes a novelty that motivates the brain to refocus. Consequently, instead of having one prime-time 1 and one prime-time 2 experience, a lesson will have as many prime-time 1 and 2 experiences as the number of varied-modality engagements introduced. In Figure 10.2, the student has prime-time 1 and prime-time 2 experiences five times. Figure 10.4 illustrates the prime-time 1 and prime-time 2 appearances in the engagement. Knowing the primacy-recency phenomenon reinforces the need for instruction to be delivered in small increments, steps, or chunks.

Reinforcing Learning With Recall, Rehearsal, and Reflection

Previously discussed, *recall* enables teachers to determine what students know, can do, and understand. It occurs through association from past experiences as well as past learning. It is through association or connections that students make personal meaning. Students come to class with beliefs and understandings in place. To build upon their prior knowledge, teachers need to determine the validity of those understandings. Recall experiences throughout the lesson allow this validation to take place so that either correct understandings are built upon or incorrect understandings are corrected before an engagement begins. This validation may also be a result of an advance organizer engagement. If incorrect

Figure 10.4 Prime-Time 1 and Prime-Time 2 Experiences in a Sequentially Developed Lesson Plan

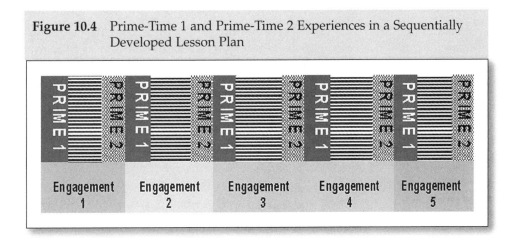

understandings or beliefs are not addressed, the result of instruction may not fit the intended target learning or enable the student to correct the misconception (Bransford et al., 2000, p. 10). Incorrect understandings easily become the basis for negative transfer, creating a more difficult scenario for the student to comprehend the intended learning (Bransford et al., 2000, p. 70).

Fisher, Frey, and Lapp (2012) suggest that teachers determine the type of background or prior knowledge that students have before continuing instruction. They offer four categories to determine the relevancy of the knowledge:

1. Representation: Is the information essential or merely interesting?

2. Transmission: Does the information require repetition or rehearsal to be understood, or is it easily explained?

3. Transferability: Is the information necessary to understand future concepts, or is it specific to one topic?

4. Endurance: Will the information be remembered or easily forgotten? (Fisher et al., 2012, p. 23)

The authors advocate the activation of background or prior knowledge through connections such as text-to-text for recalling information from a prior chapter or text-to-world if building on a recent field trip or video.

Additionally, Fisher et al. (2012) present stratgies to determine background or prior knowledge that can be used as *advance organizers.* Their strategies determine the levels of understanding that the students have and allow the teacher to know where to begin the instruction. Some examples include cloze assessments, word sorts, caption writing, and opinionaire (Fisher et al., 2012, pp. 26–28). These tasks not only indicate prior knowledge but can also signal the new learning that is forthcoming.

Rehearsal is essential to place information into long-term memory. Sousa (2001) presents two important factors for rehearsal: time and type, either rote or elaborative. The learner needs time to continually reprocess the information until meaning and relevance are attached to it (Sousa, 2001, pp. 85–86). Without meaning being attached, however, the time factor becomes moot.

Rote rehearsal processes information that must be learned in specific sequence or context such as phone numbers or steps in a procedure like scientific method or order of operations. Elaborative rehearsal is a more complex process. It uses relationships and connections to prior learning. Sousa (2001, p. 86) gives the example of rote rehearsal being used to memorize a poem and elaborative rehearsal to interpret its meaning. When more senses are used during elaborative rehearsal, the associations become stronger and are more likely to place the learning into long-term memory. A strategy for rote rehearsal includes simple repetition. Elaborative rehearsal strategies include paraphrasing, note taking, predicting, questioning, student-to-student processing, writing about math concepts, and summarizing.

Marzano (2010) refers to rehearsal as practice. He suggests that procedural knowledge or skills, strategies, or processes move through stages until they reach a level of automaticity, the point at which the skill can be completed without conscious thought (Marzano, 2010, p. 81). Strategies and processes are more complex pieces of procedural learning. He cautions against confusing necessary practice with its improper use as drill. Guided practice needs to be relevant and to help in the construction of meaning (Marzano, 2007, p. 62). In the CCSS, teachers of math will need to have students expand on their answers, requiring a deeper level of instruction than drill tasks provide.

When students learn and rehearse or practice content and skills in a variety of modes, they are more likely to remember or recall what they have learned. Jensen (1998, p. 111) refers to this phenomenon as "recall resiliency." In order to encourage meaningful rehearsal, he suggests the use of mnemonics, mind maps, drawing visual cues, opening and closing class with the same three words or concepts that relate to the day's lesson, peer teaching, and sharing.

Like the introduction of information, rehearsal needs to occur frequently in small doses (Bransford et al., 2000, p. 236). Jensen (1998, p. 109) suggests to repeat key ideas within 10 minutes of the original learning, then 48 hours later, and again in 7 days. Marzano (2003) cites the work of Nuthall (1999) to affirm the notion that multiple experiences with information are necessary to learn information sufficiently. These authors suggest that learners need at least four interactions with information to effectively learn it. In practice, this is an I-2-2-2 effect: an introduction to new material followed by three rehearsals or repetitions delivered in a different modality or form. Each rehearsal must occur no more than two days apart. With this in mind, a totally new concept should not be introduced toward the end of the week with the weekend interrupting the sequence of rehearsals.

Reflection is a metacognitive approach to learning that enables learners to recognize what they know and to focus on their levels of performance (Pellegrino, Chudowsky, & Glaser, 2001, p. 78). It is an opportunity for students to self-assess their level of understanding. Since an intense level of attention can only be managed for short periods of time, the brain needs time to make meaning, an internal operation. During this period of time, considered "downtime," reflection engagements encourage the "imprint" of new learning (Jensen, 1998, p. 46). Forms of reflection can be individual such as quick writing in learning journals or sharing with a partner as in think-pair-share. Besides placing reflective engagements within the lesson, a culminating reflection time should occur. As seen in Figure 10.2, a reflection engagement completed at the end of the lesson allows students time to review target learning and to answer essential questions. This placement further takes advantage of the prime-time 2 factor of high focus.

Assessment

The *assessment* element of the lesson plan holds great importance for student learning and the delivery of instruction. *Formative assessment*, that assessment that checks for student understanding throughout the lesson, sets the stage for the pacing of the lesson as well as the depth of understanding that can be delivered and learned. Heeding Yogi Berra's admonition, the teacher who uses formative assessment effectively in the classroom plots a course for students to arrive at a comprehensive learning destination. Effective use of this strategy includes the instructional adjustments made due to the results of the assessment.

As discussed earlier in this chapter, the mid–20th century saw a renewal in student-focused instructional delivery. Educational researchers, cognitive psychologists, and practitioners gave impetus to the growing concern about instruction, its delivery, and the results. While asssessment has always been in the educational picture to assign grades, its application, accuracy, and use of results as formative assessment have not been forefront. Benjamin Bloom and colleagues brought attention to this effective instructional strategy through their publication *Handbook on Formative and Summative Evaluation of Student Learning* in 1971 (Guskey, 2007/2008). In 1998, a *Phi Delta Kappan* article by Black and Wiliam detailed a meta-analysis of formative assessment. Popham (2008) credits this article for bringing increased and more recent impetus to the serious application of formative assessments and the essential adjustments made from the assesment results. Wiliam's (2011) book, *Embedded Formative Assessment,* expands on his original premise and presents multiple arguments for and examples of formative assessment as he defines it.

Black and Wiliam (1998) put forth their analysis of why external tests do not improve student learning. External tests refer to tests given periodically to determine if students have reached a benchmark level of understanding or other summative tests that measure a student's mastery of designated standards such as state achievement tests. From the results of these tests, teachers and curriculum leaders can revisit a school or district's curriculum or teachers in a TLC (teacher learning community) or PLC (professional learning community) can revisit a curriculum map or discuss teaching strategies to improve student learning. Although some practitioners use teacher-developed benchmark tests to adjust the intended curriculum and share teaching strategies, this type of adjustment is not immediate. While it may improve the intended curriculum or strategies for later instruction, it does not adjust for the completed instruction that is being discussed in the PLC. For maximum effectiveness, the adjustment needs to occur within minutes or days of the assessment. In the article, Black and Wiliam (1998) assert that student improvement can only take place if "teaching and learning [are] interactive" with formative assessment taking place in the classroom during instruction and causing adjustment of teaching and learning.

Since that time, others have championed the use of formative assessment. Different names or labels have appeared such as *interim assessments* that do not necessarily relate to the formative assessment process discussed above. Concern arises about the mislabeling and misuse of other forms of assessment presented as formative assessment, especially by commercial entities (Chappuis & Chappuis, 2007/2008; Popham, 2008; Tomlinson, 2007/2008). Fisher and Frey (2007) alternate the term *formative assessment* with *checking for understanding,* a term used by Madeline Hunter, a mid-20th-century educational innovator. Lorna Earl (2003) suggests that differences in assessment purpose occur when assessment is done *of* learning, *for* learning, and *as* learning (cited in Tomlinson, 2007/2008). Assessment *of* learning refers to summative assessment, to determine the level of learning attained at the end of a unit. Assessment *for* learning refers to that ongoing assessment during instruction. Each purpose has a role; each requires judicial use.

Due to the number of different definitions of formative assessment, Popham (2008) chooses to simplify the definition created by FAST SCASS (Formative Assessment for Students and Teachers State Collaboratives on Assessment and Student Standards). His definition reverberates in the definitions put forth by other researchers and educational writers:

> Formative asssessment is a *planned process* in which *assessment-elicited evidence* of students' status is used by teachers to *adjust* their *on-going instructional procedures* or by students to *adjust* their *current learning tactics*. (Popham, 2008, p. 6, emphasis added)

He explains the difference between authentic formative assessment and benchmark tests. If an assessment is not used to adjust instruction and/or learning, it is not formative. Therefore, benchmark or interim tests given periodically to determine mastery of curricular outcomes are not formative. They may influence changes in instruction or curriculum, but those changes do not occur immediately during the instruction of that unit. Further, because they are not developed to provide immediate adjustment to specific target learning, commercial assessments touted to be formative are not and cannot be (Popham, 2008, pp. 9–10).

To be truly formative, assessments take place in the classroom and are improvement focused. Renouncing the preponderance of comparative testing that students endure, Popham (2008) further emphasizes the improvement focus feature by firmly suggesting that these assessments are not graded. For instance, anonymously taken short quizzes provide a sense of what the entire class understands. Adjustments to class instruction are based on those results. One type of quiz used for this purpose is a testlet. A longer quiz can be divided into four or five separate testlets, each quiz having four or five items that cover the concepts being taught. The testlet results are aggregated to determine the students' levels of understanding. Using this method gives an accurate picture of learning progress without spending an inordinate amount of time on a test (Popham, 2008, p. 63).

As stated earlier when discussing target learning, students need to have a clear understanding of what they are to learn when being assessed (Black & Wiliam, 1998; Chappuis & Chappuis, 2007/2008; Fisher & Frey, 2007; Guskey, 2007/2008; Popham, 2008; Tomlinson, 2007/2008; Wiggins & McTighe, 1998). This caveat is a need, not an option, for learning and for assessment. Stiggins (2001) also writes that all assessment does not need to be grade or score related. It must, however, have a clear target, a focused purpose, and a proper method (Stiggins, 2001, p. 19). The feedback to students based on the results of formative assessment must be specific to the content being learned and their progress toward the learning target. Hattie (1992) considers feedback based on student work and delivered in small frequent responses to be the most powerful single modification for improving student achievement (cited in Marzano, 2003, p. 37). Hattie (2012) cautions, however, that feedback needs to be individualized. When feedback is delivered to the entire class, few students take the feedback personally.

The next engagement in the lesson plan should not be introduced until the teacher conducts a check for understanding, gives any necessary feedback if appropriate at the time, and determines that the class is ready to move ahead. Hatttie (1999) considers feedback a fundamental component of teaching that imparts information to students, assesses and evaluates the students' understanding, and then connects the next part of the instruction with the students' demonstrated understanding. Individual students with difficulties should be helped with a differentiated approach. When engagements vary in form and modality, they aid the adjustments needed for reteaching or reinforcement.

Depending on the importance of the content of each engagement, the assessment can take the form of a quick check for understanding such as walk-arounds or a more comprehensive formative assessment. Quick checks appear in several easy-to-monitor forms. A stack of red, yellow, and green cups with the green cup on the top placed on the desk serves as a visual cue to the teacher during instruction. If the student does not understand the material, the red cup is placed on top to indicate the student needs immediate help. If the student partially understands, the yellow cup goes on top to indicate a possible need for help. If the student has complete understanding, the green cup remains on top. In order to determine if a green cup student truly understands, the teacher stops occasionally and, randomly, has one of those students explain the concept being taught or the engagement being completed. When students begin to trust that the main point in the classroom is student success, the need to hide misunderstandings begins to disappear. This level of trust may take a while to establish.

A more in-depth check could be individual whiteboards or a pre-printed card response. Using the whiteboard, students write an answer and hold it up for the teacher to determine the level of understanding by the entire class. When more discrimination is needed, students can use index cards preprinted with letters *A, B, C, D, T,* and *F* and ?. The teacher projects multiple-choice or true/false statements on a screen, and students respond by holding up the card that identifies their answer. From the number of correct answers, the teacher has an idea of student understanding (Popham, 2008, p. 53). The important fact is that the assessment surveys the entire class and not one or two students.

A whip-around accomplishes a similar end. Students are asked to write three responses to a task the teacher poses that relates to the instruction. When the three responses are written, all students stand and randomly begin to share their responses one at a time. As each response is given, students check off on their list any that have been mentioned. When all three responses are checked off, the student sits. The process continues until all students are seated. During the reponse time, the teacher notes what types of responses are given and what are missing. From that whole class assessment, any necessary adjustments can be made (Fisher & Frey, 2007, pp. 34–35).

Traditional question-and-answer sessions with a few students answering do not give teachers the necessary information to determine if instruction is meeting the needs of all the students. Often referred to as "guess what is in the teacher's head," this form of intiating the question, responding to the question, evaluating the correctness of the question, and moving to the next question only indicates the understanding of one or a few students. This format precludes any definitive data to determine if adjustments need to be made (Fisher & Frey, 2007, p. 34). These authors have a variety of assessment strategies in their books for teachers to implement.

Wiliam (2011) describes a questioning method that randomizes student responses and places an evaluative function on answers. She labels the strategy, shared with her by a middle school teacher, "pose-pause-pounce-bounce." She poses a question (*pose*), waits at least five seconds (*pause*), randomly calls on a student to answer (*pounce*), and randomly asks another student to validate the previous student's answer (*bounce*). Her random selection of students to respond concurs with Wiliam's recommendation to implement a "no hands up except to *ask* a question" policy.

Popham (2008) and others believe that through the use of formative assessment, the learning process in the classroom can begin to help students to assume responsibility for their own learning if the environment in the classroom is nonthreatening. Just as teachers adjust their teaching, students adjust their learning through "learning tactics" (Popham, 2008, p. 71). This places more responsibility on students to know themselves and how they learn. As they proceed, they begin to self-assess their own type of formative learning. When this effect takes place, the classroom becomes the model that Black and Wiliam (1998) propose: "Teaching and learning are interactive."

Connections

Following the assessment portion of the lesson plan, the *connection* element creates a segue from one learning engagement to the next engagement. As a second opportunity for recall, it promotes transfer of learned material to working memory. Therefore, as a connection, the teacher refers to specific aspects of the lesson that will appear in the next engagement, creating the relationship as a "look-for."

Successful transfer does not occur naturally; it must be structured and reinforced. A learner needs to make meaning with information before it can be successfully transferred and placed in working memory and, ultimately, into long-term memory. If students do not or cannot make meaning, understanding of the information as well as memory of it will be lost (Bransford et al., 2000, p. 236).

Two aspects of instruction encourage reinforcement to create meaning: having an identified conceptual lens and integrated instruction. Through connections to the conceptual lens, chunking of information more easily occurs and, as a result, is more easily stored and applied later in new situations (Bransford et al., 2000, p. 17). Integrated instruction places students in positions to see relationships between diverse ideas and subjects. The greater the number of patterns and relationships that are created or established, the more likely the student will be able to place new information into working and long-term memory (Sousa, 2001, p. 139).

As noted in the recall part of the lesson plan, students build new knowledge on prior knowledge. That prior knowledge is the result of transfer. If the past learning helps, it is positive transfer. If prior knowledge interferes with new knowledge and causes confusion as the result of a misconception, it is negative transfer. Interestingly, the transfer–working memory process is more often provoked by environment than by conscious recall (Sousa, 2001; Wolfe, 2001). Therefore, some constructs of lessons—movement, colors, music, place—influence the type of transfer, postitive or negative. This environmentally triggered experience represents an episodic memory (Jensen, 1998).

Knowing the factors that affect transfer aids in planning the connections part of the learning engagement. Hunter (1982) and others agree that four major factors influence transfer: similarities, critical attributes, association, and context and degree (cited in Sousa, 2001, p. 143). The use of similarities is a familiar instructional practice that has positive and negative influences. Memories are stored by similarities but retrieved by differences. Therefore, when two very similar concepts are taught simultaneously, confusion and misconceptions may occur. The introduction of longitude and latitude is an example of concepts so similar that, when they are introduced during the same lesson, students often experience difficulty in differentiating between them. By the same token, use of similarities can be a powerful segue between a completed engagement and the following one (Sousa, 2001).

An understanding of the critical attributes of a concept is to be aware of the characteristics that make it unique from all others. If students understand those aspects, they are better able to avoid the confusion that may arise from exposure to concepts that are too similar. A *connection* statement could rehearse the salient characteristics of the concept practiced in the engagement and how those characteristics will be experienced in the ensuing engagement.

An active, concrete engagement helps students to understand the critical attribute concept. A person in the class decides upon some physical characteristic, color, or piece of clothing worn by students. Without revealing the choice, participants/students are called upon according to whether they have the attribute(s). If the students have it, they stand in the "yes" line. If not, they are asked to stand in the "no" line. While students are being identified, the rest of the class is to determine what the critical attributes are by looking at the students in the "yes" and "no" lines. Begin with one or two attributes. As the students are better able to discern the attributes, add another. As a rehearsal process, students should be the ones to choose the attributes.

Association factors are those that are bonded and recalled together such as Romeo and Juliet or branding trademarks like the Golden Arches or an apple with a bite out of it for Apple (Sousa, 2001, p. 144). Mnemonics, a form of association, aids in the remembering of concepts in which meaning is difficult to establish. By associating the new information with a known concept, meaning is created (Wolfe, 2001, p. 105).

The context and degree of original factors depend on how well and accurately prior knowledge is learned. Therefore, the inclusion of recall, rehearsal, and formative assessment in the learning engagement takes on a significant role.

Connection serves as a vehicle for transfer of learning. Two ways to promote transfer incorporate the use of metaphors, analogies, similes, and journal writing. Metaphors, analogies, and similes promote the transfer of abstractions. These processes can reach to the past by asking students to connect what is being learned with what has been learned or can aid prediction. Marzano et al. (2001) and Dean et al. (2012) advocate the creation of visual metaphors or nonlinguistic representations for concepts or vocabulary. In this way, the concept or word being learned has more neural connections for transfer and retrieval. At the beginning of this chapter, the quotation from Yogi Berra serves as a metaphor for the lesson plan process. He suggests a careful plan is necessary to reach a destination; the lesson plan seeks the destination of effective instruction and improved student learning.

Journal writing provides an opportunity for reflection. Although it is too extensive to serve as a simple segue or connection between engagements, it is effective as a reflection engagement to promote transfer either during or at the end of the lesson. As a reflection engagement, the prompt needs to be specifically stated, preferably connected to the essential question(s) for the lesson. It can also be used to connect the day's instruction with prior learning or to predict how the day's instruction will connect with the following lesson.

Connections between engagements create conceptual, content, and/or skill relationships that motivate transfer and meaning. The connection may be a simple statement connecting one engagement to the next or a more complex connection such as creating a metaphor for what was learned. Whichever is chosen, the overt connection is essential to help students see the purpose and relationship of the engagement that will follow.

SUMMARIZING USING THE SCHEDULE ■ FOR EFFECTIVE INSTRUCTION

The quest for improved student achievement lies within the grasp of all educators, and it materializes in the classroom. The school schedule forms an important vehicle for carrying out that quest, including the subschedules that meet the needs of diverse populations. It is, however, what occurs within the schedule that influences what all students know, do, understand, apply, and explain. Teaching bell-to-bell with an incrementally sequenced lesson plan relies on empirical research and authentic anecdotal experiences. As Schmoker (2011) reminds us, the answer is simple—active involvement of students in a rigorous curriculum; clear targets; instruction presented in small chunks or engagements; and consistent, frequent formative assessment or checks for understanding immediately adjusted as needed. A conceptual lens provides the vehicle for chunking concepts and skills, a posted target learning identifies the destination, and known essential questions light the way.

Planned with awareness of the attention focus of the students addressed, the series of engagements in the lesson plan provides six way stations to inform instructional pacing and address important learning factors. The questions following each of these factors allow the lesson planner to heighten a level of awareness.

Purpose

- How does this engagement move the student toward an understanding of the target learning?
- Is the target learning clear?
- Does it address essential learning?
- Will students be able to see the connections or the progression from this engagement to the target learning?
- How does this engagement build toward success in answering the esssential questions?

Motivation

- Does this engagement tap into students' interests or needs?
- Does this engagement actively involve students?
- Will this engagement allow students an oppportunity for success so that their success provides motivation to learn?
- Does the motivation provide intrinsic or extrinsic rewards?

Recall

- Does the recall question, cue, or visual focus on provoking the specific prior knowledge, skill, or content that will be necessary in this engagement?
- Will the recall segment provide a connection between prior knowledge and the new learning?
- Does the recall provide students with an opportunity to rehearse what has already been learned?
- Does the recall task require rote or elaborative memory of prior knowledge?
- Does the recall allow for teacher recognition of student misunderstandings?

Engagement

- Is the engagement a "chunk" of learning, a small step toward the target learning?
- Because of this engagement, will students increase their ability to answer successfully the essential questions?
- Does the engagement vary in modality from the previous and the following engagements?
- Is the student actively involved in the engagement?
- Does the engagement provide an opportunity for group discussion, solutions, or reflections?
- Does the engagement focus on the acquisition of knowledge (declarative) or skills (procedural)?
- Is a connection to students' real-life experiences embedded in the engagement?
- Can the engagement be differentiated?
- Do the engagements begin with an advance organizer and end with a reflection to take advantage of prime-time 1 and 2 learning times?

Assessment

- Will the engagement allow formative assessment to occur?
- What types of formative assessment will be used in this engagement?
- How will the instruction be adjusted if formative assessment indicates that the class or individual students do not have a solid understanding of the material?
- How will more formal or benchmark formative assessment results be used in a PLC meeting to monitor a specific course and overall student achievement?

- How can teachers' questions be improved to assess student understanding?
- What types of feedback will be provided?
- Will the feedback be immediate and encourage teaching or learning adjustment?
- What kinds of assessments will be given to determine grades versus to determine understanding?

Connections

- What type of connection best works between two engagements?
- How does the connection element of the lesson plan assist transfer of learning?
- Should this lesson include a full engagement for connections between complex concepts?
- When should a connection be a full engagement?
- What "look-fors" should be included in this connection?

As the conceptual lens for this chapter, adaptation creates an opportunity for instruction in which present practices are accommodated or new ones assimilated. Those courses that serve diverse populations must also be examined for ways instruction can be adapted to the research-based lesson plan tenets.

A thorough reading of this chapter leads to its target learning: Research aids the development of purposeful lessons and learning engagements to guide instruction. When the engagement process is implemented with effective instruction that seeks to serve how students and adults learn, the target learning of this chapter has been met.

By the end of this chapter, the engaged reader can either answer in depth each of the essential questions offered below or find the passage that cues the answer.

- How does an articulated-engagement approach to instruction enhance learning?
- How does research support the articulated-engagement lesson plan model?
- In what ways do recall, rehearsal, and reflection enhance the learning process?
- How does formative assessment influence instruction?
- How does this lesson plan meet the needs of diverse populations as well as mainstreamed students?

Most important, when each of these lesson elements is addressed, Yogi can rest easily: The reader knows the path and will get there.

11

Professional Development to Support the Comprehensive Schedule

The first step towards getting somewhere is to decide that you are not going to stay where you are.

J. Pierpont Morgan

The advent of the Common Core State Standards prompts the continued educational debate on what must be done to educate America's children. Points of view about the CCSS, both pro and con, emerge with varying points standing between the two. Nearly all, however, have some association with the belief that more student-centered instruction and ample provisions for teacher support to provide that instruction are essential to change from the status quo.

Effective and purposeful professional learning activates change from the status quo. Rather than embark on the current "hot topic," districts and schools need to evaluate their situations and communities to determine needs. Next, those defined needs require prioritizing. From those priorities, two or three feasible initiatives should be adopted, presented, and implemented, until the previously determined goals are achieved. When each goal is reached and the initiative can be sustained, the next important change item or initiative can be pursued. Research indicates that initiatives integrated with the goals or vision for the school are more effective than isolated unconnected initiatives (Wei, Darling-Hammond, Andree, Richardson, & Orphanos, 2009).

Reeves (2010, p. 27) cautions leaders to avoid the "Law of Initiative Fatigue." He is not alone. Fullan (2000) contends that only when schools choose a few selective goals or initiatives and collaboratively work on their implementation do they avoid fragmentation and overload. A selective focus allows faculties to become familiar with and practice the designated initiative. Practicing or rehearsing the initiative is as essential for the adult learner as the same strategies are for the student learner.

Because the schedule provides the fundamental platform for instruction, it is often a focus for school restructuring or, in Fullan's (2001, p. 44) words, reculturing. In this chapter, professional development focal points address the process of restructuring with an emphasis on assimilating an understanding of schedules that provide time frames to meet the instructional needs of all students and opportunities for professional learning.

ENACTING CHANGE   ■

Patience effects change. Fullan (2001) uses the word *reculturing* because true change within the system of the school requires reculturing, a change in the way processes take place. Rather than adopting a bevy of innovations, reculturing is a process that requires selectivity of new ideas and practices that fit identified needs (Fullan, 2001, p. 44). Further, reculturing or change takes time, three to six years depending on the size of the school and the complexity of the change (Fullan, 2000). Too frequently, impatience for dramatic results causes the abandonment of a solid initiative that has not had an opportunity to be institutionalized through effective implementation.

Senge et al. (2000) offer insights on the pace of change. Sustained change takes place when those affected commit to it. Successful change cannot be dictated. If, however, an environment is created that fosters reflection, provides adequate support for instruction, and encourages teachers to develop abilities, change can be nudged. When change is patiently enacted, it is more sustainable. Like effective learning engagements, change that begins small, escalates appropriately, and undergoes reflection during its process is more likely to be sustained (Senge et al., 2000, p. 273).

When frameworks for a schedule are adopted, the time frame for evaluating the schedule's success must be sufficient for all component parts to work together. The scheduling process requires time to encode and work through glitches; teachers need time to understand the possibilities for instruction and professional learning within the schedule; and instructional practices need time for evaluation, possible alteration, and implementation.

In addition to their caution regarding the number of initiatives, researchers and educational experts consistently champion the idea that people, not programs, make the difference in successful professional development. Initiatives are more easily accomplished when teachers are a part of the process, actively involved in all aspects of the school (Wei et al., 2009; Dufour, 1995; Hirsh & Killion, 2009; Reeves, 2010). Unfortunately, most teachers have limited influence in school decision making, including identification of school needs and resulting initiatives (Wei et al., 2009). To avoid Reeves's (2010) Law of Initiative Fatigue, those most responsible for carrying out the initiative should have input in selecting it. From there, the initiative serves to build teacher capacity for implementation.

To complete the process of choosing a new schedule, an effective scheduling committee reflects the makeup of the school. Based on a collaborative model and comprising elective and core teachers, diverse population teachers, parents, and administrators, the committee presents multiple points of view to identify whole-school needs. Success in this effort demands that the committee enter into a collaborative arrangement so that singular, personal agendas are not pushed before essential needs.

■ MISSION/VISION STATEMENTS

When beginning the process of determining a professional learning focus, the mission/vision statement of the school or district provides the target. If the statement created to guide the school gathers dust on a shelf or is rarely visited when professional discussions occur, it lacks clear direction and is "counterproductive" (Reeves, 2010, p. 57). Further, Reeves (2010) suggests that the change from comparative assessment between and among students to standards-based assessment challenges the way our mission/vision statements are written or put into effect.

At present, the public face of mission/vision statements is thoughtful and noble. To provide a more practical target for professional learning purposes, a different form of statement lends guidance. That statement needs specifics to take the message from lofty and ambiguous to pragmatic and explicit. By adding school-specific details to the following topics, those details provide meaning to an otherwise ambiguous ideal: evidence of results, provision of assessments, early feedback to determine the beginning effects of an initiative implementation, and timely ongoing feedback to encourage improvement or adaptation (Reeves, 2010, pp. 58–60). Eventually, the public face of a mission/vision statement should include the same type of specifics that inform the professional staff.

Danielson (2002) also endorses clearly stated mission/vision goals for a school community. While within the statements lie the philosophy of the school, she suggests the inclusion of "what we want" statements. Those statements are more specific than "students will be lifelong learners" generalities. Some of her suggestions are "high-level learning of all students [and] a culture of positive inquiry for teachers" (Danielson, 2002, p. 118).

The mission/vision statement guides the adoption of a schedule, the instruction that takes place within the time frames of that schedule, and the degree of professional learning opportunities possible. When a scheduling committee begins discussion about a new schedule, writing a mission/vision statement filled with "what we want" ideas and explicit results will add specificity to the existing mission/vision statement. The same process should take place when discussions of instruction, the needs of diverse populations, and other ventures into change occur, emphasizing the goal of learning for all.

PRINCIPAL LEADERSHIP ■

Multiple studies define the characteristics of a successful principal. The correlation of those studies affirms particularly effective principal characteristics that not only are visions for a school leader but are practiced by that leader.

To be a change agent, a successful principal mobilizes others to address tough problems (Roberts, 2000, p. 414). According to Roberts (2000), the principal leads the action to show personal engagement. Fullan (2001, p. 47) also recommends action and counsels that change is complex and "different circumstances require different strategies." To move away from the staus quo, the change agent needs to be "willing to temporarily upset the school's equilibrium" (Marzano, 2005, p. 44). Hord and Hirsh (2009, p. 22) recommend mobilizing others by placing trust in teachers, conveying to them that they can succeed, and then expecting evidence of success. But Reeves (2009) cautions about the difference between the verbalization of wanting change and implementing it. Recognizing that leaving comfortable practices behind is traumatic, he likens the change process to Kübler-Ross's (1969) stages of grief (Reeves, 2009, p. 45). Change is loss. The effective leader recognizes the resulting complexity in addressing loss while providing the basis for real collaboration and developing trust.

Although the principal carries responsibility for the final decision, suggestions and ideas from others enter into that decision. Reeves (2006, p. 28) cites Elmore's (2000) advice that one person cannot go it alone, needing to implement "distributed" leadership. When a schedule change is being considered, the constituency groups are a part of the distributed leadership to provide significant input. The principal's oversight on decisions about instruction entails a consistent focus on learning for all participants, students and teachers. By providing support for new approaches to instruction in a changing world, the principal ensures increased likelihood that those approaches will be implemented. A part of that support includes identifying time within a schedule to set the stage for collaboration and professional learning communities (PLCs). To accomplish these tasks, the design of professional development should open the door for sustained change.

REQUISITES FOR PROFESSIONAL LEARNING ■

Language changes to describe existing phenomena. Earlier, schools and districts delivered professional days or hours of staff development, also known as inservice training. Today, those occurences refer to the professional expertise of the staff with an emphasis on learning: professional development or professional learning. The change in language emphasizes the change in purpose. No longer are teachers "trained"; they are partners in learning. While this description does not fit all schools and all districts, it is the description that should be pursued.

Because the process for learning transcends age, many descriptions of a professional development meeting look amazingly like the instruction described in Chapter 10. The process for professional development described by Fogarty and Pete (2009/2010) is one. Adult learners want to be actively involved so that they have a deeper understanding of the concept and can provide authentic implementation. They learn better when the information is presented in diverse forms similar to changing modalities during engagements in the classroom. The focus of professional development works best when related to individual teaching needs, the teachers' real world. If accompanied by practical support, practice, and feedback, the new process or strategy has the potential to replace the old and become a part of the teaching repertoire. Measurable results reassure teachers as well as administration that the initiative is working.

Hirsh and Killion (2009) advise that all members share in the responsibility for implementation of the initiative and, as such, are accountable for its success. These facets become viable within the context of collaboration, the honest sharing of ideas and beliefs. The report from Stanford University on professional learning (Wei et al., 2009) reveals salient points from research:

- Effective professional development is ongoing and connected to practice, focuses on teaching and learning of specific academic content, and connects to other school initiatives.
- If the professional development initiative is sustained and intense, the potential for improved student achievement appears.
- Collaborative approaches promote school change.

Unfortunately, the above points are not the norm. Research also indicates where gaps occur:

- Professional learning for 9 of 10 teachers consists of short-term conferences, workshops, or lack of follow-up.
- For the largest effects of professional development initiatives to take hold, between 30 and 100 hours spread over 6–12 months are essential. Most professional learning experiences are much shorter, even as short as 1–2 hours.
- Few teachers report having any collaborative input in designing curriculum and sharing practices. The collaboration that does occur is weak.

Professional development may be the linchpin to reform and reculturing a school as well as the catalyst for instruction that takes place within the school. As Reeves (2010, p. 44) counsels, people, not programs, make the difference. They move the system from where it is to where it envisions to go. Consequently, the involvement of faculty in the selection of a scheduling framework is essential.

INSTRUCTION WITHIN THE SCHEDULE   ■

Once a scheduling framework is chosen, comprehensive professional development for all stakeholders is the next step. An understanding of how the schedule supports instruction and professional collaboration becomes paramount in its success. Student achievement is the beacon that guides decisions in the use of the schedule. As recent literature continues to reveal, teaching is only a part of the equation; learning is the brass ring. Chapter 10 emphasizes the importance of using instructional strategies to deliver the intended curriculum. Formative assessments throughout the lesson and periodic benchmark assessments provide data to adjust instruction.

Concern about the adoption of too many initiatives should not keep the staff from integrating initiatives that build on one another. Schedule development, instruction, and PLC initiatives logically interrelate. Each of these initiatives correlates with the other in a symbiotic relationship that strengthens the cumulative effect. To accomplish the integrated success of the initiative, all members of a school are stakeholders in attaining their success. Each has a role to play in putting the schedule into effective use. Each has a responsibility for the hard work of collaboration and is not simply a complacent member of the PLC. Each must bring thoughtful information about teaching, students, and learning to the table for discussion and develop plans of action. To meet these ends, the schedule needs to provide adequate opportunites for meeting during the school workday.

Teams or small learning communities may have opportunites to flex the schedule. If so, they will require help and support to implement the flex. Further, if flex opportunities allow extended- or variable-time class periods, teachers need ongoing support in adapting their teaching to fill the class period with active, engaged instruction. Flexing the schedule provides opportunites for classes to meet at different times, taking advantage of the varying levels of students' focus at different times of the day.

A task of the PLC is to investigate the standards that relate to the school's curriculum. Marzano (2003) suggests that teaching in-depth the entirety of standards as they exist is an impossible feat. By identifying power standards, the PLC can build common assessments and scoring guides based on those standards. Reeves (2010, pp. 29–30) presents three criteria points for identifying which standards should be identified as power standards:

- Leverage: Standards that influence more than a single discipline. Curriculum integration assumes greater importance when standards are leveraged. The PLC identifies those disciplines.
- Endurance: Length of application of the standard exists beyond a single test or assessment.
- Essential: The level of applicability of the standard to the curriculum in the next grade.

The work of the PLC is best accomplished when meetings occur within the school schedule promoting a professional atmosphere in which to discuss standards. When participants actualize the three initiatives of schedule, instruction, and PLC groups, they show evidence of the effectiveness of the integrated initiatives.

The classroom is the agar dish for student learning within the laboratory of the school as impacted by the schedule. The success of the schedule remains subject to the rich opportunities for instruction that takes place within those classrooms. Chapter 10 presents a research-based, incremental-engagement lesson plan prototype. For the successful implementation of this model, professional development is essential. Adaptive instructional strategies rely on assimilation of the engagement lesson plan concept. That assimilation begins with intense introductions to the lesson plan with successive follow-up for rehearsal. Without commitment to follow-up, the instructional initiative is doomed to failure. Reeves's (2009) observations of unsuccessful initiatives reveal that insufficient implementation rather than lack of merit causes failure. Just as with student learning, authentic implementation occurs when sufficient rehearsal of the lesson plan initiative allows it to achieve automaticity.

■ SUMMARIZING PROFESSIONAL DEVELOPMENT TO SUPPORT THE COMPREHENSIVE SCHEDULE

Without adequate professional development, worthy initiatives die before their time. Wei et al. (2009) found that teachers want the support allowed through professional development. They look to their instructional leaders to provide better experiences than the cafeteria format they now receive.

The potpourri of professional development opportunities suggests that people will eagerly take on innovative practices. That perception as well as the innovation disappears due to a lack of time-related commitment. The microwave attitude of society demands that results appear instantly. If not, the hunt is on for the next best idea. Research, however, reveals that real change does not and cannot take place for three to six years. Orchestrated professional development ensures a solid use of the time interval.

Initiative fatigue is real and capable of undermining grand visions. Initiatives should be few in number and connected to the essential needs of the school or district with others added as earlier ones are retired. The mission/vision statement of the school directs the understanding of the needs. Initiatives are chosen accordingly.

Benchmark evaluations track the progress of an initiative or its implementation. The process becomes an incremental journey sustained by ongoing professional development. Time for those experiences appears throughout the day or year: regular professional development days identified by the district, school faculty meetings, and designated PLC time.

Leadership for the implementation of the initiatives and professional learning rests with the building principal. The actions of the principal speak loudly and can be the motivating factor for the success or failure of an initiative. Although the principal is ultimately responsible for decisions, all populations within the school need to have a voice in helping to reach that decision.

Professional learning influences self-evaluation of teaching practices. A discussion guide appendix follows this chapter. When measured against the backdrop of improved student learning, classroom instruction reaffirms its vital role. The school schedule provides a framework within which the needs of diverse populations are met and effective adaptations of instruction take place. Developing that school schedule provides the first steps to move away from the staus quo and into the adventure of an instructionally rich learning environment and professional life.

Appendix: Professional Development Guide for the Entire Faculty and PLCs

Chapter 1: Schedules: The Springboard for Action

1. Study the research on change and identify implications for restructuring, altering the schedule, or addressing the needs of diverse populations.

2. Modify the list of aspects of a well-considered schedule to best reflect the school.

3. Organize a scheduling committee to include representatives of diverse populations, academies, career pathways, and small learning communities.

4. Determine if the mission/vision statement is current.

5. Revisit the mission/vision statement to identify aspects of the schedule that it reflects.

6. Develop an instrument/questionnaire to determine the faculty's awareness of how schedules impact student achievement.

7. Create an instrument to determine the role of the scheduling committee.

8. Create a rubric to assess the effectiveness of the work of the scheduling committee.

9. Include an aspect of the professional development program to explore the relationship of the teachers' contract and the school schedule.

10. Create a list of diverse populations in the school.

Chapter 2: Special Programs for Educational Success: RTI, Special Education, and ELL

1. Define the term *diverse population.*

2. Identify the cultural implications of subsets within the complexity of a school population or community.

3. Explain how the school or district defines or identifies subgroups.

4. For each of the subsets, list curriculum and logistical needs that will impact the construction of the schedule.

5. Decide how the schedule will address each of the tiers of response to intervention (RTI).

6. Prescribe the training that teachers will need to implement the three tiers of RTI.

7. Assess the school and faculty's awareness of the Individuals with Disabilities Education Act (IDEA).

8. Assess the school or faculty's degree of implementation of IDEA.

9. Assess the extent to which the schedule accommodates the implementation of IDEA.

10. Describe the status of the English language learner (ELL) in the school.

11. Determine which items listed by Rossell (2004–2005) best address the needs of students in the school.

12. Identify ELL student needs that must be met through the schedule.

13. Assess the inclusiveness of the schedule in light of IDEA recommendations.

Chapter 3: Special Programs for Educational Success: Credit Recovery, Career and Technical Education, Gifted and Talented, Advanced Placement, and International Baccalaureate

1. Describe the extent to which credit recovery can impact the graduation rate.

2. Give reasons for the school's commitment to credit recovery.

3. Describe the design of the credit recovery program that best fits the needs of students.

4. Establish benchmarks to assess the success of the credit recovery program.

5. Develop a training program for the teachers directly involved in credit recovery classes.

6. List the career and technical education (CTE) programs that exist in the school or district.

7. Describe how CTE and college prep courses can be blended.

8. Create a plan to make all teachers knowledgeable about these opportunities.

9. Appoint a committee to explore the implementation of CTE programs within magnets, houses, or academies.

10. Design an orientation program for middle school and/or ninth-grade students to learn about available CTE programs.

11. Create a curriculum map to integrate CTE programs with core subjects.

12. List course opportunities available with honors, gifted and talented, Advanced Placement, and International Baccalaureate designations.

13. Explore how each program can be integrated into the total school curriculum.

14. Determine the school/district commitment to differentiate learning or grouping opportunities for the highly able student.

15. Develop a master plan to include special programs within the organization of the school schedule.

Chapter 4: Inclusive Scheduling Frameworks: Fixed

1. List ways in which fixed frameworks are important to the culture of the school.

2. Describe how flexibility can be accomplished in a fixed schedule.

3. Determine professional development for fixed frameworks.

Frameworks	Define	Benefits for Diverse Populations	Benefits for General Population	Limitations	Potential for Implementation	Professional Development Needed
Semester 1/ Semester 2–4 × 4						
Semester 1/ Semester 2–5 × 5						
Double English/ Double Mathematics						
Quarters						
Day 1/Day 2						
Trimesters						
Credit Recovery						
Rotational						
Single Subject						
Traditional						

Chapter 5: Inclusive Scheduling Frameworks: Variable

1. List ways in which variable frameworks are important to the culture of the school.

Frameworks	Define	Benefits for Diverse Populations	Benefits for General Population	Limitations	Potential for Implementation	Professional Development Needed
Interdisciplinary– Maximum Flexibility						
Interdisciplinary– Limited Flexibility						
Interdisciplinary– Encore/ Exploratory						
Combination						

Chapter 6: Integrating Fixed and Variable Frameworks Into a Comprehensive Schedule

1. Based on Table 6.3, create one or more compatibility charts that might be implemented.

2. Provide a rationale for the frameworks selected and the compatibility between those frameworks.

3. Identify the guidelines for creating the schedule for the selections made in Numbers 1 and 2.

4. List the component parts of professional development that teachers will need to work within the selected schedule.

Chapter 7: Learning Communities and Flexibility

1. Compose a working definition of a small learning community (SLC).

2. List opportunities for teams or SLCs in Grades 5, 6, 7, and 8.

3. List opportunities for magnets, houses, academies, or SLCs in Grades 9–12.

4. Identify opportunities for interdisciplinary instruction throughout the school.

5. Create sample agendas for SLC meetings.

6. Describe how flexibility enhances SLCs.

7. Describe how flexibility and personalization are accomplished in the SLC.

8. Evaluate ways collaboration affects student achievement.

9. Identify how SLCs can reduce the dropout rate.

10. List possible career pathways for Grades 9–12.

11. Describe how career pathways enhance real-life applications of curriculum.

12. Create a Venn diagram that analyzes the characteristics of professional and small learning communities.

13. List guidelines for the creation, operation, and evaluation of professional learning communities (PLCs).

14. Plan a professional development program to prepare teachers to function as members of a PLC.

15. Outline a professional development program to prepare teacher leaders for a PLC program.

16. Define flexibility within the parameters of the instructional program.

17. Create an addition to the mission/vision statement that includes flexibility and personalization.

18. Create a guide to implement the frameworks for flexibility.

19. Create a rubric to evaluate the use of the frameworks of flexibility.

20. Design a professional development program to implement the flex/advisory or intervention period.

Chapter 8: Steps in Building a Middle School Schedule

1. Analyze the significance of each of the nine steps.

2. Determine the steps that will need the greatest attention.

3. Develop a plan to implement each of the nine steps.

4. Develop a plan to assess the middle-grades schedule that the committee creates.

5. Evaluate the schedule to identify opportunities for flexibility.

6. Outline major aspects of a professional development program to implement the schedule.

Chapter 9: Steps in Building a High School Schedule

1. Analyze the significance of each of the 18 steps.

2. Determine the steps that will need the greatest attention.

3. Develop a plan to implement each of the 18 steps.

4. Develop a plan to assess the high school schedule that the committee creates.

5. Evaluate the schedule to identify opportunities for small learning communities and flexibility.

6. Create a subcommittee to develop and review department summaries, the full-time-equivalent distribution chart, and the table of teachers' assignments for equity and consistency within the teachers' contract.

7. Outline major aspects of a professional development program to implement the schedule.

Chapter 10: Using the Schedule for Effective Instruction

1. List opportunities in the current school schedule for diverse populations to implement variable-length time periods.

2. Assess knowledge of the faculty on the topics of cognitive psychology, brain-research studies, teaching and learning strategies, and other best practices.

3. Use the professional learning community model to investigate the correlation between the above topics and student achievement.

4. Determine to what extent written curriculum guides exist for each content area.

5. Create a coordinating council of instructional coaches to develop professional development related to teaching in variable-length time periods.

6. Plan a professional development program to introduce conceptual lens, target learning, and essential questions.

7. Develop a series of follow-up sessions to monitor implementation of conceptual lens, target learning, and essential questions.

8. Plan a professional development program to address the specifics of the lesson plan prototype and learning engagements.

9. Using the bell-to-bell sequence of engagements, explain the relationship of the engagements to the conceptual lens, target learning, and essential questions.

10. Develop a series of follow-up questions or a rubric to monitor implementation of the lesson plan prototype and learning engagements within all class time frames.

11. By department or within the PLC, teachers create a database of sample engagements to be used in courses offered by that department.

12. Within a PLC format, faculty members will reflect on and discuss the traits of a good engagement, formative assessment, and connection.

13. Within the PLC discussion, address the following questions:

    a. How does an articulated-engagement approach to instruction enhance learning?

    b. How does research support the articulated-engagement lesson plan model?

    c. In what ways do recall, rehearsal, and reflection enhance the learning process?

    d. How do formative assessment and feedback impact instruction?

    e. How does this lesson plan model meet the needs of diverse populations as well as mainstream students?

Chapter 11: Professional Development to Support the Comprehensive Schedule

1. Identify why professional development is essential to support the comprehensive schedule.

2. List specific professional development activities to implement, maintain, or assess the schedule.

3. List faculty expectations of the scheduling committee.

4. List faculty expectations of those responsible for building the schedule.

5. List implications of the Common Core State Standards for the school schedule.

6. Identify a series of steps for the introduction of a program initiative.

7. Decide in what ways scheduling committee members can be the agents of change.

8. Invite a guest speaker to address the concept of change or a specific initiative.

9. Within the PLC, team, or department, reflect on the message of the guest speaker.

10. List the desirable norms of faculty members when presented with a new initiative or change concept.

11. Create benchmarks to assess the implementation of a change.

12. Analyze or modify the mission/vision statement whenever necessary.

13. Identify the relationship between the chosen elements of a schedule and the amended mission/vision statement.

14. List teacher expectations of the principal in the change process.

15. Evaluate how distributed leadership is implemented in the school or district.

16. Identify the relationship between the principal's role in professional development and supervision of the instructional program.

17. Consider how professional development should meet the needs of the adult learner.

18. Create a Venn diagram to compare and contrast professional development with student learning.

19. Identify how the school schedule can enhance learning for all students, including diverse populations.

20. Define how learning is the "brass ring" of professional development.

21. Consider how collaboration affects the effectiveness of the school schedule.

References

Allen, J. (2004). *Tools for teaching content literacy.* Portland, ME: Stenhouse.

Allensworth, E. M., & Easton, J. Q. (2007). *What matters for staying on track and graduation in Chicago public high schools.* Chicago: Consortium on Chicago School Research and the University of Chicago. Retrieved March 18, 2009, from http://ccsr.uchicago.edu/content/publications.php?pub_id=116

Alliance for Excellent Education. (2007, October). The high cost of high school dropouts: What the nation pays for inadequate high schools. *Issue Brief.* Retrieved August 29, 2011, from http://www.all4ed.org/files/archive/publications/HighCost.pdf

Arhar, J. M. (1992). Interdisciplinary teaming and the social bonding of middle level students. In J. Irvine (Ed.), *Transforming middle level education: Perspectives and possibilities* (pp. 139–161). Boston: Allyn & Bacon.

Armstrong, T. (2006). *The best schools: How human development should inform educational practice.* Alexandria, VA: Association for Supervision and Curriculum Development.

Association for Supervision and Curriculum Development. (2011). *A lexicon of learning.* Retrieved August 20, 2011, from http://www.ascd.org/Publications/Lexicon-of-Learning/l.aspx

Ausubel, D. P. (1968). *Educational psychology: A cognitive view.* New York: Holt, Rinehart & Winston.

Baker, K., & de Kanter, A. (1983). *Bilingual educaton: A reappraisal of federal policy.* Lexington, MA: Lexington Books.

Batalova, J., & McHugh, M. (2010). *Number and growth of students in U.S. schools in need of English instruction.* Washington DC: Migration Policy Institute. Retrieved August 22, 2011, from http://www.migrationinformation.org/integration/ellcenter.cfm

Beers, K. (2003). *When kids can't read: What teachers can do.* Portsmouth, NH: Heinemann.

Bergmann, S. (2001). Comprehensive guidance and support services. In T. O. Erb (Ed.), *This we believe . . . and now we must act* (pp. 108–115). Westerville, OH: National Middle School Association.

Black, P., & Wiliam, D. (1998). Inside the black box: Raising standards through classroom assessment. *Phi Delta Kappan, 80*(2), 139–148.

Bloom, B. S., Hastings, J. T., & Madaus, G. F. (1971). *Handbook on formative and summative evaluation of student learning.* New York: McGraw-Hill.

Blythe, T. A., Allen, D., & Powell, B. S. (1999). *Looking together at student work: A companion guide to assessing student learning.* New York: Teachers College Press.

Blythe, T. A., Allen, D., & Powell, B. S. (2008). *Looking together at student work: A companion guide to assessing student learning* (2nd ed.). New York: Teachers College Press.

Boykin, A. W., & Noguera, P. (2011). *Creating the opportunity to learn.* Alexandria, VA: Association for Supervision and Curriculum Development.

Bransford, J. B., Brown, A. L., & Cocking, R. R. (Eds.). (2000). *How people learn: Brain, mind, experience, and school* (Expanded ed.). Washington DC: National Academies Press.

Brooks, J. G., & Brooks, M. G. (1993). *In search of understanding: The case for constructivist classrooms.* Alexandria, VA: Association for Supervision and Curriculum Development.

Brough, J. A., Bergmann, S., & Holt, L. (2006). *Teach me, I dare you.* Larchmont, NY: Eye on Education.

Brown-Chidsey, R. (2007). No more "waiting to fail." *Educational Leadership, 67*(1), 40–46.

Buffum, A. M., Mattos, M., & Webber, C. (2010). The why behind it. *Educational Leadership, 68*(2), 10–16.

Butrymowicz, S. (2010). The answer sheet (V. Strauss, producer). *Washington Post,* August 12. Retrieved August 7, 2011, from http://voices.washingtonpost .com/answer-sheet/guest-bloggers/arc-ed-credit-recovery-program.html

Calderon, M., Slavin, R., & Sanchez, M. (2011). Effective instruction for English learners. *Immigrant Children, 21*(1), 103–127. Retrieved August 22, 2011, from http:// futureofchildren.org/futureofchildren/publications/docs/21_01_05.pdf

Callahan, C. (2003). *Advanced Placement and International Baccalaureate programs for talented students in American high schools: A focus on science and mathematics (Conclusions).* Retrieved October 11, 2011, from http://www.gifted.uconn .edu/nrcgt/callahan.html

Callahan, C. T., Tomlinson, C. A., Reis, S. N., & Kaplan, S. N. (2000, June). TIMSS and high-ability students: Message of doom or opportunity for reflection. *Phi Delta Kappan, 81*(10), 787–790.

Calvin, W. (1996). *How brains think.* New York: Basic Books.

Chappuis, S., & Chappuis, J. (2007/2008). The best value in formative assessment. *Educational Leadership, 65*(4), 14–18.

Clark, K. (2009). The case for structured English immersion. *Educational Leadership, 66*(7), 42–46.

Collier, L. (2011, November). The need for teacher communities: An interview with Linda Darling-Hammond. *Council Chronicle, 21*(2), 12–14.

Cotton, K. (2001). *New small learning communities: Findings from recent literature.* Northwest Regional Educational Laboratory, School Improvement Program.

Daniel, L. (2007). *Flexible scheduling.* Retrieved December 5, 2011, from http:// www.nmsa.org/Research/ResearchSummaries/FlexibleScheduling/ tabid/1140/Default.aspx

Danielson, C. (2002). *Enhancing student achievement: A framework for school improvement.* Alexandria, VA: Association for Supervision and Curriculum Development.

Darling-Hammond, L. (1995, September 22). *Restructuring schools for student success.* Retrieved February 2, 2005, from http://www.highbeam.com/library

Dean, C. B., Hubbell, E. R., Pitler, H., & Stone, B. (2012). *Classroom instruction that works* (2nd ed.). Alexandria, VA: Association for Supervision and Curriculum Development.

Dessoff, A. (2009, October). *Reaching graduation with credit recovery.* Retrieved August 7, 2011, from http://www.districtadministration.com/viewarticle .aspc?articleid=2165

Dewey, J. (1938). *Experience and education.* Kappa Delta Pi Lecture Series. New York: Collier Books.

Dolan, W. (1994). *Restructuring our schools: A primer on systemic change.* Kansas City, KA: Systems & Organization.

DuFour, R. (1995). Restructuring is not enough. *Eduational Leadership, 52*(7), 33–36.

DuFour, R. (2004, May). *What is a "professional learning community"?* Retrieved August 11, 2011, from http://pdonline.ascd.org/pd_online/secondary_ reading/el200405_dufour.html

Dwek, C. S. (2006). *Mindset: The new psychology of success*. New York: Ballantine Books.

Earl, L. (2003). *Assessment as learning: Using classroom assessment to maximize student learning*. Thousand Oaks, CA: Corwin.

Editorial Projects in Education. (2007, June 12). Diplomas count: Ready for what? Preparing students for college, careers, and life after high school. *Education Week, 26*(40).

Education World. (2000, June 28). Retrieved August 14, 2011, from http://www.educationworld.com/a_curr246.shtml

Elmore, R. (2000). *Building a new structure for school leadership*. Washington DC: Albert Shanker Institute.

Erickson, H. (2001). *Stirring the head, heart, and soul: Redefining curriculum and instruction* (2nd ed.). Thousand Oaks, CA: Corwin.

Fisher, D., & Frey, N. (2007). *Checking for understanding: Formative assessment techniques for your classroom*. Alexandria, VA: Association for Supervision and Curriculum Development.

Fisher, D., &. Frey, N. (2008). Releasing responsibility. *Educational Leadership, 66*(3), 32–37.

Fisher, D., Frey, N., & Lapp, D. (2012). Building and activating students' background knowledge: It's what they already know that counts. *Middle School Journal, 43*(3), 22–31.

Fitzgerald, R. (1996). Brain-compatible teaching in a block schedule. *The School Administrator, 53*(8), 20–24.

Fogarty, R., & Pete, B. (2009/2010). Professional learning 101: A syllabus of seven protocols. *Phi Delta Kappan, 91*(4), 32–34.

Foster, C. (2012, February). *Will your students be prepared…or just educated?* Retrieved February 7, 2012, from Middle E-Connections: amle@amle.com

Fredricks, J. M., McColskey, W., Meli, J., Montrosse, B., Mordica, J., & Mooney, K. (2011, January). *Measuring student engagement in upper elementary through high school: A description of 21 instruments*. Retrieved January 9, 2012, from http://ies.ed.gov/ncee/edlabs/regions/southeast/pdf/REL_2011098.pdf

Frey, N., Fisher, D., & Everlove, S. (2009). *Productive group work*. Alexandria, VA: Association for Supervision and Curriculum Development.

Fullan, M. (2000). The three stories of education reform. *Phi Delta Kappan, 81*, 581–584.

Fullan, M. (2001). *Leading in a culture of change*. San Francisco: Jossey-Bass.

Gallagher, K. (2010). Reversing readicide. *Educational Leadership, 67*(6), 36–41.

Garcia, E. E., Jensen, B. T., & Scribner, K. P. (2009). The demographic imperative. *Edcuational Leadership, 66*(7), 8–13.

George, P. S., & Alexander, W. (1993). *The exemplary middle school* (2nd ed.). Orlando, FL: Harcourt Brace.

Gere, A. (2010). Taking initiative. *Principal Leadership, 11*(3), 36–42.

Glatthorn, A. A., & Jailall, J. (2000). Curriculum for the new millennium. In R. S. Brandt (Ed.), *Education in a new era* (pp. 97–121). Alexandria, VA: Association for Supervision and Curriculum Development.

Glenn, D. (2010, May 9). *Carol Dwek's attitude: It's not about how smart you are*. Retrieved January 23, 2012, from http://chronicle.com/article/Carol-Dweks-Attitude/65405

Gootman, E., & Coutts, S. (2008). Lacking credits, some students learn a short cut. *New York Times*, April 11. Retrieved August 7, 2011, from http://www.nytimes.com/2008/04/11/education/11graduation.html

Guskey, T. R. (2007/2008, December/January). The rest of the story. *Educational Leadership*, 28–35.

Hackmann, D. G., Petzko, V. N., & Valentine, J. W. (2002). Beyond interdisciplinary teaming: Findings amid implications of the NASSP national middle level study. *NASSP Bulletin, 86*, 33–47.

Hackmann, D. G., & Valentine, J. W. (1998, May). Designing an effective middle level schedule. *Middle School Journal, 29*(5), 3–13.

Hadi-Tabassum, S. (2004–2005). The balancing act of bilingual immersion. *Educational Leadership, 62*(4), 50–54.

Harry, B., & Klingner, J. (2007). Discarding the deficit model. *Educational Leadership, 64*(5), 16–21.

Hattie, J. A. (1992). Measuring the effects of schooling. *Australian Journal of Education, 36*(1), 5–13.

Hattie, J. (1999, August 2). *Influences on student learning.* Inaugural lecture: Professor of Education, University of Auckland.

Hattie, J. (2008). *Visible learning: A synthesis of over 800 meta-analyses relating to achievement.* New York: Routledge.

Hattie, J. (2009, September 8). *Visible learning, tomorrow's schools: The mindsets that make the difference.* Guest lecture at the Treasury, Wellington, NZ. Retrieved May 10, 2012, from http://www.treasury.govt.nz/publications/media-speeches/guestlectures/pdfs/tgls-hattie.pdf

Hattie, J. (2012). *Visible learning for teachers: Maximizing impact on learning* (p. 255). New York: Routledge.

Hayes-Jacobs, H. (1997). *Mapping the big picture: Integrating curriculum and assessment K–12.* Alexandria, VA: Association for Supervision and Curriculum Development.

Hersh, R. H. (2009). A well-rounded education for a flat world. *Educational Leadership, 67*(1), 50–53.

Hines, R. A. (2001, December). *Inclusion in middle schools.* Retrieved March 2, 2005, from http://ceep.crc.uiuc.edu/

Hirsch, E. D. (2008). An epoch-making report, but what about the early grades? *Education Week, 27*(34), 30–31, 40.

Hirsh, S., & Killion, J. (2009). When educators learn, students learn. *Phi Delta Kappan, 90*(7), 464–469.

Hoachlander, G. (2008). Bringing industry to the classroom. *Educational Leadership, 65*(8), 22–27.

Holloway, J. (2003). Grouping gifted students. *Educational Leadership, 61*(2), 89–91.

Hord, S. H., & Hirsh, S. (2009). The principal's role in supporting learning communities. *Educational Leadership, 86*(5), 22–23.

Howell, R. J., Patton, S. L., & Deiotte, M. T. (2008). *Understanding response to intervention: A practical guide to systemic implementation.* Bloomington, IN: Solution Tree.

Hunter, M. (1982). *Mastery teaching.* El Segundo, CA: T.I.P. Publications.

Institute for Research and Policy on Acceleration, National Association for Gifted Children, and Council of State Directors of Programs for the Gifted. (2009, November). *Guidelines for developing an academic acceleration policy.* Retrieved September 16, 2011, from http://www.nagc.org/uloadedFiles/Advocacy/Acceleration%20Policy%20Guidelines.pdf

Jackson, A. W., & Davis, G. A. (2000). *Turning points 2000: Educating adolescents of the 21st century.* New York: Teachers College Press.

Jensen, E. (1998). *Teaching with the brain in mind.* Alexandria, VA: Association for Supervision and Curriculum Development.

Johnson, D. W., & Johnson, R. T. (1995). Cooperative learning. In J. H. Block, S. T. Everson, & T. R. Guskey (Eds.), *School improvement programs* (pp. 25–56). New York: Scholastic.

Kemple, J. J. (with Scott-Clayton, J.). (2004, March). *Career academies: Impacts on labor market outcomes and educational attainment.* Retrieved August 31, 2011, from http://www.mdrc.org/publications/366/overview.html

Kemple, J. J., & Snipes, J. C. (2000, February). *Career academies: Impact on students' engagement and performance in high school.* Retrieved August 31, 2011, from http://www.mdrc.org/publications/41/execsum.html

Klingner, J. K., & Artiles, A. J. (2003). When should bilingual students be in special education? *Educational Leadership, 61*(2), 66–71.

Kübler-Ross, E. (1969). *On death and dying: What the dying have to teach doctors, teachers, nurses, and their own family members.* New York: Touchstone.

Kulik, J. A. (1993, Spring). *An analysis of the research on ability grouping.* Retrieved September 29, 2011, from http://www.gifted.uconn.edu/nrcgt/newsletter/spring93/sprng935.html

Lee, V. E. M., & Smith, J. B. (1995, October). Effects of high school restructuring and size on early gains in achievement and engagement. *Sociology of Education, 68,* 241–270.

Letgers, N. (1999). *Teacher collaboration in a restructuring urban high school.* Center for Research on the Education of Students Placed at Risk.

Little, J. (1990). The persistence of privacy: Autonomy and initiative in teachers' professional relations. *Teachers College Record, 91* (4), 509–536.

Little, M., & Dieker, L. (2009). Two are better than one. *Principal Leadership, 9*(8), 43–46.

Lortie, D. (1975). *Schoolteacher: A sociological study.* Chicago: University of Chicago Press.

Loveless, T. (2008). *High-achieving students in the era of NCLB: An analysis of NAEP data.* Thomas B. Fordham Institute.

MacIver, D. J., & Plank, S. B. (September, 1996). *Creating a motivational climate conducive to talent development middle schools. Report No. 4: The Talent Development Middle School.* Baltimore: CRESPAR, Johns Hopkins University.

Macklein, M. (2006, March 20). Advanced Placement: A detour for college fast track? *USA Today.* Retrieved October 11, 2011, from http://www.usatoday.com/news/education/2006–03–20-ap-main_X.htm

Martin, J. L., & Morrow, C. (1997). *Moving toward interdisciplinary curriculum. Trainer's manual for a guidebook: Middle school edition.* Texas Education Agency.

Marzano, R. J. (2000). 20th century advances in instruction. In R. Brandt (Ed.), *Education in a new era* (pp. 67–95). Alexandria, VA: Association for Supervision and Curriculum Development.

Marzano, R. J. (2003). *What works in schools: Translating research into action.* Alexandria, VA: Association for Supervision and Curriculum Development.

Marzano, R. (2005). *School leadership that works: From research to results.* Alexandria, VA: Association for Supervision and Curriculum Development.

Marzano, R. (2007). *The art and science of teaching: A comprehensive framework for effective instruction.* Alexandria, VA: Association for Supervision and Curriculum Development.

Marzano, R. J. (2009). Helping students process information. *Educational Leadership, 67*(2), 86–87.

Marzano, R. (2010). When practice makes perfect . . . sense. *Educational Leadership, 68* (3), 81–83.

Marzano, R. J., Pickering, D. J., & Pollock, J. E. (2001). *Classroom instruction that works: Research-based strategies for increasing student achievement.* Alexandria, VA: Association for Supervision and Curriculum Development.

Merenbloom, E. Y., & Kalina, B. A. (2007). *Making creative schedules work in middle and high schools.* Thousand Oaks, CA: Corwin.

Mizell, H. P. (2004, October 1). *Still crazy after all these years: Grade configuration and the education of young adolescents.* Retrieved November 28, 2011, from http://www.middleweb.com/mw/resources/HMgradeconfig.pdf

Mora, J. (2009). From the ballot box to the classroom. *Educational Leadership, 66*(7), 14–19.

National Association for Gifted Children. (2009a, March). *Grouping (Position Paper).* Retrieved September 16, 2011, from http://nagc.org/uploadedFiles/Information_and_Resources/Postition_Paper/Grouping.pdf

National Association for Gifted Children. (2009b, November). *Response to intervention for gifted children: The association for the gifted, a division of the Council for Exceptional Children: Position Paper.* Retrieved September 16, 2011, from http://www.nagc.org/uploadedFiles/RtI.pdf

National Association for Gifted Children. (2009c, March). *Twice exceptionality (Position Paper).* Retrieved September 16, 2011, from http://www.nagc.org/uploadedFiles/information_and_Resources_Position_Papers_twice%20exceptionality%20position%20paper.pdf

National Association for Gifted Children. (n.d.). *Pullout programs/specialized classes: What the research says.* Retrieved September 16, 2011, from http://nagc.org/index.aspx?id=3420

National Association of Secondary School Principals. (1996). *Breaking ranks: Changing an American institution.* Reston, VA: Author.

National Association of Secondary School Principals. (2002). *What the research shows: Breaking ranks in action.* Reston, VA: Author.

National Association of Secondary School Principals. (2004). *Breaking ranks II: Strategies for leading high school reform.* Reston, VA: Author.

National Association of Secondary School Principals. (2006). *Breaking ranks in the middle: Strategies for leading middle level reform.* Reston, VA: Author.

National Association of State Directors of Special Education. (2008). *Response to intervention: Blueprints for implementation.* Retrieved August 11, 2011, from http://www.nasdse.org/Portals/)/SCHOOL.pdf

National Council of Teachers of English. (2005). *Standards for middle and high school literacy coaches and subject matter teachers (Draft).* Retrieved April 2005 from http://www.ncte.org/collections/literacycoach

National Forum to Accelerate Middle-Grades Reform. (2004, June). Policy statement. *Small Schools and Small Learning Communities, 4.* Retrieved June 9, 2012, from http://www.middlegradesforum.org/images/stories/SmallCommunities.pdf

National Governors Association Center for Best Practices, Council of Chief State School Officers. (2010). *Common Core State Standards: English language arts standards.* Washington, DC: Author. Retrieved July 17, 2012, from http://www.corestandards.org/

Nelson, W. (1998, May). The naked truth about school reform in Minnesota. *Phi Delta Kappan,* 682.

Nuthall, G. (1999). The way students learn: Acquiring knowledge from an integrated science and social studies unit. *The Elementary School Journal, 99*(4), 303–341.

Oakes, J. (2005). *Keeping track: How schools structure inequality.* New Haven, CT: Yale University Press.

Pellegrino, J. C., Chudowsky, N., & Glaser, R. (Eds.). (2001). *Knowing what students know: The science and design of educational assessment.* Washington, DC: National Academy Press.

Piaget, J. (1971). *Genetic epistemology* (E. Duckworth, Trans.). New York: Norton.

Plank, D. (2011, August 31). English-language learners: One size does not fit all. *Education Week, 31*(2), 20–21.

Popham, W. (2008). *Transformative assessment.* Alexandria, VA: Association for Supervision and Curriculum Development.

Protheroe, N. (2009, July). Using data to reduce the drop-out rate. *Principal's Research Review, 4*(4), pp. 1–7.

Protheroe, N. (2011, March). Implementing and sustaining school improvement. *Principal's Research Review, 6*(2), 7.

Rance-Roney, J. (2009). Best practices for adolescent ELLs. *Educational Leadership, 66*(7), 32–37.

Reeves, D. B. (2006). *The learning leader: How to focus school improvement for better results.* Alexandria, VA: Association for Supervision and Curriculum Development.

Reeves, D. B. (2009). *Leading change in your school: How to conquer myths, build commitment, and get results.* Alexandria, VA: Association for Supervision and Curriculum Development.

Reeves, D. B. (2010). *Transforming professional development into student results.* Alexandria, Virginia: Association for Supervision and Curriculum Development.

Renzulli, J. S. (1978, November). *What makes giftedness? Reexamining a definition.* Retrieved October 16, 2011, from http://www.kappanmagazine.org/Content/92/8/81.full.pdf-html?sid=d9962791-f2a5–43eb-af6e-8cbec11e93e1

Richardson, J. (2011). The ultimate practitioner. *Phi Delta Kappan, 93*(1), 27–32.

Roberts, C. (2000). Leading without control: Moving beyond the "Principal Do-Right" model of educational leadership. In P. C. M. Senge (Ed.), *Schools that learn: A fifth discipline fieldbook for educators, parents, and everyone who cares about education* (pp. 411–418). New York: Doubleday Dell.

Roderick, M. (1993). *The path to dropping out: Evidence for intervention.* Westport, CT: Auburn House.

Rogers, K. (1991). *The relationship of grouping practices to the education of the gifted and talented learner.* Retrieved September 29, 2011, from http://gifted.uconn.edu/nrcgt/rogers.html

Rogers, K. (1993, September). *Grouping the gifted and talented: Questions and answers.* Retrieved September 29, 2011, from http://www.davidsongifted.org/db/Articles_id_10173.aspx

Rogers, K. (2002). Grouping the gifted and talented. *Roper Review, 24*(4), 103–107.

Rossell, C. (2004–2005). Teaching English through English. *Educational Leadership, 62*(4), 32–36.

Rouse, C. E. (2005). *Labor market consequences of an inadequate education.* New York: Columbia University.

Russell, P. (1979). *The brain book.* New York: E. P. Dutton.

Samuels, C. (2011, March 2). *Education Week spotlight.* Retrieved August 6, 2011, from http://www.edweek.org/ew/articles/2011/03/02/22rti-overview.h30.html

Saunders, M. H., & Hamilton, E. (2010, September 27). *Linking learning to life: A high school transformation effort* (E. staff ed.). Retrieved August 31, 2011, from http://www.edutopia.org/stw-career-technical-education-research-roundup

Schaefer, R. J. (1971). Retrospect and prospect. In *The curriculum: Retrospect and prospect: Seventieth yearbook of the National Society for the Study of Education* (Part I, pp. 3–25). Chicago: University of Chicago Press.

Schmoker, M. J. (2006). *Results now: How we can achieve unprecedented improvements in teaching and learning.* Alexandria, VA: Association for Supervision and Curriculum Development.

Schmoker, M. J. (2011). *Focus: Evaluating the essentials to radically improve student learning.* Alexandria, VA: Association for Supervision and Curriculum Development.

Senge, P., Cambron-McCabe, N., Lucas, T., Smith, B., Dutton, J., & Kleiner, A. (2000). *Schools that learn: A fifth discipline fieldbook for educators, parents, and everyone who cares about education.* New York: Doubleday.

Smith, B. L. (2001). *The challenge of learning communities as a growing national movement.* Providence, RI: Association of American Colleges and Universities, Conference on Learning Communities.

Sousa, D. A. (2001). *How the brain learns: A classroom teacher's guide.* Thousand Oaks, CA: Corwin.

Sparks, S. (2011, November 28). *Study links academic setbacks to middle school transition* (E. Week, producer). Retrieved November 28, 2011, from http://www.edweek.org/ew/articles/2011/11/28/13structure.h31.html

Sprenger, M. (1999). *Learning and memory: The brain in action.* Alexandria, VA: Association for Supervision and Curriculum Development.

Stern, D. (2010, September 27). *From vocational education to career-technical education: A capsule history and summary of research.* Retrieved August 31, 2011, from http://www.edutopia.org/stw-career-technical-education-research-roundup

Sternberg, R. (2008). Excellence for all. *Educational Leadership, 66*(2), 15–19.

Stiggins, R. (2001). *Student-involved classroom assessment* (3rd ed.). Columbus, OH: Prentice Hall.

Sylwester, R. (1995). *A celebration of neurons: An educator's guide to the human brain.* Alexandria, VA: Association for Supervision and Curriculum Development.

Sylwester, R. (2011, October). *Creating an appropriate 21st century education: The roles of cognitive neuroscience and computer technology.* Retrieved October 31, 2011, from http://i-a-e.org/newsletters/IAE-Newsletter-2011-75.html

Taba, H. (1966). *Teaching strategies and cognitive functioning in elementary school children (Cooperative research project).* Washington, DC: Office of Education, U.S. Department of Health, Education, and Welfare.

Thomas, W. P., & Collier, V. P. (2003). The multiple benefits of dual language. *Educational Leadership, 61*(2), 61–64.

Tomas Rivera Policy Institute. (2006, March). *Equity in offering Advanced Placement courses in California high schools: Gaining or losing ground.* Retrieved October 10, 2011, from http://www.trpi.org/PDFs/ap_2006.pdf

Tomlinson, C. A. (1999). *The differentiated classroom: Responding to the needs of all learners.* Alexandria, VA: Association for Supervision and Curriculum Development.

Tomlinson, C. A. (2001). *How to differentiate instruction in mixed-ability classrooms.* Alexandria, VA: Association for Supervision and Curriculum Development.

Tomlinson, C. A. (2007/2008). Learning to love assessment. *Educational Leadership, 65*(4), 8–13.

Tomlinson, C. A., & Imbeau, M. B. (2010). *Leading and managing a differentiated classroom.* Alexandria, VA: Association for Supervision and Curriculum Development.

Vars, G. F. (1993). *Interdisciplinary teaching: Why and how.* Columbus, OH: National Middle School Association.

Villa, R., & Thousand, J. (2003). Making inclusive education work. *Educational Leadership, 61*(2), 19–23.

Voltz, D. L., Sims, M. J., & Nelson, B. (2010). *Connecting teachers, students, and standards: Strategies for success in diverse and inclusive classrooms.* Alexandria, VA: Association for Supervision and Curriculum Development.

Walberg, H. J. (1997). Uncompetitive American schools: Causes and cures. In *Brookings papers on educational policy.* Washington DC: The Brookings Institution.

Weber, M. (2009, June). *Special education law: Challenges old and new* (P. D. Kappan, producer). Retrieved August 19, 2011, from http://www.pdkmembers_online/publications/archive/pdf/k0906web.pdf

Wei, R. C., Darling-Hammond, L., Andree, A., Richardson, N., & Orphanos, S. (2009). *Professional learning in the learning profession: A status report on teacher development in the United States and abroad.* National Staff Development Council and The School Redesign Network at Stanford University.

Wiggins, G., & McTighe, J. (1998). *Understanding by design.* Alexandria, VA: Association for Supervision and Curriculum Development.

Wiggins, G., & McTighe, J. (2002). *Understanding by design: Teaching and assessing for in-depth, engaging, and effective learning.* San Antonio, TX: Association for Supervision and Curriculum Development.

Wilhelm, J. D. (2009). Change we can believe in: Real literacy for real learning. *Middle Ground, 12*(4), 12–13.

Wiliam, D. (2011). *Embedded formative assessment.* Bloomington, IN: Solution Tree Press.

Williams, R. B., & Dunn, S. E. (2000). *Brain-compatible learning for the block.* Thousand Oaks, CA: Corwin.

Wise, B. (2008). High schools at the tipping point. *Educational Leadership, 65*(8), 8–13.

Wolfe, P. (2001). *Brain matters: Translating research in classroom practice.* Alexandria, VA: Association for Supervision and Curriculum Development.

Zemelman, S., Daniels, H., & Hyde, A. (1998). *Best practice: New standards for teaching and learning in America's schools.* Portsmouth, NH: Heinemann.

Index

NOTE: Page numbers with figures and tables are identified as (fig.) and (table).